DELUGE

DELUGE

DELUGE

GAZA AND ISRAEL
FROM CRISIS TO CATACLYSM

EDITED BY
JAMIE STERN-WEINER

O/R

OR Books

New York · London

Published by OR Books, New York and London

Visit our website at www.orbooks.com

All rights information: rights@orbooks.com

First printing 2024

Library of Congress Cataloging-in-Publication Data: A catalog record for this book is available from the Library of Congress.

British Library Cataloging in Publication Data: A catalog record for this book is available from the British Library.

Typeset by Lapiz Digital.

paperback ISBN 978-1-68219-619-9 • ebook ISBN 978-1-68219-620-5

"What was will not be"

—Israeli Minister of Energy and
Infrastructure Israel Katz

On October 7, 2023, Hamas-led militants from Gaza attacked civilian communities and military installations in southern Israel.

Hamas called the operation Al-Aqsa Deluge.

Contents

PART III. SOLIDARITIES

Foreword

Avi Shlaim

The powerful military offensive launched by Israel on the Gaza Strip in October 2023, or Operation Swords of Iron to give it its official name, was a major landmark in the blood-soaked history of the Israeli-Palestinian conflict. It was an instant, almost Pavlovian response to the Hamas attack on Israel on October 7. That attack caught Israel by complete surprise, and it was devastating in its consequences, killing about 300 Israeli soldiers, massacring more than 800 civilians, and taking some 250 hostages. Whereas previous Hamas attacks involved the firing of rockets from the Gaza Strip on southern Israel, this was a ground incursion into Israeli territory made possible by breaking down the fence with which Israel had surrounded Gaza. The murderous Hamas attack did not come out of the blue as many believed. It was a response to Israel's illegal and exceptionally brutal military occupation of the Palestinian territories since June 1967, as well as the suffocating economic blockade that Israel had imposed on Gaza since 2006. Israel, however, treated it as an unprovoked terrorist attack that gave it a blank check to use military force on an unprecedented scale to exact revenge and to crush the enemy.

Israel is no stranger to the use of military force in dealing with its neighbors. It is a country that lives by the sword. Under international law, states are allowed to use military force in self-defense as a last resort; Israel often employs force as a first resort. Some of its wars with the Arabs have been "wars of no choice," like the first Arab-Israeli war of 1948; others have been "wars of choice," like the Suez War of 1956 and the invasion of Lebanon in 1982. Wars are usually followed by the search for a diplomatic resolution of the conflict. When one examines Israel's record in dealing with the Arabs as a whole, however, the use of force appears to be the preferred instrument of statecraft. Indeed, all too often, instead of war being the pursuit of politics by other means, Israeli diplomacy is the pursuit of war by other means.

When talking about the Arab-Israeli conflict, one needs to distinguish between two levels: the interstate level and the Israeli-Palestinian level. The interstate level refers to the relations between Israel and the neighboring Arab states. The Israeli-Palestinian level refers to the relations between Israel and the Palestinian people who are a non-state actor. In essence this is a clash between two national movements over the same piece of land. This is the heart and core of the conflict. Historically, Israel has preferred to negotiate with conservative Arab leaders, like President Anwar Sadat of Egypt and King Hussein of Jordan, rather than with the leaders of the Palestinian national movement.

The Oslo Accord of September 1993 was an exception to this rule. It was an agreement between the Palestine Liberation Organization (PLO) and Israel, the first agreement between the two principal parties to the conflict. As such it may deserve the overused term "historic," although it did not touch the root cause of the conflict. All the key issues in dispute, the "final status issues" as they are sometimes called, were deferred to negotiations in the last year of the stipulated five-year transition period. These are the status of Jerusalem, the right of return of the Palestinian refugees expelled from their homes in 1948, the status of the Jewish settlements on occupied Palestinian land, and the borders of the Palestinian entity. All these issues remain unresolved to this day. Palestinian frustration with the lack of political progress toward independence sparked two *intifadas*, or uprisings, one in 1987 and the second in 2000. Israel, under the Labor government that signed the Oslo agreement, opted to repackage rather than to end the occupation. Under the Likud governments that followed, Israel reneged on the promise to exchange land for peace. Under both Labor and Likud, Israel seemed intent on "managing" rather than resolving the conflict with the Palestinians.

In 2005 a right-wing Likud government, under the leadership of Ariel Sharon, decided to withdraw unilaterally from the Gaza Strip. This was part of a broader strategy designed to defeat the Palestinian struggle for national liberation by separating the West Bank from the Gaza Strip. Hamas, the Islamic Resistance Movement, won a decisive victory in the Palestinian legislative elections of January 2006 and proceeded to form a unified Palestinian government, but Israel continued to practice the imperial tactic of divide and rule. Once in power, Hamas lowered its sights from a unitary, Islamic Palestinian state from the Jordan River to the Mediterranean Sea to a Palestinian state along the 1967 lines.

All of Hamas's peace overtures were rebuffed by Israel and its Western allies. Israel, the US, and the European Union persisted in viewing Hamas as a terrorist organization despite its clean victory in the 2006 elections. It is no exaggeration to say that Israel blocked every avenue to a peaceful settlement of the conflict. Prime Minister Ehud Barak did offer to the Palestinians a two-state solution in 2000 and so did Ehud Olmert in 2008, but the terms they offered did not meet the minimal Palestinian demands. These demands, it is important to stress, were anchored in UN resolutions and a broad international consensus.

Deadlock on the diplomatic front led to periodic clashes between Hamas and Israel. This is not a conflict between two roughly equal parties but asymmetric warfare between a small paramilitary force and one of the most powerful militaries in the world, armed to the teeth with the most advanced American weaponry. The result was low-intensity (but for people in Gaza, still devastating) conflict which took the form of primitive missiles fired from inside the Gaza Strip on settlements in southern Israel and Israel Defense Forces (IDF) counter-insurgency operations designed to weaken but not to destroy Hamas. From time to time, Israel would move beyond aerial bombardment to ground invasion of the enclave. It launched major military offensives into Gaza in 2008–2009, 2012, 2014, 2021, 2022, and 2023.

Israeli leaders used to call these recurrent IDF incursions into Gaza "mowing the lawn." This was the metaphor to describe Israel's strategy against Hamas. The strategy did not seek to defeat Hamas, let alone drive it from power. On the contrary, the aim was to allow Hamas to govern Gaza but to isolate and weaken it, and to reduce its influence on the West Bank. Israel's overarching political objective was to keep the Palestinian Authority and the Hamas government geographically separate so as to prevent the emergence of a unified leadership. In this context, Israel's periodic offensives were designed to degrade the military capability of Hamas, to enhance Israeli deterrence, and to turn the civilian population of Gaza against its rulers. In short, it was a strategy of managing the conflict, of avoiding peace talks, of using the Palestinian Authority in Ramallah as a sub-contractor for Israeli security on the West Bank, and of containing Palestinian resistance within the open-air prison of the Gaza Strip.

This strategy lay in tatters following the Hamas attack on a military base and Israeli civilians around the Gaza Strip on October 7, 2023. The scale and ferocity of the attack clearly demonstrated that Hamas was not deterred by the military might of the IDF. The cruelty and savagery that accompanied the killing of civilians shook Israeli society to the core. Cries for revenge reverberated throughout the land. What were previously viewed as annoying pinpricks were overnight transformed into an existential threat. Despite deep political cleavages inside Israeli society, a consensus emerged that Hamas had to be destroyed and that the threat to Israel's security emanating from the Gaza Strip had to be removed once and for all.

The change in the popular mood was reflected in an abrupt change in government policy. The three declared war aims of the Israeli government in Operation Swords of Iron were: to destroy Hamas as a political and military organization, to bring back the hostages, and to prevent the Gaza Strip from posing a threat to Israeli security ever again. After October 7, there was no more talk about mowing the lawn. What has not changed is the Israeli addiction to occupation, its hugely exaggerated trust in the utility of military force, and its dogged refusal to give peace a chance. The simple truth that without peace they cannot have security was lost on the government and the great majority of Israelis.

The chapters in this volume were written while Israel's war on Gaza was still in progress. The aim of the volume is to place this war in its proper historical context and to provide a preliminary assessment of the many different aspects of the war. When one initiates a war, one knows how it will start but one does not know how it will end. Here we are trying to explore how and why the war started and to examine developments in its initial stage. We cannot predict how the war will end nor what its long-term consequences might be. What is clear beyond doubt, however, is that this war constitutes a turning point in the history of the Israeli-Palestinian conflict. Collectively, we hope to have shed some light in this volume on what is one of the most protracted, bitter, and intractable conflicts of modern times.

Avi Shlaim
Oxford
December 2023

Acknowledgments

The editor is grateful for the assistance of Yaniv Cogan, Fionn Dempsey, Norman G. Finkelstein, Célestine Fünfgeld, Alex Nunns, Mouin Rabbani, Avi Shlaim, and the OR Books team.

Some Key Dates

- **November 1917:** British foreign secretary Lord Balfour declares, "His Majesty's Government view with favour the establishment in Palestine of a national home for the Jewish people."
- **1936–1939:** The Arab Revolt in Palestine.
- **November 1947:** The United Nations (UN) General Assembly adopts Resolution 181 (II), which approves the partition of Palestine into an Arab and a Jewish state.
- **May 14, 1948:** Establishment of the State of Israel.
- **May 15, 1948–January 1949:** The first Arab-Israeli war (the War of Independence/*Nakba*). Israel expands its territory and drives some 750,000 Palestinians into exile. About 250,000 Palestinians flee to Gaza, which comes under Egyptian administrative control.
- **December 1948:** The UN General Assembly adopts Resolution 194 (III), which resolves "that the [Palestinian] refugees wishing to return to their homes and live at peace with their neighbours should be permitted to do so at the earliest practical date."
- **February–July 1949:** Arab-Israeli armistice agreements establish demarcation boundaries. They eventually come to be internationally accepted as Israel's legal borders.
- **October 1956:** Britain, France, and Israel invade Egypt. Israeli forces occupy Gaza and carry out summary executions as well as large-scale massacres. The UN estimates that

between 447 and 550 civilians are killed in the first three weeks of Israel's occupation of Gaza.

- **June 5–10, 1967:** Israel engages in armed hostilities with Egypt, Jordan, and Syria, and achieves a resounding military victory. The West Bank, including East Jerusalem, and Gaza Strip, as well as the Syrian Golan Heights and Egyptian Sinai, come under Israeli military occupation.
- **November 22, 1967:** The UN Security Council adopts Resolution 242. This comes to be called the "land for peace" formula for resolving the conflict: Israel must fully withdraw from the territories it occupied in the 1967 war, while neighboring Arab states must unequivocally establish peaceful relations with Israel.
- **1971:** To crush resistance in Gaza, Israel displaces thousands of Gaza residents and bulldozes broad paths through the Strip.
- **June 1982:** Israel invades Lebanon to destroy the Palestine Liberation Organization (PLO). Up to 20,000 Palestinian and Lebanese, overwhelmingly civilians, are killed.
- **December 1987:** The first Palestinian intifada (uprising) breaks out in Gaza. Palestinians across the occupied Palestinian territories enter into mass civil revolt against Israel's occupation.
- **February 1988:** Hamas, the Islamic Resistance Movement, issues its first communiqué. The group is established as the militant arm of the Muslim Brotherhood in Palestine.
- **November 1988:** The PLO officially recognizes the State of Israel beside a Palestinian state in the West Bank, including East Jerusalem, and Gaza.
- **September 1993:** The PLO "recognizes the right of the State of Israel to exist in peace and security" while Israel

"recognize[s] the PLO as the representative of the Palestinian people." This begins the "Oslo peace process."

- **August–September 2005:** Israel unilaterally evacuates all settlements and military bases from Gaza (the "disengagement") but retains control over Gaza's borders, waters, airspace, and population registry.

- **January 2006**: Hamas wins a majority of seats in PA legislative elections. Israel imposes an economic blockade on Gaza, while the US and EU apply sanctions to the new government.

- **June 2007**: Hamas consolidates its control of the Gaza Strip, while Israel tightens the blockade.

- **December 27, 2008–January 18, 2009:** Israel unleashes "Operation Cast Lead" in Gaza. Thirteen Israelis and approximately 1,400 Palestinians are killed.

- **July 8–August 26, 2014:** Israel unleashes "Operation Protective Edge" in Gaza. About 2,200 Palestinians and 73 Israelis are killed. Eighteen thousand homes in Gaza and one house in Israel are destroyed.

- **May 2017**: Hamas publishes a "Document of General Principles and Policies" to supersede its Charter. The Document designates establishing a Palestinian state alongside Israel, with the return of Palestinian refugees, "a formula of national consensus."

- **March 2018**: Tens of thousands of people in Gaza begin weekly demonstrations against the siege and for their rights as refugees. Between March 30 and December 31, 2018, at least 189 demonstrators are killed and 6,103 injured by live ammunition.

- **May 2021**: Hamas fires rockets from Gaza, citing Israeli encroachments in East Jerusalem. More than 250 people in Gaza and 13 in Israel are killed in the ensuing escalation, which ends with a ceasefire after eleven days.

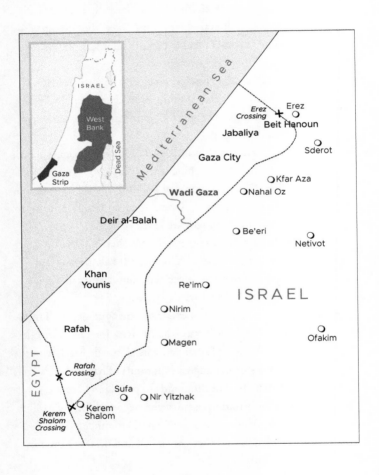

Introduction

On October 7, 2023, hundreds of Palestinian militants burst the gates of Gaza, overwhelmed military installations, and rampaged across southern Israel. The operation was shocking in its boldness, the ensuing massacre for its brutality. But the conditions that led to the Hamas attack were long-standing. Gaza is a speck of coastline that is among the most densely populated areas on earth. Some 75 percent of its inhabitants are refugees driven from their homes to make way for the State of Israel in 1948, and their descendants. Israel occupied the Strip in 1967 and de facto annexed it without extending rights of citizenship to the inhabitants. After Palestinians revolted against Israeli military rule, in 1987 (the first intifada), Israel crushed the uprising and then strengthened its grip on Gaza through various forms of confinement. By 2004, the head of Israel's National Security Council could describe Gaza as "a huge concentration camp."[1] In January 2006, the Islamic Resistance Movement, Hamas, won democratic elections in Gaza and the West Bank. Israel and its allies responded by subjecting the occupied Palestinian population—already enduring the "worst economic depression in modern history"—to "possibly the most rigorous form of international sanctions imposed in modern times."[2] After Hamas consolidated control in Gaza the following year, Israel tightened the screws further as it put Gaza under a comprehensive closure that has been enforced with varying degrees of intensity ever since.[3]

The siege extinguished Gaza's economy and reduced its people to penury. "The idea is to put the Palestinians on a diet," a senior Israeli official explained, "but not to make them die of hunger."[4] The unemployment rate soared to among the highest in the world, four-fifths of the population were forced to rely on humanitarian assistance, three-quarters became dependent on food aid, more than half faced "acute food insecurity," one in ten children were stunted by malnutrition, and over 96 percent of potable water became unsafe for human consumption.[5]

The head of the United Nations (UN) agency for Palestinian refugees, UNRWA, observed in 2008 that

> Gaza is on the threshold of becoming the first territory to be intentionally reduced to a state of abject destitution, with the knowledge, acquiescence and—some would say—encouragement of the international community.[6]

The UN warned in 2015 that the cumulative impact of this induced "humanitarian implosion" might render Gaza "unlivable" within a half-decade. Israeli military intelligence agreed, whereas a subsequent UN analysis judged the projection overly optimistic.[7]

Long before October 2023, then, Israel had turned Gaza into what the *Economist* termed a "human rubbish heap," the *Ha'aretz* editorial board a "ghetto," the International Committee of the Red Cross a "sinking ship."[8] It had reduced Gaza to what the UN high commissioner for human rights called a "toxic slum," in which above two million people were "caged . . . from birth to death."[9] An Israeli officer stationed on the Gaza border distilled his mission there: "No development, no prosperity, only humanitarian dependency."[10] He might have added, *forever.*

Many in Gaza did not share this vision for their future, and so Israel found it prudent to periodically massacre them— what Israeli officials termed "mowing the lawn."[11] Some of these onslaughts responded to resistance emanating from Gaza; armed, as when Hamas fired projectiles into Israel in May 2021 following settler encroachments in occupied East Jerusalem, or unarmed, as in early 2018, when Palestinians demonstrated nonviolently along Gaza's perimeter fence—scores were killed and thousands injured by Israeli snipers arrayed on the other side.[12] But Israel's most devastating offensives, in 2008 and 2014, were motivated by broader political objectives: to inspire fear in the Arab world and to thwart Hamas "peace offensives" that threatened to make Israel's rejectionist diplomatic posture—its refusal to withdraw from Palestinian territory in exchange for peace—untenable.[13] In the 2014 assault alone, approximately 1,600 civilians in Gaza were killed, including 550 children, and 18,000 homes were destroyed.[14]

Expulsion. Annexation. Siege. Massacre. Injustice layered on injustice, atrocity compounding atrocity, sedimented savagery amounting in sum to a colossal crime against humanity— culminating in the blockade and bombardment of a refugee population, confined in a concentration camp, *one-half of whom were children*.[15] It would surprise if suffering of this severity were a recipe for long-term stability. Israeli officials knew the "humanitarian condition in Gaza" was "progressively deteriorating"—this being the intended outcome of Israeli policy—and could predict that, "if it blows up, it'll be in Israel's direction."[16] But they apparently believed that by oscillating "between [military] operations and providing that level of aid to Gaza" sufficient to prevent its complete "collapse," Palestinian eruptions could be contained within tolerable limits. Hamas will "rise up from time to time and hit us," Israel's former national security advisor acknowledged in 2018, but "[i]t can't cause us any real damage."[17] If the timing, scale, and character of the October 7 attack came as a shock, the fact that people in Gaza would strike out at some point and in some fashion was not just predictable but priced in to Israel's "conflict management" policy. Indeed, a former deputy to Israel's national security advisor found in the Hamas-led assault, not proof of Gazans' irrational barbarism, but confirmation of a historical universal: "Eventually the oppressed will rise against their oppressor."[18]

If the "root causes"[19] of the Gaza catastrophe were familiar, and if the resort to terrorism by Israel as well as Hamas had ample precedent, still, four critical aspects of the crisis marked a departure:

First, there was a radical intensification in the magnitude of death and destruction inflicted. The authorities in Israel reported that Hamas-led militants killed some 1,200 people on October 7, including more than 800 civilians, and took 250 more captive. If these figures are correct, this means Palestinians killed more Israelis in one day than during the entire second intifada (inclusive of the bloody suicide bombings).[20] At the time of writing, allegations that Hamas forces engaged in widespread mutilation, beheading, and rape had not been substantiated. If those claims prove accurate, this would constitute another grim novelty from an organization that has historically eschewed such tactics.

In retaliation for the Hamas operation and massacre, Israel turned Gaza into a howling wasteland. Over two months, Israeli forces killed more than 17,000 people, including more than 7,700 children.[21] That's almost as many children as were killed across all the world's conflict zones over the previous three years combined.[22] Gazan hospitals developed the acronym "WCNSF"—Wounded Child No Surviving Family—as hundreds of extended family units were wiped out.[23] Nearly 85 percent of the population was internally displaced. More than 60 percent of homes were damaged or destroyed.[24] Northern Gaza became "an uninhabitable moonscape" as broad swathes of the territory were erased. "Beit Hanoun is not only dead," a correspondent for *Le Monde* reported in November, referring to a northern town, "Beit Hanoun no longer exists."[25] In what might have been a first in the annals of modern warfare, Israeli forces systematically targeted hospitals as they "completely obliterated" Gaza's "healthcare infrastructure."[26] At the same time, Israel targeted water and sewage facilities and employed "starvation of civilians as a method of warfare" as it prevented deliveries of food, fuel, water, medicines, and electricity to the battered enclave.[27] Inevitably, by mid-December, half the population of Gaza faced "severe hunger" while disease and lack of medical treatment threatened to increase the death toll by "multiples."[28]

Second, this ramping up of violence reflected a shift in Israel's strategy. Before October 7, Israel sought to manage its conflict with the Palestinians by deploying economic "carrots" alongside military "sticks" to co-opt as well as deter Palestinian resistance. In the West Bank, many Palestinians came to acquire a material investment in the status quo.[29] The emphasis in Gaza lay more on the "sticks"—those periodic bloodlettings—but there, too, a class of profiteers had congealed, even under the harsh blockade. Crucially, in the years leading up to 2023, Israeli planners thought that Hamas would prioritize control of a territory and ability to govern it over resistance. Hamas's responsibility for providing public services in Gaza, together with its dependence on Israel for access to the resources needed to discharge this obligation, would induce the movement to abandon armed struggle and acquiesce in Israel's overarching control.

The October 7 attack was an emphatic refusal of this role. Hamas would not become another Palestinian Authority, policing unlawfully annexed Palestinian territory on Israel's behalf. Even as the Hamas assault made Israel's conflict management approach a dead letter, the unqualified support extended by the US and EU in its wake gave Israel an opportunity to, as one member of Israel's war cabinet declared, "change the . . . strategic reality."[30] Israel's strategy accordingly shifted from mowing the lawn in Gaza to salting the earth; from perpetually deferring the Gaza question to definitively resolving it.[31] To this end, Israel systematically destroyed the prerequisites for civilization in Gaza and sought to render the territory uninhabitable, while mobilizing US influence to persuade Egypt to accept masses of Gazan refugees. The refusal of Egypt and other Arab states to cooperate, together with mounting international pressure to limit the humanitarian disaster, may have precluded Israel from achieving these maximal objectives. But with half of Gaza reduced to rubble, half the population crammed into the southern city of Rafah, and Hamas not yet militarily vanquished, it was wholly unclear, at the time of writing, what a viable "day after" might look like.[32]

Third, the conflict may now have entered a zero-sum phase. The mainstream Palestinian leadership has for decades sought a two-state settlement of the conflict, while Hamas also attempted, after its election in 2006, to achieve this.[33] Meanwhile, previous escalations in Gaza ended with the prospect, albeit never fulfilled, that the siege would be lifted and the possibility, however remote, that some kind of modus vivendi might be found. But after October 7, it is hard to foresee any Israeli government negotiating with Hamas on anything more substantial than a prisoner exchange. Hamas, for its part, may no longer be prepared to coexist with the State of Israel. On the one hand, Israel's genocidal war will have multiplied ten-fold the bitterness and rage in Gaza, which was already substantial. On the other hand, if Hamas had previously reconciled to Israel's existence as an immutable reality, the gravity of Israel's operational and intelligence failures on October 7, together with Hamas's impressive military performance, may have convinced them that Israel's defeat is an option.

Finally, if there appears little short-term prospect of peace taking root in Gaza's scorched soil, seeds of hope did sprout elsewhere, as a solidarity movement of unprecedented size and vigor sprang to Gaza's defense. In Western Europe and North America, massive demonstrations mobilized for week after week opposing Israel's onslaught. Progressive Jews were in the militant vanguard. In the US and Britain, public opinion backed an immediate ceasefire in Gaza, even as not one major political party endorsed this position.[34] And right in the heart of the political establishment, from the European Union to the US State Department and White House, hundreds of officials risked their careers to demand an end to complicity in Israel's war crimes.[35] In 2023, Gaza became a symbol for injustice, inequality, and the hypocrisies of power writ large, and around this symbol, the glimmer of a New International could be espied. If the Gaza cataclysm resonated so widely, especially among the young, it might be because, in this age of yawning inequality, hollowed-out democracy, and a futureless future circumscribed by economic stagnation and climate crisis, the global "99 percent" saw in Gazans' plight an extreme version of their own.

***

Contributions to this book were finalized in early December 2023. Figures provided for casualties and destruction are those reported by the United Nations on December 9.

PART I
CONTEXTS

"We are fighting human animals and we are acting accordingly"

—Israeli Defense Minister Yoav Gallant

1

Israel's War on Gaza

Avi Shlaim

When Israel withdrew from Gaza in 2005, it turned the tiny enclave into an open-air prison. Israel's response to the Hamas attack of October 7, 2023—the incessant bombardment of Gaza by land, sea, and air—turned this open-air prison into an open graveyard, a pile of rubble, a desolate wasteland.

António Guterres, the secretary-general of the United Nations (UN), said in his address to the Security Council that the Hamas attack, in which 1,200 Israelis were killed and 250 taken hostage, did not happen in a vacuum. "The Palestinian people have been subjected to fifty-six years of suffocating occupation," he noted. He immediately added that "the grievances of the Palestinian people cannot justify the appalling attacks by Hamas. And those appalling attacks cannot justify the collective punishment of the Palestinian people."

Gilad Erdan, Israel's ambassador to the UN, responded with a vicious personal attack on the secretary-general, claiming, falsely, that he accused Israel of blood libel, calling for his

Avi Shlaim is an emeritus professor of international relations at Oxford University, a fellow of the British Academy, and the author of *The Iron Wall: Israel and the Arab World* (Penguin, 2014) and *Israel and Palestine: Reappraisals, Revisions, Refutations* (Verso, 2009).

resignation, and topping it off with a call on members of the UN to stop funding the organization. Israeli antagonism to the UN and obstruction of its work is nothing new, but the contrast between the decency and humanity of the secretary-general and the rudeness and crudeness of the Israeli representative was particularly striking on this occasion.

I propose to follow in the footsteps of the secretary-general by stating the obvious: the Israel-Hamas conflict did not begin on October 7. It has to be placed in its proper historical context. The Gaza Strip is the name given to the southern part of the coastal plain of Palestine, adjoining Egypt. It was part of Palestine during the British Mandate which ended in May 1948. Under the 1947 UN partition plan this area was to form part of the Palestinian Arab state but this state did not materialize. During the 1948 war for Palestine the Egyptian army captured this semi-desert strip.

The 1949 Israeli-Egyptian Armistice Agreement left this area on the Egyptian side of the new international border. Egypt did not annex the territory but kept it under military rule, pending resolution of the Arab-Israeli conflict.

The Strip is 25 miles long and 4 to 9 miles wide with a total area of 141 square miles. In the course of the 1948 war more than 200,000 Palestinian refugees were added to a population of around 80,000, creating a massive humanitarian problem. UNRWA (the UN Relief and Works Agency) was set up to provide food, education, and health services to the refugees. Israel occupied the Gaza Strip in the course of the Suez War of October–November 1956 but was forced by international pressure to vacate it in March 1957. A large number of civilians were killed, and atrocities were committed by the Israel Defense Forces (IDF) during its short-lived occupation of the territory in what was a foretaste of things to come.

In June 1967, Israel occupied the Gaza Strip, the West Bank, including East Jerusalem, the Golan Heights, and the Sinai Peninsula. In August 2005, Israel withdrew its soldiers and settlers from the Gaza Strip. Israeli spokespersons claimed that by withdrawing they gave the Gazans an opportunity to turn the enclave into the Singapore of the Middle East. This claim is utterly preposterous when compared with the grim reality, but it is quite typical of Israeli propaganda. The reality is that between 1967 and 2005, a classic colonial situation prevailed in the Gaza Strip. A few thousand Israeli settlers controlled 25 percent of the territory, 40 percent of the arable land, and the largest share of the desperately scarce water resources.

The Gaza Strip is not backward and impoverished because its residents are lazy but because Israel's rapacious colonial regime did not give it a chance to flourish. Economic progress was thwarted by a deliberate Israeli strategy of "de-development." Sara Roy, a Jewish scholar at Harvard, the daughter of Holocaust survivors, is the leading expert on the Gaza Strip. She has written four books on Gaza (as well as a chapter in this volume). The first and ground-breaking book was called *The Gaza Strip: The Political Economy of De-development*. In this book she coined the term and formulated the pivotal concept of de-development. Her powerful thesis is that the dire state of Gaza is not the result of objective conditions but of a deliberate Israeli policy of keeping it under-developed and dependent. Despite considerable opposition from the scholarly community when she first introduced the concept, it has become widely used and part of the lexicon in political science and other disciplines. The book shows in detail the various measures by which Israel systematically thwarted the growth of industry in the Gaza Strip and exploited the enclave as a source of cheap labor as well as a market for its own goods.

There were three principal reasons for the decision of the right-wing Likud government, headed by Ariel Sharon, to withdraw from Gaza in 2005. One is that Hamas, the Islamic Resistance Movement, launched attacks against Israel's settlers and soldiers and, as a result, the price of occupying Gaza outstripped the benefits. The game was no longer worth the candle. A second aim of the move was to sabotage the Oslo peace process. As Dov Weissglas, Sharon's chief of staff, explained in an interview with *Ha'aretz* on October 8, 2004:

> The significance is the freezing of the political process. And when you freeze that process you prevent the establishment of a Palestinian state and you prevent a discussion about the refugees, the borders and Jerusalem. Effectively, this whole package that is called the Palestinian state, with all that it entails, has been removed from our agenda indefinitely . . . The disengagement is actually formaldehyde. It supplies the amount of formaldehyde that's necessary so that there will not be a political process with the Palestinians.

The third reason for disengagement had to do with demography. Palestinians have a higher birth rate than Israelis and this is perceived as a threat, a "demographic time bomb" as some Israelis call it. To preserve the slim Jewish majority in areas claimed by Israel, the Likud government decided to withdraw unilaterally from Gaza. By withdrawing from Gaza, it removed, or thought it removed, in one stroke, 1.4 million Palestinians from the overall demographic equation. Sharon claimed that by withdrawing from Gaza, his government was making a contribution toward peace with the Palestinians. But this was a unilateral Israeli move undertaken solely in what was considered to be the Israeli national interest. The nature of the move was revealed by its official name: "the unilateral disengagement from Gaza." Disengagement from Gaza was not the prelude to further withdrawals from the West Bank and it most emphatically was not a contribution to peace. The houses that were abandoned in Gaza were demolished by bulldozers in what amounted to a scorched earth policy. The controlling consideration behind the move was to divert resources from Gaza in order to safeguard and consolidate the more significant Israeli settlements in the West Bank.

In the year after withdrawing its 8,000 settlers from Gaza, the Likud government introduced 12,000 new settlers into the West Bank. Today, there are over 700,000 settlers in the West Bank, including East Jerusalem. The 2005 move was not coordinated with the Palestinian Authority (PA). The long-term aim of the Sharon government was to redraw *unilaterally* the borders of Greater Israel. One step in this overall strategy was the disengagement from Gaza. The other step was the building of the so-called security barrier on the West Bank. The security barrier was in fact as much about land-grabbing as it was about security. It was said to be a temporary security measure, but it was intended to delineate the final borders of Greater Israel.

The two moves were anchored in a fundamental rejection of Palestinian national rights. They reflected a determination to prevent the Palestinians from ever achieving independence on their own land. Denying access between the Gaza Strip and the West Bank was a means of obstructing a unified Palestinian struggle for independence. At the tactical level, withdrawing from Gaza enabled the Israeli Air Force to bomb the territory at will, something they could not do when Israeli settlers lived there.

Following the Israeli withdrawal from Gaza, Hamas moderated its program and turned to the ballot box as the road to power. Its 1988 Charter was antisemitic and called for a unitary Islamic state from the Jordan River to the Mediterranean Sea. But in its platform for the January 2006 elections, it tacitly accepted Israel's existence and lowered its sights to an independent Palestinian state along the 1967 lines. However, Hamas did not agree to sign a formal peace treaty with Israel, and it insisted on the right of return of the 1948 refugees, widely seen as a codeword for dismantling Israel as a Jewish state. Hamas won a clear victory in a fair and free election not just in Gaza, but in the West Bank as well. Having won an absolute majority of seats in the Palestinian Legislative Council, Hamas proceeded to form a government in accordance with customary democratic procedure. The Hamas victory came as an unpleasant surprise for Israel and its Western supporters. Israel refused to recognize the new government and resorted to economic warfare to undermine it. The United States (US) and European Union, to their eternal shame, followed Israel's example in refusing to recognize the democratically elected government and joined Israel in economic warfare to undermine it.

This is just one example, one example among many, of Western hypocrisy on Israel-Palestine. The Western leaders claim that they believe in democracy and that their objective around the world is democracy-promotion. They invaded Iraq in 2003 in the name of democracy and ended up by destroying the country and causing hundreds of thousands of casualties. The Western military interventions in Afghanistan, Syria, and Libya also used democracy as a camouflage for imperial ambitions and all of them ended in dismal failure. Democracy needs to be built by the people from the ground up; it cannot be imposed by a foreign army from the barrel of a tank.

Palestine was a shining example of democracy in action. With the possible exception of Lebanon, it was the only genuine as opposed to sham democracy in the Arab world. Under the incredibly difficult conditions imposed by coercive military occupation, the Palestinians succeeded in building a democratic political system. The Palestinian people had spoken, but Israel and its Western allies refused to recognize the result of the election because the people had voted for the "wrong" party.

In March 2007, Hamas formed a national unity government with Fatah, the mainstream party that came second in the ballot box. It was a moderate government which consisted mainly of technocrats rather than politicians. Hamas invited its coalition partner to negotiate with Israel a long-term *hudna*, or truce. Much more significant than the offer of a long-term hudna was Hamas's acceptance of a two-state settlement (with the implicit de facto recognition of Israel). This acceptance was already hinted at in the Cairo Declaration of 2005, the "Prisoners' Document" of 2006, and the Mecca Accord between Hamas and Fatah of 2007. Hamas all but explicitly endorsed a two-state settlement and, as the then UN Middle East Envoy Álvaro de Soto observed, it could have evolved further—if only its overtures had not met with flat dismissal and rejection from Israel and its allies. Nevertheless, Hamas leaders continued to make it clear, in countless subsequent statements, that they would accept a Palestinian state based on the 1967 borders.

Not content with dismissing Hamas's call for a hudna and its offer of negotiations for a two-state settlement, Israel entered into a plot to topple the national unity government and to oust Hamas from power. In 2008, a leak of memos from the Israel-Palestinian Authority negotiations showed that Israel and the US armed and trained the security forces of President Mahmoud Abbas with the aim of overthrowing the unity government. Later, the "Palestine Papers," a cache of 1,600 diplomatic documents leaked to Al Jazeera, provided more details. They revealed that a secret committee was formed called the Gaza Security Committee. It had four members: Israel, the United States, Fatah, and Egyptian intelligence. The aim of this committee was to isolate and weaken Hamas and to help Fatah stage a coup in order to recapture power.

Hamas decided to pre-empt the Fatah coup. It seized power violently in Gaza in June 2007. Since then, the two branches of the Palestinian national movement have been divided with Hamas ruling over the Gaza Strip from Gaza City and the Palestinian Authority, dominated by Fatah, governing the West Bank from Ramallah. The Palestinian Authority, funded mainly by the European Union and to a lesser extent by the United States, functions essentially as a sub-contractor for Israeli security. It is corrupt, incompetent, and impotent. As a result, it enjoys little legitimacy in the West Bank and even less in the Gaza Strip.

Israel's response to the Hamas seizure of power was to intensify a blockade on Gaza. The US, United Kingdom (UK), and other European allies participated in this cruel blockade. The blockade has now been in force for seventeen years. It inflicts daily hardship on the inhabitants of the Strip. It involves Israeli control not only of the imports but also of all exports from Gaza, including agricultural goods. The blockade of Gaza is not only cruel and inhumane but plainly illegal. A blockade is a form of collective punishment which is explicitly proscribed by international law. And yet the international community has totally failed to hold Israel to account for this and the rest of its illegal actions. Israel denies that it is an occupying power of the Gaza Strip. However, the UN, the International Committee of the Red Cross (ICRC), Amnesty International, and Human Rights Watch have all concluded that Israel remains in "effective occupation" despite its physical withdrawal because it continues to control access to the territory by land, sea, and air.

Having been denied the fruits of its electoral victory, Hamas resorted to the weapon of the weak, to what Israel calls terrorism, and this took the form of rocket attacks from Gaza on southern Israel. The IDF retaliated by bombing Gaza; a tit-for-tat ensued and the inevitable escalation of hostilities. In June 2008, Egypt brokered a ceasefire between Israel and Hamas. The ceasefire worked remarkably well. In the six months before June, the average number of rockets fired on Israel was 179. In the following months, the average fell to three rockets a month. On November 4, 2008, the IDF launched a raid into Gaza, killed six Hamas fighters, and killed the ceasefire, leading to an immediate resumption of hostilities. Hamas offered to renew the ceasefire on its original terms, which included the easing of the blockade. Israel refused the offer and prepared to renew the fight. In general, Hamas has a much better record than Israel of observing ceasefires.

Israel launched its first major military offensive in Gaza on December 27, 2008, naming it Operation Cast Lead. The reason given for the attack was self-defense. Israel, like any other country, it was claimed, has the right to defend itself and to protect its citizens. In other words, Israel claimed the right to self-defense against the people it occupied and oppressed. However, if all Israel wanted was to protect its citizens, it did not have to resort to force. All it had to do was to follow Hamas's good example and observe the ceasefire. Israel repeatedly invokes its right to self-defense but under international law self-defense does not apply if you are an illegal military occupier.

Operation Cast Lead was also the first major Israeli assault on the people of Gaza, and I use the words "people of Gaza" deliberately. Israel claims that Hamas uses civilians as human shields and that this makes them legitimate military targets. In a crowded enclave, however, it is inevitable that some Hamas command centers, tunnels, and weapons stores are located near civilian buildings. That is not the same as using civilians as human shields. Many of the Israeli claims that Hamas uses schools, hospitals, mosques, and UNRWA buildings as cover for its operations have turned out to be untrue. On the other hand, the claim that the IDF goes to great lengths to avoid hurting innocent civilians is flatly contradicted by the evidence. Its offensive inflicted very heavy casualties and massive damage to the civilian infrastructure. It established a pattern of regular incursions to hit Hamas, incursions that invariably rain down death and destruction on the civilian population.

The United Nations Human Rights Council appointed a commission of inquiry into Operation Cast Lead. It was headed by the eminent South African Judge Richard Goldstone. The Goldstone team noted that both sides were guilty of war crimes but reserved its severest criticisms for Israel because of the scale and seriousness of its war crimes. To give just one example, Goldstone and his colleagues found seven incidents in which Israeli soldiers shot civilians leaving their homes, holding a white flag.

The conclusion of the report was that the attacks in 2008–2009 were directed, at least in part, at the people of Gaza as a whole. It was "a deliberately disproportionate attack designed to punish, humiliate, and terrorize a civilian population." During the second Lebanon war of 2006 the IDF chief of general staff Gadi Eizenkot enunciated a policy of deliberately harming enemy civilians which became known as the "Dahiya Doctrine." The doctrine was named after the Dahiya neighborhood of Beirut, where Hezbollah was headquartered during the war. It encompassed the destruction of civilian infrastructure in order to deny its use to the enemy and it endorsed the use of "disproportionate force" to achieve that end. Israel has repeatedly applied this criminal doctrine in Gaza to devastating humanitarian effect.

Operation Cast Lead was followed by further Israeli attacks on the Gaza Strip in 2012, 2014, 2018, 2021, 2022, and mid-2023. Operation Swords of Iron is the eighth Israeli military offensive in Gaza in fifteen years, and it is by far the most lethal and destructive. After two months of fighting, the Palestinian death toll had risen to at least 17,700, including 7,729 children and 5,153 women, with over 48,700 injured—more than the total of the previous military offensives combined. A further 265 Palestinians were killed on the West Bank by the Israeli military and armed settlers. Nearly 1.9 million people in Gaza, equivalent to 85 percent of a population of 2.3 million, were internally displaced. Heavy IDF bombardment reduced entire neighborhoods to rubble and inflicted catastrophic damage on the civilian infrastructure and economy of Gaza. UN staff who assist the Palestinians were another casualty of this savage Israeli offensive. More than 130 UNRWA teachers, health workers, and aid workers were killed—the highest number in any conflict in the UN's history.

The United Nations Office for the Coordination of Humanitarian Affairs (OCHA) estimated that Israeli attacks destroyed more than 52,000 housing units and damaged more than 253,000. At least 60 percent of Gaza's homes were damaged or destroyed. By November 12, OCHA reported, 279 educational facilities had been damaged, more than 51 percent of the total, with none of Gaza's 625,000 students able to access education. More than half of Gaza's hospitals and nearly two-thirds of primary healthcare centers were out of service and 53 ambulances damaged. All thirteen hospitals in Gaza City and northern Gaza had received evacuation orders from the Israeli military. Water consumption had fallen by 90 percent since the war started. People were queuing for an average of four to six hours to receive half the normal bread ration. Around 390,000 jobs had been lost since the start of the war. Before the war the jobless rate already stood at 46 percent, rising to 70 percent among youth. The socio-economic impact of the war has been nothing short of catastrophic. It is difficult to avoid the conclusion that, as in Operation Cast Lead, Operation Swords of Iron is "a deliberately disproportionate attack designed to punish, humiliate, and terrorize a civilian population."

Israeli generals frequently use the same phrase to describe their recurrent operations in Gaza: "mowing the lawn." What this means is that they have no political solution to the problem of Gaza. So every few years they move in with foot soldiers, tanks, artillery, navy, and aircraft, smash up the place, degrade the military capabilities of Hamas, pulverize the civilian infra- structure, and then go home and leave the political problem completely unresolved.

"Mowing the lawn" is a chilling metaphor because it describes a mechanical action that you do periodically every few years and with no end in sight. Under this template, there is no end to the bloodshed, and the next war is always around the corner. This is not a policy for dealing with Gaza; it is a non-policy. To put it differently, it is an inappropriate military response to what essentially is a political problem.

There is a popular Israeli saying: if force does not work, use more force. This is an asinine idea: if force does not work, it is because it is an unsuitable instrument for dealing with the problem at hand. It can also be counterproductive. Israel's dis- proportionate, excessive use of military force in the past ended up encouraging the rise of Hezbollah in Lebanon and of Hamas in the Gaza Strip. Israel's policy of assassinating Hamas leaders with the aim of decapitating the organization has never worked. The dead leaders are quickly replaced by younger leaders who are usually more militant.

The government formed by Benjamin Netanyahu at the end of 2022 was the most radical, right-wing, xenophobic, expan- sionist, overtly racist, and the most incompetent government in Israel's history. It was also the most explicitly pro-settler, Jewish supremacist government. The policy guidelines of this government assert that "the Jewish people have an exclusive and inalienable right to all parts of the Land of Israel." In other words, only Jews have a right to the whole Land of Israel which includes the West Bank. Palestinians have no national rights. This extreme and uncompromising position makes bloodshed inevitable because it leaves the Palestinians no peaceful avenue for realizing their right to national self-determination.

After October 7, Israel announced a new war aim, namely, to eliminate Hamas altogether as a political and military force. Israeli leaders began to speak of "dismantling Hamas once and for all" or "eradicating" Hamas. To anyone familiar with the history of Israel-Gaza relations, this aim comes as a surprise. It definitely represents an abrupt reversal of Netanyahu's previous policy. Whereas some Israeli leaders prefer having a unified collaborator PA administration in Gaza and the West Bank, Netanyahu was content with the status quo of different regimes in Gaza and the West Bank. Here is what he reportedly said to his Likud colleagues in March 2019: "Anyone who wants to thwart the establishment of a Palestinian state has to support bolstering Hamas and transferring money to Hamas . . . This is part of our strategy—to isolate the Palestinians in Gaza from the Palestinians in the West Bank."

On October 7, the cynical policy of Netanyahu, of preserving the status quo in the occupied territories by a tactic of divide and rule, collapsed spectacularly. His policy was to keep the Palestinian Authority weak, to allow Israel a free hand to do whatever it liked on the West Bank, and to keep the Palestinians in Gaza cooped up in the open-air prison. It was a policy of containment that ultimately failed to contain.

On October 7, the inmates broke out of the prison. In the words of Norman Finkelstein, the breakout was akin to a slave rebellion. Fighters of Hamas and Islamic Jihad broke down the fence and went on a killing spree in southern Israel. First, they attacked a military base, then kibbutzim and settlements around the borders of Gaza. They killed about 350 soldiers, more than 800 civilians, and the carnage was accompanied by terrible atrocities. They also took 250 hostages, both soldiers and civilians. This was a game-changer: the first time Hamas conducted a large-scale attack by land inside Israel. It was a horrific and totally unexpected attack that traumatized the whole of Israeli society.

On the Israeli side, this was more than an intelligence failure; it was a policy failure of the highest magnitude. For years Netanyahu had been saying to the Israeli public that the Palestinians are finished, that they are defeated, that Israelis can do whatever they like on the West Bank, that they can forget Gaza, and achieve peace with the Arab states without making any concessions to the Palestinians.

The 2020–2021 Abraham Accords between Israel and Bahrain, the United Arab Emirates (UAE), Morocco, and Sudan seemed to vindicate Netanyahu. They yielded what he wanted: peace for peace without Israel having to make any concessions on the Palestinian issue. The Accords were a betrayal of the collective Arab position on the Palestinian issue. This position was adopted by the Arab League summit in Beirut in March 2002, and it became known as the Arab Peace Initiative. It offered Israel peace and normalization with all twenty-two members of the Arab League in return for agreeing to an independent Palestinian state along the 1967 lines with a capital city in East Jerusalem. Israel ignored the offer. The Abraham Accords amounted to a very different kind of deal for Israel and a stab in the back to the Palestinian national movement. They were sponsored by the United States as part of a misguided policy of promoting stability in the Middle East by cooperating with authoritarian Arab regimes and Israel while bypassing the Palestinians.

The Hamas attack announced loud and clear that the Palestinian issue is not dead and that Palestinian resistance to the Israeli occupation is far from over. One of its aims was to deter Saudi Arabia from concluding a peace treaty with Israel. Under strong American pressure, Saudi Arabia came very close to signing an Abraham Accord with Israel. In the Arab world, as in the West, there is a disconnect between the governments and the people on Israel-Palestine. The governments value their relationship with America and Israel; the Arab street remains strongly pro-Palestinian regardless of the shifting geopolitics of the region. The Hamas attack, by rekindling popular support for the Palestinian cause throughout the Arab and Islamic worlds, forced the Saudis to think again.

The October 7 attack also highlighted the contrast between the craven subservience of the PA to Israel and America and the Islamic resistance to the occupation spearheaded by Hamas. The PA had been totally ineffective in protecting the people of the West Bank against Israeli land grabs, ethnic cleansing, escalating settler violence, and ever-increasing provocations in and around the al-Aqsa mosque in the Old City of Jerusalem, one of the three holiest sites of Islam alongside Mecca and Medina. Al-Aqsa is of the greatest importance to Muslims as a religious symbol and this is precisely why the encroachment by the Netanyahu government and its Jewish fundamentalist followers is so incendiary. By its attack on October 7, Hamas signaled to Israel that these provocations will no longer be tolerated. It was for this reason too that the operation was named the Al-Aqsa Deluge. All in all, it was a powerful assertion of Palestinian agency and leadership in the ongoing struggle against the Israeli occupation.

The Hamas attack left Netanyahu's entire policy in tatters, and he will probably pay the political price for the intelligence and security failures. Before October 7 there was massive protest in Israel against his plan for judicial overhaul. The protest did not cease altogether following the Hamas attack but the situation in Gaza became the dominant issue. It did not take long for families of the hostages to start a vigil outside the prime minister's residence in Jerusalem. After the dust settles, all the anger will be redirected at Netanyahu. In the face of mounting international calls for an immediate ceasefire, he remains defiant. He knows that once the war against Hamas comes to an end, his days in office will be numbered. Politically speaking, Netanyahu looks like a dead man walking.

What is clear is that Netanyahu's new policy of eradicating Hamas has no chance of succeeding. Hamas has a military wing, the Izz ad-Din al-Qassam Brigades, which commits terrorist acts when it targets Israeli civilians. Even if all its commanders were killed, they would be quickly replaced by new recruits and more militant ones. But Hamas is also a political party with institutions and a social movement with many branches such as a women's association and a students' association. It is part of the fabric of Palestinian society. What is more: Hamas is a set of ideas, including the idea of freedom and self-determination for the Palestinian people. Military force can decimate an organization, but it cannot kill an idea.

With characteristic hubris, Netanyahu announced that he was determined to destroy Hamas not only to ensure his own country's security but also to free the people of Gaza from Hamas's tyranny. Israel's indiscriminate use of force, however, does not weaken Hamas; it strengthens it. By relying on brute military force alone, Israel weakens those Palestinian leaders who advocate for negotiations and believe that Palestinians need only behave nicely for the world to sit up and listen. Nor is Hamas identical to ISIS, as Netanyahu and an ever-increasing number of his ministers keep claiming. ISIS is a jihadist organization with a nihilist global agenda. Hamas, by contrast, is a regional organization with a limited and legitimate political agenda.

On June 2, 1948, Sir John Troutbeck, a senior official in the Foreign Office, wrote a memo to Foreign Secretary Ernest Bevin. He complained that by their support for the creation of Israel, the Americans helped to create a "gangster state with a thoroughly unscrupulous set of leaders." Whether Israel behaves like a gangster state is open to debate, but Netanyahu is without doubt a thoroughly unscrupulous leader. As he directed Israel's 2023 assault on Gaza, Netanyahu was also on trial for three serious corruption charges, and he knew that if convicted, he might end up in prison. The imperative of personal political survival helped to shape his conduct of the war.

Yet Netanyahu's motives for prolonging the war in Gaza went deeper than self-preservation. His life's mission has been to defeat the Palestinian national movement and to prevent the emergence of an independent Palestinian State alongside Israel. He grew up in a fiercely nationalistic Jewish home. His father, Benzion Netanyahu, was the political secretary of Ze'ev Jabotinsky, the spiritual father of the Israeli Right and the chief architect of the strategy of the "iron wall." In 1923, Jabotinsky published an article under the title "On the Iron Wall (We and the Arabs)." In it he argued that the Zionist goal of an independent Jewish state in Palestine could only be achieved unilaterally and by military force. A Jewish state could only be established not by negotiations with the Arabs of Palestine but behind an iron wall of Jewish military power. The essence of the strategy was negotiations from strength. Once the Arabs gave up hope of defeating the Jews on the battlefield, then would come the time for stage two, for negotiating with them about their status and rights in Palestine. Israeli prime minister Yitzhak Rabin moved from stage one to stage two of the strategy by signing the

Oslo Accord with the PLO in 1993 though he never conceded any Palestinian national rights.

Netanyahu came to power in 1996, following the assassination of Rabin, with the explicit mission of subverting the Oslo Accords and preventing the establishment of a Palestinian state. He was fixated on the first part of the iron wall strategy, on accumulating more and more military power, and avoiding stage two, negotiations of any kind. Until October 7, his strategy was to drive a firm wedge between Gaza and the West Bank and to allow a weak Hamas to govern Gaza. After October 7, he was determined to destroy Hamas but without allowing the PA to extend its writ to Gaza because that would strengthen the case for a two-state solution. This amounted to a crude version of Jabotinsky's strategy, using Jewish military power not to resolve the conflict but to keep the Palestinians in the West Bank and Gaza in a permanent state of subordination to a Jewish supremacist state. Netanyahu's declared aim is to ensure security for Israel for the long-term. His undeclared aim is to end forever the prospect of Palestinian independence.

One disturbing aspect of the Israeli response to the horrific Hamas attack is the dehumanizing of the Palestinian people. This is nothing new. On one occasion, Netanyahu famously suggested that it was Haj Amin al-Husseini, the leader of the Palestinian National Movement, who suggested to Hitler that instead of expelling the Jews from Germany, he should exterminate them. One of Netanyahu's most often repeated, and most morally repugnant, claims is that Palestinian nationalism is a direct continuation of Nazi antisemitism.

Today, many Israeli ministers depict the Palestinians as Nazis. Yoav Galant, the defense minister, referred to the enemy as "human animals," and used this view to justify the inhuman siege that he imposed, the cutting off of electricity, food, water, and fuel to 2.3 million people. Particularly chilling in its cruelty, given the huge number of children killed, was the statement by Israeli president Isaac Herzog that the "entire nation" of Gaza "is responsible." Dehumanizing an entire people can have serious political consequences even if they are unintended. The Nazi dehumanization of the Jews was a major factor in paving the way for the death camps. Israeli demonization of the Palestinians is a similarly dangerous dynamic that can be used to justify the ethnic cleansing of Gaza.

The Western response to the crisis in Gaza has comprised the usual hypocrisy and brazen double standards, but this time taken to a new level. The Western love of Israel has always been accompanied by the denial of Palestinian history and humanity. Deep concern for Israel's security is reiterated all the time by all Western leaders, but no thought is spared for Palestinian security, let alone Palestinian rights. Evidently, the Palestinians are the children of a lesser God.

In the immediate aftermath of the Hamas attack, Western leaders undertook a pilgrimage to Jerusalem to demonstrate that they are standing by Israel. Palestinian resistance to the occupation, the most prolonged and brutal military occupation of modern times, has been decontextualized and de-historicized. The Palestinians are engaged in an anti-colonial struggle, possibly the last anti-colonial struggle in today's world. But their struggle is widely attributed by Western commentators to religious fanaticism and irrational hatred of Jews rather than to the normal, universal desire of all people to live in freedom and dignity on their land.

The Western stand with Israel carries an echo of the habitual colonial tendency to treat struggles for national liberation as proof of the savagery, barbarism, and terrorism of the indigenous population. This is how the "civilized world" responded to the liberation struggles of South Africans, Algerians, Kenyans, and Vietnamese. And this is how some Western leaders look upon Palestinian resistance today.

The US and UK have given Israel not only moral but material and military support as well as diplomatic protection. President Joe Biden said that the attack of October 7 was the worst attack on the Jewish people since the Holocaust. This is to trivialize the Holocaust. America sent two aircraft carriers to the Eastern Mediterranean and beefed up its forces in Saudi Arabia, Iraq, and Jordan. By shielding Israel from Hezbollah and Iran, the US enabled Israel to carry on with the mass slaughter in Gaza. In effect, America and Britain gave Israel warrant to pursue its war on Gaza despite the humanitarian catastrophe it caused. They called for "humanitarian pauses" when what was desperately needed was a complete ceasefire. The seven-day pause in the fighting made it possible to send some humanitarian aid into Gaza and for the freeing by Hamas of some of the hostages in return for the release of three times the number of Palestinians from Israeli prisons. But as soon as the pause expired, on December 1, the IDF intensified the bombardment, killing 700 people in one day and exacerbating the utterly horrendous humanitarian crisis.

A UAE draft resolution to the Security Council for an immediate humanitarian ceasefire was defeated by an American veto on December 8, although it had the support of thirteen members with only the UK abstaining. Since 1948, the US has used its veto thirty-four times to defeat resolutions critical of Israel. The majority of these resolutions were drafted to provide a framework for resolving the Israel-Palestine conflict. The veto of the UAE draft resolution was widely denounced, especially in the global south, as tantamount to a free pass for Israel to continue the butchery and destruction of Gaza.

In his October 28 address to the nation, Netanyahu said that Israelis were fighting their second war of independence. This is preposterous: no one is threatening Israel's independence or existence today. It is Israel which is denying freedom and independence to the Palestinians. The statement may also have carried a veiled threat. In 1948 what Israelis call their "War of Independence" was accompanied by the Nakba, the catastrophe, the ethnic cleansing of Palestine. There have been ample signs that the Netanyahu government is in fact actively planning a second Nakba.

A leaked report of Israel's intelligence ministry, dated October 13, outlined three alternatives "to bring about a significant change in the civilian reality in the Gaza Strip in light of the Hamas crimes that led to the 'Iron Swords' war." The alternative deemed by the document's authors to best serve Israeli security involves moving Gaza's civilian population to tent cities in northern Sinai, then building permanent cities and an undefined humanitarian corridor. A security zone would be established inside Israel, on the border with Egypt, to block the displaced Palestinians from entering. The report did not say what would become of Gaza once its population is cleared out. History tells us that once Israel drives Palestinians from their homes, it does not allow them to return. This is what happened in the 1948 war and in the 1967 war and, despite strong Egyptian opposition, it could happen again.

These are not isolated actions but part of a pattern. They all serve the ultimate goal that the Zionist movement had set itself from the start: to build a Jewish state on as large a part of Palestine as possible with as few Arabs within its borders as possible. Operation Swords of Iron marks a new and utterly ruthless step in this direction. As Ahdaf Soueif, the Egyptian-British novelist, observed in the *Guardian* on December 4, 2023, "[w]hat the global south has known for 100 years, the people of the global north are understanding now: that the Zionists want all the land, with no Palestinian people, and will stop at nothing to get it."

In 1876, Liberal opposition leader William Gladstone published a pamphlet denouncing atrocities committed by soldiers of the Ottoman Empire against civilians in Bulgaria. Gladstone's indictment seared itself in my memory since I was an eighteen-year-old schoolboy in London doing A-level British History. The key passage went as follows: "Let the Turks now carry away their abuses in the only possible manner, namely by carrying off themselves. Their Zaphtiehs and their Mudirs, their Bimbashis and their Yuzbachis, their Kaimakams and their Pashas, one and all, bag and baggage, shall, I hope, clear out from the province they have desolated and profaned." This is rather how I feel about the atrocities perpetrated by the IDF in the Gaza province today.

"You wanted hell— you will get hell"

—Israeli Coordinator of Government in the Territories Major General Ghassan Alian

2

Econocide in Gaza

Sara Roy

On November 14, 2023, several weeks after the start of the horrifying conflict in Gaza, a colleague received this message from a friend of hers who lives in Rafah in the southern Gaza Strip: "There is really no water or bread. It has stopped completely due to the lack of fuel. We are now in famine and there is no drinking water or salt water. If it continues for 3 days, we will actually die." Two days later, on November 16, the World Food Programme reported:

> Supplies of food and water are practically non-existent in Gaza and only a fraction of what is needed is arriving through the borders. With winter fast approaching, unsafe and overcrowded shelters, and the lack of clean water, civilians are facing the immediate possibility of starvation . . . There is no way to meet current hunger needs with one operational border crossing . . . Fuel shortages have triggered a crippling halt in bread production across all 130 bakeries in Gaza. Bread, a staple food for people in Gaza, is scarce or non-existent . . . The

Sara Roy is an associate of the Center for Middle Eastern Studies at Harvard University. Her most recent book is *Unsilencing Gaza: Reflections on Resistance* (Pluto Press, 2021).

food infrastructure in Gaza is no longer functional . . . Local
markets have shut down completely . . . [L]ife in Gaza [is at]
a standstill . . . People are going hungry.[1]

After nearly forty years of engagement with Palestinian-
Israeli crisis, studying the impact of the occupation on Gaza's
economy and society, I am not altogether surprised by the catastrophic events described above. That Gaza now finds itself
devastated and dismembered, with the majority of its population internally displaced, on the verge of starvation and
expulsion, is the deadliest expression to date of longstanding
Israeli policies of separation, isolation, and closure. I have
examined these policies in great detail in my writings, ana-
lyzing how they deliberately aimed to weaken, undermine,
and hollow out Gaza's economy over time. This gave rise to
my concept of de-development, which, simply put, deprives
the economy of its productive capacity and any possibility of
meaningful structural growth. In effect, de-development describes the systematic dismantling of a normal economy and
its rational functioning.

A crucial point in the trajectory of Israeli policy was the
imposition of a total economic blockade (or siege) of Gaza
by land, sea, and air. The blockade effectively began following Hamas's victory in the Palestinian legislative elections in
January 2006 and was tightened after Hamas's takeover of the
Gaza Strip in June 2007. In the seventeen years since it was
imposed, the blockade has proven to be the single most damaging measure affecting Gaza's economy and society. The impact
has been devastating. With the blockade the logical endpoint
of de-development was arguably reached: an economy internally disabled, unable to function without external sources of
support. According to a confidential document produced by an
international organization in 2015,

> Gaza has not been a functioning economy since 2007. Without external aid there simply would not be a functioning economy in Gaza, and public or other basic services would not be provided to the population.

In this way, the blockade starkly revealed a reality, long obscured, that had characterized Gaza's economy since 1967 when the occupation began: Gaza's was never a normal economy, and was never allowed to be.

The blockade, like other Israeli measures, must be understood not as a singular, decontextualized event imposed in response to other precipitating and decontextualized events—but as part of a policy framework that long preceded its implementation. In fact, the blockade, which is really an intensified military closure, was consistent with, and a more acute expression of, Israel's separation and closure policy in Gaza that began in 1991 and was formalized in 1993. Gaza has been under a form of closure—restricting and periodically prohibiting trade and the movement of Gaza's labor force and general population—for over three decades, a structure that has never been lifted. All that has changed in the period since it was imposed is the closure's intensity.

The total siege of Gaza that was imposed following the horrifying murders of Israelis by Hamas militants on October 7, 2023, was part of that same policy continuum of separation and closure—clearly, its most extreme and pernicious form—characterized by the destruction of Gaza's infrastructure (especially housing) and the denial of food, water, electricity, and fuel to its population. This speaks to a process which I term *econocide*: the wholesale destruction of an economy and its constituent parts, particularly a clearly defined economic identity and an organized and functioning economic community.[2] It is the logical extension of de-development—destruction. Without doubt, Gaza's economy has been destroyed.

The Gaza blockade in context: A policy trajectory
Although it is not possible here to detail the long and painful
history of the past decades and the various political and economic policies that emerged therein, certain points are critical
to an understanding of the Gaza blockade.[3]

—De-development and the "peace process"
Often lost from view is the reality of occupation—which now
spans three quarters of Israel's entire history—as the primary
factor defining (and delimiting) Gaza's tragic situation. The
Oslo "peace process" of the 1990s enabled Israel to claim that
it was mitigating if not ending the occupation. (It is worth noting that the term "occupation" appears nowhere in any of the
Oslo agreements, which also fail to acknowledge Israel as an
occupying power.) In fact, the Oslo process was doing the exact
opposite: deepening Israel's control of the territories through a
variety of policies—including territorial fragmentation and the
large-scale expropriation of Arab land and other resources—
intended to ensure Israel's continued presence and preclude the
establishment of a Palestinian state. In this way, the historical
contest over territory was replaced by a policy of separation,
isolation, and containment. Israeli policy now goes well beyond
occupation to total annexation of the West Bank and almost
total ruination in Gaza.

The political and economic illusions created by the Oslo
process and negotiation framework—supported by a com-
pliant Palestinian Authority (PA) and donor community—
led to a range of economic programs and initiatives promoting "economic peace" under occupation. By conflating
freedom with free trade, economic peace as conceived by
Oslo's architects held that economic change must precede
political change, creating a context conducive to future political compromise. In other words, the "economic returns of

cooperation will outweigh the benefits of resistance," or, as Israeli prime minister Benjamin Netanyahu explained in November 2009, "development does not solve problems, it mitigates them and makes them more accessible for solution and creates a stronger political base." In effect, this policy saw any form of economic improvement as an alternative to ending the occupation and the dispossession that accompanies it. The persistence of this failed approach could be seen in US secretary of state John Kerry's 2013 attempt to restart Israeli-Palestinian peace negotiations by "promot[ing] economic development and . . . remov[ing] some of the bottlenecks and barriers that exist with respect to commerce in the West Bank." In this way, he said, economic growth "will help us be able to provide a climate . . . an atmosphere, within which people have greater confidence about moving forward."

Yet the economic peace approach did not fundamentally differ from Israeli policies dating back to the early years of occupation. These policies aimed to extinguish Palestinian political demands and aspirations through limited economic gains under an occupation that continued to extract Palestinian resources. Oslo was simply a more sophisticated expression of this deception. Some of the industrial estates, infrastructural change, trade, and institutional development that attended the Oslo process did deliver limited change and transient periods of economic growth. But they could not be sustained given the (structural) context of increasingly oppressive Israeli control, restrictions (notably a strengthened closure regime), and assault.

The damage wrought by the Oslo "peace process" was profound, and perhaps nowhere more striking than in Gaza. Throughout my near four decades of research on the Gaza Strip, I have encountered two recurring themes. The first is Israel's desire to rid itself of any responsibility for Gaza while retaining control of it—a clear outcome, if not a goal, of the Oslo process. Continued control is essential since, as the late Tanya Reinhardt argued, Israel cannot free Gaza if it wants to rule the West Bank, its principal objective. This is because a free Gaza would be able to establish direct ties with the Arab (and possibly Western) world and become, once again, a center of resistance to Israeli occupation. By extension, in destroying Gaza, as it is doing at present, Israel believes it is eliminating any resistance to its annexation of the West Bank.

The second theme centers on Israel's desire to "exchange" Gaza, as it were, for full and internationally (i.e., American) sanctioned control of the West Bank, something, arguably, Israel achieved after October 7. This would prevent the creation of a Palestinian state and secure Israel's continued occupation. This increasingly evident goal, institutionalized during the Oslo period and shared by successive Israeli governments throughout the second intifada, involved an encircled, noncontiguous, and fragmented Palestinian entity under Israeli control on less than half the West Bank, with the remaining majority effectively annexed. A critical feature of the policy was the isolation, encirclement, and weakening of the Gaza Strip, which would similarly remain under Israeli dominance. Basically, the objective was to eliminate Palestinian control over the whole of the West Bank and East Jerusalem and sever most ties between these areas and Gaza. In order to implement this reality, Israel needed to attenuate Palestinian demands and to create a malleable leadership willing to accept such an outcome. It attempted to do this primarily by economic cooptation in the West Bank and, in the Gaza Strip, by economic deprivation, demographic isolation, and physical as well as institutional destruction.

—Gaza "disengagement"

A critical turning point for the conflict generally and Gaza specifically came in 2005 with then Israeli prime minister Ariel Sharon's so-called disengagement from the Gaza Strip. This involved the redeployment of the Israeli army outside Gaza's borders and the evacuation of all Israeli settlements, even as Israel maintained complete and direct control over Gaza's borders, airspace, water, and maritime access. This policy laid the framework for a new unilateral approach and exposed the "peace" negotiations as a means of buying time to entrench Israeli occupation rather than a sincere attempt to end it. In a now famous October 2004 interview with Israeli newspaper *Ha'aretz*, Sharon's close advisor Dov Weissglas, who handled some of the negotiations, explained the rationale behind the Gaza disengagement:

> I found a device . . . to ensure that there will be no stopwatch here. That there will be no timetable to implement the settlers' nightmare. I have postponed the nightmare indefinitely. Because what I effectively agreed to with the Americans was that part of the settlements would not be dealt with at all, and the rest will not be dealt with until the Palestinians turn into Finns. . . . The significance is the freezing of the political process. And when you freeze that process you prevent the establishment of a Palestinian state and you prevent a discussion about refugees, the borders, and Jerusalem. Effectively, this whole package that is called the Palestinian state, with all that it entails, has been removed from our agenda indefinitely. And all this with authority and permission. All with a presidential blessing and the ratification of both houses of Congress.

In a 2006 meeting with a high-level Israeli official who played a key role in designing the Gaza disengagement plan, a colleague of mine was told the following: "The next two years will be crucial for Israel. Our goals are very clear—more settlements in the West Bank and the increased cantonization of the West Bank. We want to see three major cantons in the West Bank and the fourth will be Gaza." These goals were subsequently achieved.

Israel's 2005 disengagement from the Gaza Strip effectively completed the implementation of Oslo's 1994 Gaza and Jericho First plan, which also aimed to turn Gaza into an imprisoned and diminished canton (in the guise of the envisioned provisional Palestinian state) and isolate it from the West Bank. This in turn freed Israel to pursue, in one form or another, its de facto annexation of the West Bank, which it has largely accomplished in the two decades since the first Oslo accord was signed. Shlomo Ben-Ami, a former Israeli foreign minister, put it this way: "To believe that we ended the occupation in Gaza while still occupying the West Bank is to assume that Gaza is not part of a Palestinian entity." It is precisely this assumption that has long informed Israeli policy toward Gaza, especially after 2005.

The Gaza disengagement plan should thus be understood as part of the continuum that began at least with the Oslo process and arguably with earlier government initiatives. The core goals were the same: to internally divide, separate, and isolate the Palestinians—demographically, economically, and politically—so as to ensure Israel's full control—both direct (West Bank) and indirect (Gaza Strip)—over *all* Palestinian lands and resources. The ultimate goal is to safeguard a Jewish majority in an expanded Israel and to preclude any political process (and any diplomatic pressure to initiate that process) that would result in the establishment of a Palestinian state.

Indeed, the disengagement plan, by formally separating the territories into two entities each with a separate status, divided the Palestinian people, separated families, and made it difficult if not impossible for Gazans to access a range of services, including health and education. By destroying the national collective and with it, political unity, separation further diminished organized resistance to the occupation regime. Separation also removed the geographical basis of a national economy, denied people access to all of their lands, prevented them from exploiting their natural resources, and severed the Palestinian economy from the global one. It also impeded institution-building and other developmental processes and was an important factor facilitating Israel's many attacks on Gaza. This is why, in practice, the evacuation of Gaza's Israeli settlements and the subsequent "restoration" of nearly one-third of the Strip's land to Palestinian use had no meaningful impact on the local economy.

As the historical center of political resistance and a dynamic source of conflict, Gaza represents a political challenge and threat that goes well beyond—and long precedes—the establishment of Hamas. Israel understood this, which is why Gaza was sealed and cut off from the West Bank in 2005 and a more devastating blockade was imposed the following year.

Paradigm shifts

The lack of territorial contiguity between Gaza and the West Bank, the geographic distance between them, and the absence of any "safe passage" are what make Gaza's total separation and isolation possible. The severing of Gaza reflects just one of several critical paradigm shifts that emerged over the last three decades. These shifts profoundly changed the way the Israeli-Palestinian conflict is understood, with crucial consequences for both territories. With regard to Gaza, these transformational shifts accelerated its de-development, unviability, and now desolation.

Gaza's isolation, which came to define the post-Oslo status quo, itself derives from another defining paradigm shift: the steady, seamless normalization of the occupation over the last three decades—the way it has come to be seen as natural, manageable, and routine, and has been largely acceded to by key international actors.

Indeed, in the more than three decades since the Oslo agreements were signed, it became clear that the occupation was not going to be stopped. If the occupation has changed over time, it is in the extent of its expansion and the tightening of its grip. The most obvious indication of its entrenchment is the relentless growth of Israeli settlements and of their infrastructure (including a settlement road network from which Palestinians are effectively barred). Many if not most Israelis, largely untouched by the everyday realities of the occupation, accept—even embrace—a status quo seen as stable and permanent (although this may be changing after October 7). In this way, peace and occupation stopped being viewed as incompatible. On the contrary, peace could be achieved in the presence of occupation, which some even saw as necessary for achieving peace. As Alon Liel, Israel's former ambassador to South Africa, stated over ten years ago:

> It seems that we Israelis have come to the conclusion that we no longer need peace. Behind the separation wall and with the army's might, we are more or less safe without peace. The economy is growing, and Tel Aviv is booming. The occupation is not a source of great moral discomfort to us. Except for the minority which does combat military service, the military oppression of Palestinians is out of sight and out of mind for the average Israeli. Many of us tend to believe that the conflict can be managed forever and Israel no longer has a "Palestine problem."

This normalization of the occupation assumes a different but extremely compelling form in the Gaza Strip. With its 2005 disengagement, Israel claims that it no longer occupies Gaza.

The claim is patently contrary to international law and has never been formally accepted by the international community. In practice, however, Gaza's status as an occupied territory ceased to be a matter of much international concern. Instead, after 2006, the focus of attention shifted to Gaza's enforced isolation, containment, and punishment.

Following Hamas's assumption of power, the Israeli-Palestinian conflict was reshaped to center on Gaza and on Israel's hostile relationship with Hamas. On September 19, 2007, for example, the Israeli government designated Gaza a "hostile territory." The new designation had severe economic implications. It also transformed the way the occupation was perceived: instead of a political and legal issue of international legitimacy, it became a simple border dispute where the rules of war, not of occupation, apply. This represented another critical paradigm shift in the way the Israeli-Palestinian conflict is understood. The new interpretation has been made explicit with regard to Gaza, where Israel affirms that its sole post-disengagement obligations to Gaza's people "are those mandated by the law of armed conflict, which continues to apply, so long as the violent conflict between the Israeli military and armed groups in Gaza continues."

Hence, the Israeli government has explicitly referred to its intensified closure or blockade policy in Gaza as a form of "economic warfare." Aspects of this warfare included Israel's 2007 termination of the customs code (needed for imports into Gaza) and the Israeli-created and controlled buffer zones cutting into Gaza's northern and eastern perimeters, which account for at least 48 percent of Gaza's cultivable land. These measures were intentionally designed to undermine and deplete Gaza's economy and productive capacity as part of Israel's policy to bring down the Hamas regime (and punish Gazans for supporting Hamas) while promoting the PA in the West Bank.

The West came largely to accept Israel's recasting of its relationship with Gaza from one between occupier and occupied to one between warring parties. This has facilitated Israeli attacks on Gaza and rendered illegitimate, or irrelevant, any notion of freedom or democracy for Palestinians. Raji Sourani, an internationally recognized human rights lawyer, and the late Eyad el-Sarraj, a well-known psychiatrist, noted some time ago that "[i]mpunity has become so pervasive and violations of international law so routine, that Israel now feels comfortable admitting publicly that its closure policy targets the civilian population."

The growing obsolescence of occupation as an analytical and legal framework led to another important paradigm shift: from ongoing occupation to outright annexation and imposed sovereignty with regard to the West Bank, and from ongoing occupation to isolation and disablement with regard to Gaza.

The shift in the analytical framework for Gaza from occupied territory to an entity governed by the rules of war had important consequences in terms of Israeli policy toward the Palestinian economy. In the first two decades of occupation, Israel sought to control and dominate the Palestinian economy, shaping it to serve its own interests. Israel's current policy in Gaza, by contrast, attacks the economic structure with the aim of permanently disabling it. In the process, the population is transformed from a people with national, political, and economic rights into a humanitarian problem.

In a November 2008 cable from the US embassy in Tel Aviv released by WikiLeaks, US officials wrote: "As part of their overall embargo plan against Gaza, Israeli officials have confirmed (to US embassy economic officers) on multiple occasions that they intend to keep the Gazan economy on the brink of collapse without quite pushing it over the edge," with the aim of having Gaza's economy "functioning at the lowest level possible consistent with avoiding a humanitarian crisis." Confirming this analysis, the Israeli human rights organization Gisha noted that following Hamas's 2007 takeover of Gaza, the entry of goods into the Strip was limited to a "humanitarian minimum" that included only those goods considered "essential to the survival of the civilian population."

Indeed, senior army officers developed "mathematical formulas to monitor foodstuffs and other basic goods entering the Strip. . . . The formulas used coefficients and a formulation for 'breathing space,' a term used by . . . authorities to refer to the number of days remaining until a certain supply runs out in Gaza, to determine allowed quantities." In other words, the military used these formulas "to determine the quantity and types of food Gaza residents would be allowed to consume."

Given the policy of economic warfare against Gaza, it was but a short step from the goal of Gaza's isolation and disablement to that of its abstraction and deletion, which is being carried out at present. Israeli policy also shifted from addressing the economy in some manner (whether positively or negatively) to dispensing with the concept of an economy altogether. That is, rather than weaken Gaza's economy through punishing closures and other restrictions, as had long been the case, the Israeli government imposed a blockade that treats the economy as totally irrelevant.

Perhaps the most dramatic expression of Gaza's economic nullification was the Israeli Supreme Court's decision in November 2007 to approve fuel cuts to Gaza—deemed permissible since it would not harm the population's "essential humanitarian needs." This was followed in January 2008 by the court's approval of electricity cuts and in May 2008 by a lowering of acceptable levels for fuel and electricity. The court did "not accept the petitioners' argument that 'market forces' should be allowed to play their role in Gaza with regard to fuel consumption." Hence, once the government decides how much fuel it will allow into Gaza, the economy (e.g., market forces) has no role.

The endpoint of Israel's policy continuum as applied to Gaza is the transformation of Palestinians, especially Gazans, into intruders in their own land, without claims, living in submission and dependence in a place where true civilians, let alone innocents, no longer exist. Within this construct, Palestinians are at best reduced to a "humanitarian issue," a demographic presence in impoverished enclaves without economic or political rights and dependent on the "goodwill" of the international community. At worst, they are rendered disposable, a status made manifest in the killing of over 17,700 Palestinians in the weeks following October 7.

Impact of the blockade
In its 2011 report on poverty in Gaza and the West Bank, the World Bank summarized Palestine's reality:

> Following the second intifada of 2000, the Palestinian economy began to resemble no other in the world. Limited say over economic policies and trade, the extent of dependence on Israel and international aid and a regime of internal and external closures has created an economy characterized by extreme fluctuations in growth and employment and an increasing divergence between the two territories: the West Bank a fragmented archipelago; and Gaza an increasingly isolated island.

Although closure has a long history in Gaza dating back to 1991 when it was first imposed, it was made more acute after 2000 with the start of the second intifada. Closure was tightened further after the 2005 disengagement, deepening the separation between the Strip and the West Bank. Another damaging feature was the intermittent closure of the Rafah crossing between Gaza and Egypt to the movement of goods (though not people). Still, it was not until 2006, after Hamas's electoral victory and the escalated conflict between the Israeli military and armed groups in Gaza (triggered by the capture of Israeli soldier Gilad Shalit by Hamas operatives in June 2006), that heightened restrictions were imposed on imports and exports as well as on the movement of people, including Gaza's labor force. With the further intensification of closure after Hamas's takeover of the Strip in June 2007 and the establishment of Hamas's de facto government, Gaza's isolation was complete.

Gaza's small economy has always been heavily dependent on trade with the West Bank and Israel and on employment in Israel. With the comprehensive blockade of 2006–2007, onerous restrictions were imposed particularly on trade. Imports were severely restricted[4] and exports—e.g., agricultural produce, furniture, textiles, and processed food—were almost totally eliminated, which was especially destructive to Gaza's economy. The movement of people was similarly restricted. Normal trade ended completely with Israel's cancellation of the customs code, making the importation of anything (except humanitarian goods) and the export of finished products virtually impossible. By September 2008, the normally restrained World Bank wrote that Gaza had been "starkly transform[ed] from a potential trade route to a walled hub of humanitarian donations." Indeed, the blockade has proved to be most ruinous for Gaza, ending the functioning of the formal economy.

Over the ensuing decade and a half, certain restrictions were eased, particularly on imports and on the movement of Gazan labor into Israel. Nevertheless, the changes introduced and formalized by the draconian blockade catalyzed a new phase of economic decline, which was accelerated by the 2008–2009 assault on Gaza known as Operation Cast Lead, and its many sequels. This decline has been characterized most dramatically by the erosion of Gaza's private sector (spurred by the lack of investment, the inability to acquire needed inputs, and high transaction costs) and already repressed productive base (leading to high levels of unemployment and impoverishment), the termination of all direct transactions between Israeli and Gaza banks (leading to massive cash shortages and other financial constraints further weakening private sector activity and trade), and heightened restrictions on the movement of people between Gaza, the West Bank, and Israel. A 2015 study found that, "[by 2013] the Palestinian economy had been hollowed out." Furthermore,

> the siege, along with three Israeli incursions in five years, have robbed Gaza of its energy and entrepreneurial resources. [By 2014] per capita income [was] lower than it was twenty years ago, having fallen from $1,347 in 1994 to an estimated $1,100 in 2014. With its population unable to move freely between Gaza and the West Bank, or to trade freely, it can only survive through external financial assistance.[5]

Almost ten years later, just prior to October 7, per capita income in Gaza remained below its 1994 level.

While it is beyond the scope of this chapter to detail the blockade's devastating sectoral impact, certain facts are revealing. On the eve of the current conflict, unemployment affected close to 50 percent of Gaza's labor force overall and 62 percent of young people (fifteen to twenty-nine years old). That is to say that "almost every second economically active Gazan [was] out of work," according to the World Labour Organization, a rate that is among the highest in the world. Between 63 and 66 percent of the population suffered from food insecurity (referring to people without access to enough food to meet their minimum dietary needs) and between 75 and 80 percent relied on humanitarian assistance to survive. It is noteworthy that this situation obtained despite the absence of a natural disaster or food shortage. By early November 2023, "multidimensional poverty ha[d] increased" and will no doubt deepen as the conflict continues. By the third week of the war, "nearly all of the Gazan population . . . was estimated to have become multidimensionally poor," meaning that "almost all of the 2.3 million Palestinians residing in the enclave . . . require basic support for survival."[6]

On blockades and barriers and other forms of defeat
Gaza has been under occupation for fifty-six years and subject to increasingly severe trade and mobility restrictions for thirty-two consecutive years. It has been virtually severed from its natural and international markets for eighteen consecutive years, and dependent on external assistance by key donor states for the PA's recurring budget operations (rather than for development) for twenty-three consecutive years.

Long before October 7, 2023, Gaza had been removed as an integral part of Palestine (increasingly excluded from projections for Palestine as a whole), eliminating any possibility of a larger Palestinian economy capable of sustained growth and development—in other words, an economy that could support a sovereign Palestinian state. Without an economy able to stand on its own, any Palestinian state would be "limited to the height of its residential buildings and the depth of its graves," as the deputy mayor of Jerusalem Meron Benvenisti said many years ago, in words now eerily prescient.

Debilitating Gaza's economy is the key to debilitating Palestine's economy—and sovereignty—as a whole. Israel's current war on Gaza, as already stated, has transformed debility into destruction by denying people food, water, electricity, and fuel; razing or damaging over 60 percent of Gaza's housing stock; and internally displacing nearly 85 percent of Gaza's people. Just one month into the conflict, 182,000 jobs were estimated to have been lost in Gaza.[7]

Gaza has long been fenced in, walled off, encircled, and blockaded. A security fence around Gaza was first erected in 1994, completed in 1996, and complemented by a one-kilometer buffer zone inside Gaza meant to prevent Palestinians from approaching the border with Israel undetected. After Israel's 2005 redeployment from Gaza a series of enhanced security barriers were erected. According to *Ha'aretz*:

> Israel invested nearly four billion shekels in building the underground barrier between it and the Gaza Strip . . . This was one of the largest engineering projects in Israeli history and took three and a half years to build. Six cement manufacturing facilities were built along the border just for this purpose. More than two million cubic meters of cement was poured dozens of meters deep in the earth, to the level of the groundwater—enough cement to "to build a road from Israel to Bulgaria," the Defense Ministry said.
>
> Israel managed to defend itself from threats from Gaza, by doing the same thing over and over again. It identified a threat from the sea and erected a barrier. It identified a threat from the ground and erected a barrier. It identified a threat from the air and erected a barrier. It identified a threat from underground and erected a barrier.[8]

Yet, these structures of enclosure, isolation, and concealment could not protect Israelis who, horrifically, lost their lives in the carnage of October 7. The walls meant to protect them also confine them, begging the question, is it possible for Israel to live without barriers? Perhaps the answer lies in something my late friend and Gaza activist, Mary Khass, told me over thirty years ago: "There is no freedom if you are an occupier."

"Shujaiya—rest in peace!"

—Deputy Commander of Israel Defense
Forces Battalion 749, while demolishing thirty
houses in the Gaza City district of Shujaiya

Is Hamas to Blame for the Failure to Resolve the Israel-Palestine Conflict?

Colter Louwerse

> "*If Israel recognizes our rights and pledges to withdraw from all occupied lands, Hamas and the Palestinian people will decide to halt armed resistance*"
> — Hamas chairman Khalid Meshal[1]

> "*[An extended truce or calm] harms the Israel strategic goal, empowers Hamas, and gives the impression that Israel recognizes the movement*"
> — Israeli foreign minister Tzipi Livni[2]

After Hamas-led militants massacred hundreds of Israelis on October 7, prominent observers argued that the group's

---

Colter Louwerse is an academic researcher focused on the diplomatic history of the Palestine Question. His Ph.D. dissertation, *The Struggle for Palestinian Rights: The Palestinian Campaign for Self-Determination and Statehood at the United Nations, 1967-1989*, shed new evidentiary light on the relationship between Palestinian popular struggle, diplomacy, and development of proposals for "resolving" the Israeli-Palestinian conflict under international auspices.

ideological intransigence left Israel with no option but to eliminate it.[3] US president Joe Biden rejected calls to "stop the war" because "[a]s long as Hamas clings to its ideology of destruction, a cease-fire is not peace."[4] Senator Bernie Sanders dismissed the prospect of "a permanent ceasefire with an organization like Hamas which is dedicated to destroying the State of Israel."[5] "People who are calling for a ceasefire now," former US secretary of state Hillary Clinton asserted, "don't understand Hamas." The group "will sabotage any efforts to forge a lasting peace, and will never stop attacking Israel."[6] The practical corollary of this reasoning was set out with disarming frankness by the *Economist*. In an editorial published November 2, the august journal acknowledged that "Israel is inflicting terrible civilian casualties" in Gaza, accepted that Israel "has unleashed a ferocious bombardment against the people of Gaza," recognized that a prolongation of Israel's offensive would cause "the deaths of thousands of innocent people" in Gaza—and concluded that "Israel must fight on," because "while Hamas runs Gaza, peace is impossible."[7] Given its lethal-cum-genocidal implications,[8] the claim that no lasting truce or peace agreement with Hamas is possible merits careful scrutiny.

Attempts to blame Palestinian recalcitrance for the intractability of the Israel-Palestine conflict are not new. On the contrary, Israeli spokespeople long ago elevated into a public relations mantra the aphorism of Abba Eban, Israel's one-time foreign minister: "The Palestinians have never missed an opportunity to miss an opportunity" for peace.[9] The main problem with this claim is that it is flatly contradicted by the historical record. Palestinian leaders have sought for decades to resolve the conflict on terms approved by the international community. By contrast, Israel and the United States have consistently rejected those terms in favor of Israel's territorial expansion. Furthermore, Israeli military offensives have often been directed not at combatting Palestinian terrorism but, on the contrary, at dispelling the "threat" of a peace agreement. Whenever Palestinian leaders moved toward accepting the international consensus framework for resolving the conflict, Israel responded with violence calibrated to force them back into militant rejectionism.

Preventing peace with the PLO
During the June 1967 Arab-Israel War, Israel came into military occupation of the Palestinian West Bank, including East Jerusalem, and Gaza Strip. (Israel also occupied the Egyptian Sinai, Syrian Golan Heights, and two islands in the Gulf of Aqaba.) Already by the mid-1970s, the international community converged on a framework for resolving the festering conflict. This framework comprised two elements rooted in fundamental principles of international law. The first called for Israel's full withdrawal from the occupied Palestinian and other Arab territories in exchange for Palestinian-Arab recognition of Israel. The second called for establishing an independent State of Palestine on the Palestinian territories from which Israel would withdraw, i.e., the West Bank and Gaza, as well as a "just resolution" of the Palestinian refugee question.[10] *Land for peace* and *Palestinian self-determination* secured through a *two-state settlement*: these principles for a reasonable if imperfect resolution of the Israel-Palestine conflict were eventually endorsed by an overwhelming consensus at the International Court of Justice (ICJ), in the political organs of the United Nations (UN), and of respected human rights organizations.[11]

In the immediate aftermath of the June 1967 war, both Israel and the Palestine Liberation Organization (PLO) rejected a two-state settlement. Preferring territorial expansion over peace, Israel pursued an "insatiable quest for Lebensraum" in the occupied Palestinian territories.[12] It began establishing illegal settlements in 1967 and unlawfully annexed East Jerusalem in 1980.[13] Palestinians under Israeli occupation were controlled through "brute force, repression and fear, collaboration and treachery, beatings and torture chambers."[14] Israel's defiance of UN efforts to facilitate a negotiated resolution of the conflict was underwritten by Washington, which, impressed by Israel's decisive victory over Arab nationalism in 1967, adopted Israel as its key "strategic asset" in the Middle East.[15] Under the direction of Secretary of State Henry Kissinger, the United States extended unqualified support for Israel's rejection of any peace plan requiring its full withdrawal from occupied territory.[16]

Israel's rejectionism was at first mirrored by Palestinian leaders.[17] In the late-1960s, the PLO was unwilling to recognize the legitimacy of a Jewish state established through the systematic dispossession of the Palestinian people and situated on over three-quarters of historic Palestine. The diverse factions which together comprised the PLO cleaved to the "unifying" political program articulated in the organization's 1969 Charter. This called for "the retrieval of Palestine" and its "liberation through armed struggle."[18] PLO chairman Yasser Arafat and the moderate leadership, however, quickly discerned that mobilizing international support on behalf of the Palestinian national cause would be possible only if the PLO came to terms with Israeli sovereignty. From the early 1970s, the PLO began cautiously signaling to Washington its willingness to negotiate on the basis of the crystallizing two-state consensus.[19] After the October 1973 Arab-Israeli war swung "the tide of international opinion" in Palestine's favor, Arafat seized the moment to thrust the Palestinian case before the UN General Assembly, ambiguously offering Israel "the gun or the olive branch."[20] Pretenses to the contrary notwithstanding, Western officials understood Arafat's speech as inaugurating a Palestinian push for peace.[21] At a landmark October 1974 Arab League Summit at Rabat, a "strikingly moderate" Arafat had privately indicated to the assembled heads of state that he was "ready to accept a peace settlement" and to "recognize Israel."[22]

Arafat took his olive branch to the UN Security Council one year later. In January 1976, the PLO tacitly supported an Arab and Non-Aligned draft resolution endorsing a two-state settlement of the Arab-Israel conflict. The PLO publicly welcomed the draft resolution as "consonant with a just peace" while, in private, Palestinian representatives conveyed to American and UN officials their acceptance of Israeli sovereignty as a "major concession."[23] This far-reaching Palestinian peace offer was supported by *all* the frontline Arab "confrontation" states—Egypt, Syria, Jordan—as well as the Soviet Union.[24] The resolution was also approved by majority on the Security Council. But Israel refused to participate in the debate, angrily resolving "never to negotiate" with "terrorist organizations," and the US killed the draft by voting it down. The PLO ambassador was left to bitterly condemn this "tyranny of the veto."[25]

US and Israeli intransigence did not deflect the PLO from its moderate trajectory. On the contrary, the January 1976 draft resolution was just the first of many Palestinian offers to negotiate a two-state settlement, all of which were rejected by Washington. In 1977, Arafat painstakingly negotiated formal PLO recognition of Israel with the administration of US president Jimmy Carter. The talks collapsed when Carter refused to offer reciprocal American recognition of Palestinian self-determination.[26] In July 1979, the PLO promoted its own Security Council resolution that explicitly reconciled Israeli sovereignty with Palestinian self-determination.[27] This Palestinian initiative marked, in the words of one European ambassador to the UN, "potentially the biggest breakthrough" in peace efforts "since 1948."[28] Washington again threatened its "tyranny of the veto" and the resolution was shelved. In April 1980, the

PLO, supported by the Arab states, tabled a Security Council resolution that reproduced almost verbatim the January 1976 draft. The US vetoed it again.[29] In July 1982, the PLO affirmed its "full support" for a French and Egyptian Security Council resolution calling for "mutual" Israeli-Palestinian recognition. Faced with unrelenting American-Israeli opposition, the draft never reached a vote.[30]

Already forty years ago, then, Western observers concluded that Palestinian leaders wanted a diplomatic settlement whereas Israeli rejectionism posed the primary obstacle to peace. In 1981, the entire US intelligence community—including the Central Intelligence Agency (CIA), State Department, and Department of Defense—converged on these judgments:

1. In exchange for independent Palestinian statehood, Arafat and the core Palestinian leadership was "prepared to recognize Israel's right to exist," "could probably enforce the discipline necessary to obtain acceptance of this within the PLO," and "would also agree to a process leading to more formal recognition."[31]

2. Israeli politicians from Likud on the right to Labor on the left were united in "broad agreement" that there should be "no total withdrawal [by Israel] to the pre-June 1967 borders and no negotiating with the PLO." "Even if the PLO were to modify its charter to recognize Israel and to renounce terrorism," Israel "would still oppose negotiations with the PLO."[32]

The PLO and all Arab states support the international consensus two-state settlement; Israel and the US obstinately reject it. This fundamental impasse persists into the present and explains why the Israel-Palestine conflict continues.

Thwarting Palestinian moderation

Israel did not rely solely on Washington's Security Council veto to pre-empt, discredit, and deflect the pestiferous onslaught of Palestinian peace offers. In the 1970s and 1980s, Israel conducted so-called "reprisals" against the PLO in Lebanon that were vastly disproportionate to Palestinian attacks, wildly indiscriminate, and all too often targeted at civilians.[33] Western observers commented at the time on a most cynical aspect of this "retaliatory" policy: Israeli assaults on Palestinian and Lebanese civilians increasingly responded not to Palestinian terrorism but, on the contrary, to Palestinian *moderation*.[34] Israel's reaction to the PLO's January 1976 peace initiative was illustrative of this dynamic. Two days after the Security Council decided to include the PLO in its deliberations on the Arab and Non-Aligned draft resolution, Israeli warplanes bombed Palestinian refugee camps in South Lebanon. The strikes killed dozens, including many civilians. Israeli officials admitted the bloody assault was "preventive, not punitive" while the CIA regarded it as a "reflection of Israeli anger" over the Security Council's decision to hear the Arab peace plan.[35]

In fact, the massacre was not an emotional outburst but reflected a strategic logic that manifested repeatedly over the following six years. When Israel greeted the PLO's July 1979 peace proposal with another round of "particularly bloody" and "unprovoked" airstrikes—twenty-two men, women, and children were killed—US officials took note of the pattern.[36] "Israeli actions in Lebanon," they concluded, "are designed to weaken the position of moderate Palestinians and drive them into extremist attitudes which will effectively prevent the US from doing business with them."[37] The logic was straightforward, if perverse: people are unlikely to desire peace with you if you murder their families, and that's a good thing, if you aim to acquire territory, not peace. This macabre strategy culminated in Israel's June 1982 invasion of Lebanon.

Successive Palestinian peace initiatives had by then corroded the legitimacy of Israel's rejectionist posture and raised the prospect that Israel would be pressured into relinquishing the West Bank and Gaza Strip. In 1980, the governments of Western Europe began to reward Palestinian moderation by drifting toward the UN consensus on Palestinian rights.[38] Still more ominously, the Arab League issued a peace plan the following year offering recognition of Israel in exchange for Palestinian statehood.[39] Most disturbing of all, the PLO signed a US-brokered ceasefire in July 1981 and proved "scrupulous" in adhering to it.[40] Halting attacks across Israel's northern border, Arafat sent word to Western officials that the PLO was, "in unequivocal terms," prepared "to live in peace with Israel."[41]

These developments elicited panic in Israel. The US envoy responsible for negotiating the PLO ceasefire warned that Israeli officials were "almost paranoic" about the diminished violence.[42] Israeli defense minister Ariel Sharon feared that, by substituting the image of the PLO "diplomat" for that of the PLO "terrorist," Arafat might unleash a tide of global, and even American, pressure for Palestinian statehood. "Paradoxically, the fact that the PLO . . . restrained itself and observed the cease-fire for a year was the greatest threat of all to Israel," a prominent Israeli political sociologist concludes. "[A]fter all, someone might draw the conclusion that the organization could be a partner for peace."[43] Indeed, the word "ceasefire" was such a "negative codeword" for Israel's "neurotic" officials that many refused even to utter it in the presence of their American counterparts.[44] Perhaps "what the US ought to be doing," one high-level American official mused, "was sending Israel, not supplies of arms, but loads of Valium."[45]

In order to thwart these "Palestinian peace offensives" that threatened to foist on Israel a diplomatic settlement of the conflict, Israel resolved to "wipe out" the PLO in Beirut.[46] From July 1981, Israel persistently sought to "goad the PLO into breaching the ceasefire" and thereby to "manufacture" a "propaganda base" for war.[47] Israeli forces bombarded Lebanese villages indiscriminately, exploded car bombs in Beirut's crowded city center, and only narrowly aborted a scheme to bomb Beirut's stadium sky-high, liquidating the PLO leadership in one fell swoop.[48] When Arafat finally succumbed to the relentless pressure and authorized retaliatory rocket fire, in May 1982, the Israeli army steamrolled into Lebanon in the name of "rooting out Palestinian terror," killing as many as 20,000 Palestinian and Lebanese, overwhelmingly civilians.[49] Having been privy to Israel's repudiation of UN efforts to consolidate the ceasefire, Britain's Secretary of State for Foreign and Commonwealth Affairs Francis Pym observed in the opening week of the war that "Israel's . . . prime objective" was "not security of [its] northern border" but the *elimination of inconvenient Palestinian claims*—"inconvenient" because validated by an ever-widening international consensus.[50]

Israel's operation to smash the moderate PLO leadership in Lebanon was therefore directed not at *combating* Palestinian terrorism, but at *fomenting* and *provoking* it. This was widely recognized by informed Western observers. "The Israeli government will undoubtedly see its invasion as a clear military and political success," Britain's Joint Intelligence Committee (JIC) reported several weeks into the war. "There must now be a greater risk of terrorist acts, especially against American and Israeli targets"—and "any PLO terrorism will give Israel a propaganda success."[51] After the invasion, the PLO's moderate leadership faced internal revolt over Arafat's "failure . . . to mobilize international support behind a negotiated solution to the Palestinian issue."[52] The CIA found "the Israelis . . . pleased" with this dissension:

> the unrest will produce a more militant PLO, raising the chances for increased terrorist attacks on Israeli targets throughout the world. Nonetheless, Israel realizes that a return to terrorism will decrease the PLO's acceptability as a negotiating partner and thereby further erode international pressure on Israel to deal with the Palestinians.[53]

Though Arafat retained his leadership role, the Lebanon war dealt the Palestinian national movement a shattering blow. Displaced to far-off Tunis, riven by factionalism, and politically overshadowed by regional conflicts, the 1980s saw the PLO in steady decline. The outbreak of the first Palestinian intifada in December 1987 pulled Arafat's chestnuts from the fire. Despairing of liberation from without, Palestinians under occupation took the national struggle into their own hands. First in Gaza, then across the occupied territories, Palestinians entered into mass, unarmed civil revolt against Israel's military rule.[54] Israel's policy of "force, might, and beatings" to suppress the uprising provoked international indignation and rejuvenated support for Palestinian self-determination.[55] Arafat sought to capitalize on this newfound political urgency by launching another peace offensive. In December 1988, Arafat renounced "all forms of terrorism" and affirmed Israel's "right . . . to exist."[56] US officials groused that, by once-and-for-all burying the US-Israeli pretext for refusing to negotiate, Arafat had inaugurated a "new and rather nightmarish era" in which Palestinian claims could no longer be dismissed.[57] To deflate international pressure for a Palestinian state, the US and Israel were henceforth compelled to adjust their approach: instead of sidelining the PLO or battering it into extremism, they now sought to co-opt the Palestinian leadership and, thereby, to pacify it.

In 1993, with the intifada sputtering under Israel Defense Forces (IDF) repression, Arafat and Israel's prime minister Yitzhak Rabin shook hands on the White House lawn as they inaugurated what became known as the "Oslo peace process." For the PLO, this was a Faustian pact: the Palestinian leadership-in-exile was permitted to return and set up a subordinate administration in the occupied territories, where it would serve as "Israel's enforcer."[58] This newly established Palestinian Authority (PA) would "rule . . . by their own methods," Rabin explained to a meeting of the Israeli Labor Party, "freeing . . . Israeli soldiers from having to do what they will do."[59] "The [Oslo] agreement leaves us with the territory and them with the populated areas," Oslo's legal architect likewise enthused. "[I]t even leaves them with the dirty work of patrolling the cities and refugee camps."[60]

Worse still, the PLO embarked on negotiations conducted outside the framework of international law, absent a protective UN forum, and without having received any US or Israeli guarantees that talks would be directed toward achieving Palestinian self-determination. The results were predictable. The PLO unilaterally recognized Israel and committed to negotiations "mediated" by Israel's primary ally and patron. In exchange, Israeli leaders made no commitments on the terms of a final agreement and continued to reject any prospect of a Palestinian state, while the number of Israeli settlers in the occupied territories ballooned by more than 50 percent between 1993 and 2001.[61] When Palestinian and Israeli leaders eventually met to hash out a final deal, in 2000 and again in 2007, Israeli offers fell short of even the minimum requirements under international law.[62] Palestinian representatives were willing to compromise on the terms of the international consensus. But when they refused to entirely sign away the internationally validated rights of the Palestinian people, American "mediators" erupted in fury. "This isn't the Security Council here. This isn't the UN General Assembly," President Bill Clinton fumed in 2000. "I'm the president of the United States."[63]

Since 2014, even the pretense of diplomatic negotiations has been abandoned as Israel brazenly trumpets its opposition to Palestinian statehood.[64] The leading Israeli human rights organization, B'Tselem, affirms that "the West Bank has been annexed in practice."[65] Israel's government, formed after the November 2022 elections, is formally committed to "promote and develop [Jewish] settlement" in the West Bank, to which, it stipulates, "[t]he Jewish people have an exclusive and indisputable right."[66] All this time, the PA has run the negotiations treadmill. It has talked—pleaded—with its oppressor for three decades, longer than any other anti-colonial movement in history. Meanwhile, Israel steadily consolidated its grip on the occupied territories, incorporated ever larger tracts of Palestinian land, implanted hundreds of thousands of Jewish colonists, and squeezed Palestinians into ever smaller concentrations hemmed in on all sides by Israeli military and settler infrastructure.[67] Palestinian independence has never been farther from reach.

Hamas redux

The PLO not only accepted, but compromised well beyond, the requirements of international law and the international consensus for resolving the conflict. Can the same be said of the Hamas authorities in Gaza? In fact, Hamas has substantially retraced the PLO's political trajectory while attempting to avoid replicating the PLO's mistakes. At its inception in 1988, Hamas rejected the international two-state consensus. Its founding covenant, like that of the PLO before it, looked forward to "a decisive battle of liberation" for the whole of Palestine.[68] The Islamist movement's attitude began to shift, however, when Israel unilaterally redeployed its troops to the perimeter of Gaza in August 2005, removing civilian settlers from the Strip while retaining control over Gaza's borders, airspace, and waters.[69] A few months later, in January 2006, Palestinians across the occupied territories held a carefully monitored, "completely honest and fair" election.[70] Hamas had previously opposed elections on the grounds that the PA, like the Oslo process which created it, was illegitimate. But this time, Hamas unexpectedly decided to participate. Even more unexpectedly, it won: in what was widely interpreted as a protest vote against the PA's corruption as well as collaboration with Israel, a plurality of Palestinians gave Hamas a majority of seats in the legislature.[71]

Newly burdened with administrative responsibility and eager to obtain international legitimacy, Hamas repeatedly signaled that it was ready to moderate its program to achieve a negotiated settlement with Israel. "If Israel withdraws to the 1967 borders," Hamas leader Khalid Meshal asserted in February 2006, "there could be peace and security in the region." "If Israel declares that it will give the Palestinian people a state," added Hamas prime minister Ismail Haniyeh, "then we are ready to recognize them."[72] Hamas officials subsequently proposed a "long-term truce" that would be "automatically renewed," securing space to "negotiate a lasting peace" including resolution of "important issues like the right of return and the release of prisoners."[73] "Hamas' conditions are almost too good to be true," asserted a former deputy head of Israeli intelligence. "Refugees and right of return and Jerusalem can wait for some other process; Hamas will suffice with the 1967 borders, more or less, and in return will guarantee peace and quiet for ten, 25 or 30 years of good neighborly relations and confidence-building."[74] In January 2007, Mishal acknowledged that a viable peace settlement would leave Israel intact—"the first time," asserted Israel's leading newspaper *Ha'aretz*, "that a

Hamas official has raised the possibility of full and official recognition of Israel."[75]

Two years later, Hamas sent letters to the newly elected US president Barack Obama, committing itself to "a just resolution to the conflict not in contradiction with the international community and enlightened opinion as expressed in the International Court of Justice, the United Nations General Assembly, and leading human rights organizations."[76] The letter was delivered amidst a new spate of public statements from top officials asserting Hamas's commitment to negotiated peace: "If our demand is met and a Palestinian state is established," affirmed one high-ranking figure, "we will recognize Israel."[77] Over the following decade, Hamas reiterated to the point of tedium its support for negotiations based on the international consensus two-state settlement.[78] Ambiguities notwithstanding, the organization's overarching trajectory toward the two-state settlement was unmistakable. "Hamas has been carefully and consciously adjusting its political program for years," argued a US government agency study in 2009, "and has sent repeated signals that it is ready to begin a process of coexisting with Israel."[79] "The leadership of Hamas knows that they have no capability of destroying Israel," a former head of Israel's Mossad intelligence agency affirmed in 2016. "Hamas is now searching for ways and means of dialoguing with Israel."[80]

It might be objected that, even as Hamas offered a long-term ceasefire in exchange for a state on the West Bank and Gaza, it still refused to countenance a permanent peace with or to formally recognize Israel. But Hamas has also stated that, "regardless of its ideology or principles," it would abide by a two-state settlement if this was approved by a popular referendum of the Palestinian people or adopted by a legitimately representative government.[81] This pragmatic compromise was formalized by Hamas's adoption of a new covenant in 2017. Supplanting the "outdated" as well as antisemitic original, Hamas's "de-facto" new Charter stipulated that, whereas Hamas itself would not recognize Israel, the movement would accept the reality of Israel within its pre-June 1967 borders as "a formula of national consensus."[82] This positioned Hamas closer to the international consensus framework for resolving the conflict than every mainstream political party in Israel.

It might also be contended that the above survey overlooks Hamas statements rejecting co-existence with Israel or that it naively takes Hamas overtures at face value. But putting aside the fact that Hamas has demonstrated itself willing and able to uphold past diplomatic agreements with Israel,[83] the crucial point is this: *at no point in the last fifteen years have Israel or the United States ever so much as seriously considered testing Hamas's offers to negotiate a peaceful end to the conflict.* It bears emphasis that Hamas's moderate overtures represented its opening offer, issued without any guarantee of reciprocation from Washington or Tel Aviv. If Hamas refused to unilaterally recognize Israel, this likely reflected a rational aversion to replicating what Hamas considers a cardinal PLO error: unconditionally recognizing Israel, and negotiating on this basis for three decades, only to receive worse-than-nothing in return. "Having witnessed the sorry fate of the PLO," a leading scholar of the movement queried, "what is Hamas's incentive to follow suit?"[84] Hamas nevertheless showed potential to "evolve in a pragmatic direction that would allow for a two-state solution," UN Middle East envoy Álvaro de Soto observed.[85] Yet, reprising their treatment of the PLO three decades prior, Israel and its allies responded to evidence of Hamas's political moderation not as an opportunity to pursue but a dire threat to avert.

As soon as Hamas was elected, the US and Israel moved to punish Palestinians for their democratic choice. "If we were going to push for an election," US senator Hillary Clinton rued, "we should have made sure to determine who was going to win."[86] With Egyptian complicity, and US backing, Israel imposed a suffocating blockade on Gaza—an illegal policy of collective punishment and probable crime against humanity.[87] Following Israel's lead, the Middle East Quartet—comprising the US, UN, European Union, and Russia—put forth three "unattainable preconditions" for Hamas's entry into the peace process: renunciation of violence, respect for past agreements, and recognition of Israel.[88] Putting aside the fact that Israel reserves the right to use violence with impunity, runs rough-shod over past agreements, and flagrantly denies the Palestinian right to sovereignty, Israel ensured that nothing was done to incentivize Hamas to make concessions. Instead, the specter of Hamas "terrorists" ruling Gaza provided Israel with a conven-ient dual alibi for its refusal to negotiate Palestinian independ-ence. On the one hand, how could Israel be expected to parlay with an organization committed to its destruction?[89] On the other hand, how could Israel reach a deal with the PA if it did not represent all Palestinians?[90]

Whenever Hamas deviated from its assigned role as terror-ist spoiler—for instance, by affirming moderate positions or by forming a unity government with the PA—it became necessary to discipline the organization using the standard methods.[91] Consider the build-up to and aftermath of the January 2006 Palestinian elections, during which Hamas adhered to a unilat-eral ceasefire with Israel. Israeli military officers "readily" credited the "sharp decline in violence" primarily to Hamas's "restraint," observed the International Crisis Group, even as "Israel refused to negotiate a reciprocal and comprehensive cessation of hostili-ties" or to terminate "attacks, including assassinations."[92] When Hamas won the election, it wrote to the Middle East Quartet expressing its wish to achieve a "negotiated settlement with Israel" and, in a letter to President George W. Bush, offered to accept "a Palestinian state in the 1967 borders" along with "a truce for many years."[93] Israel responded with a sharp escalation in violence. Pummeling Gaza with indiscriminate shelling in June, the IDF killed a Palestinian family picnicking on a beach, driving Hamas to abandon the ceasefire it had "largely maintained for sixteen months."[94] Israel then abducted dozens of Hamas parliamentarians, including a third of the Palestinian cabinet.[95] The following year, the US and Israel orchestrated a Fatah-led coup in Gaza which Hamas pre-empted, fragmenting Palestinian politics and precluding Hamas's integration into the peace process.[96]

The "cycle of violence" came full circle in 2008. That June, Israel and Hamas agreed to another ceasefire. Though its terms were contested, its essence was straightforward: Hamas would not fire rockets, and Israel would lift its devastating siege.[97] Hamas was subsequently "careful to maintain the ceasefire," Israel's quasi-official Intelligence and Terrorism Information Center observed, resulting in what a Defense Ministry official conceded was "a large measure of peace and quiet to Israeli communities near Gaza."[98] Informed observers intuited that Hamas had signed the ceasefire to prepare the ground for a renewed peace offensive. Hamas "recognized . . . [it's] ideological goal is not attainable" and was "ready and willing to see the establishment of a Palestinian state in the temporary borders of 1967," asserted former Israeli intelligence chief Ephraim Halevy, but "Israel, for reasons of its own, did not want to turn the ceasefire into the start of a diplomatic process with Hamas."[99] Just barely easing its suffocating siege, Israel exploited the truce to refine plans—first developed in 2007—for an aggressive assault against the Strip.[100] The moment of opportunity presented itself on November 4: with Americans transfixed by their presidential election, Israel raided Gaza, killing six Palestinians.[101] When Hamas responded with rocket fire, the IDF seized on the pretext to terminate the truce: ignoring Hamas offers to re-establish the ceasefire, on December 27 Israel dropped over a hundred tons of bombs on Gaza, killing hundreds.[102] The bombardment violated a "48-hour lull" in hostilities, a senior UN official reported, during which "it was obvious that Hamas was trying, again, to observe that truce to get this back under control."[103] Israel then visited upon Gaza what Amnesty International described as "22 days of death and destruction," killing some 1,400 people, up to four-fifths of whom were civilians.[104]

The same blood-drenched process was repeated twice more. In 2012, Israel triggered another military operation after it assassinated its own Palestinian "subcontractor" in Gaza, who "hours before" had "received the draft of a permanent truce agreement with Israel."[105] The operation killed some 170 Palestinians.[106] In April 2014, with yet another fragile ceasefire in place, Hamas joined a Palestinian unity government that signed up to the Quartet's three demands, including recognition of Israel.[107] For once, the US and Europe signaled cautious support, sparking angry denunciations from Israel.[108] When a rogue Hamas cell abducted three Israeli teenagers in June, Israeli prime minister Benjamin Netanyahu seized the opportunity to torpedo the hated unity government. Though the Israeli government quickly realized the teenagers were dead, it pretended otherwise, citing their rescue as a pretext to rampage through the West Bank, targeting Hamas and provoking rocket fire.[109] As Israeli warplanes pounded Gaza, killing dozens, Hamas proposed a far-reaching ten-year ceasefire. Hamas demanded that Israel lift the siege on Gaza in accordance with international law and release Palestinian prisoners arrested in the preceding weeks, but dropped its traditional quid pro quo of a full Israeli withdrawal to the pre-June 1967 borders. Israel ignored the offer.[110] Unleashing Operation Protective Edge, the IDF massacred some 2,250 Palestinians, mostly civilians, including 550 children.[111]

Ceasefire, Palestinian peace offer, brutal Israeli military assault—the parallels to Israel's 1982 invasion of Lebanon scarcely require further elucidation. "What has been will be again, what has been done will be done again; there is nothing new under the sun."[112]

Roads not taken

Conventional wisdom in the West posits that the massacre of Israeli civilians on October 7 traces back to Hamas's irremediable "ideology of destruction," necessitating that the group be militarily destroyed. But the historical record compels a different view. The Hamas-led massacre was a predictable and avoidable political response to Israel's denial of Palestinian statehood and violation of human dignity in Gaza. In its treatment of the PLO and then Hamas, Israel has consistently rejected the international consensus framework for resolving the conflict while thwarting any attempt by Palestinian representatives to reach a diplomatic settlement within that framework. To neutralize these Palestinian "peace offensives," Israel sought first to bypass Palestinian leaders as interlocutors, then to violently provoke them, and finally to co-opt and contain them. Israel followed this playbook with both the PLO and Hamas, in roughly the same sequence. In each case, Israel initially refused even to engage with Palestinian overtures. When moderate PLO and Hamas pronouncements threatened to win them international legitimacy, and thereby to undermine the tenability of Israel's non-engagement policy, Israel in both cases conducted brutal military attacks aimed at derailing Palestinian diplomacy. Finally, Israel sought to maneuver both the PLO and Hamas into positions of subordinacy. Each organization found itself responsible for administering occupied territory and dependent on Israel for the resources and stability needed to do so. Israel thereby sought to reconcile the PLO and Hamas to its regime of domination over the Palestinian people without having to make any political or territorial concessions.

In the West Bank, Israel's policy proved remarkably successful. By subcontracting the task of repression to the PA, Israel eroded the Palestinian leadership's legitimacy and thus its desire as well as capacity to mobilize popular resistance to Israel's occupation. By 2023, Israel believed that it had engineered a similar equilibrium in Gaza, with Hamas administering a besieged prison camp on Israel's behalf. It seemed, at first glance, that Hamas had been "pacified": insofar as the Islamist movement prioritized its rule in Gaza, its resistance could be "contained."[113] It is now evident that this Israeli assessment was complacent. Fenced off from any diplomatic horizon and trapped within an unbearable and interminable siege, Hamas resolved to disrupt Israel's equilibrium and violently refocus international attention on Palestine.

The bottom line is this. If, over the past half-century, Israel and its allies had desisted for but a moment in not merely missing, but actively *spurning* and *sabotaging* prospects for a just resolution to the Palestine Question, the 2023 massacre of Israeli civilians and incipient genocide in Gaza need never have happened. Indeed, the Israel-Palestine conflict would almost certainly have been resolved decades ago.

"Remember . . . Amalek"

—Israeli Prime Minister
Benjamin Netanyahu

Rule Number One of Nonviolent Resistance: It Can't Work If It's Misrepresented as Violent

R. J.

The actions of Hamas on October 7, 2023, were universally condemned in the United States. The denunciation focused on Hamas's brutal treatment of civilians in southern Israel— conduct that this author likewise deplores. But implicit in much of the criticism was also the following accusatory question: *Why didn't Gazans use nonviolent protest to achieve their goals?* This rebuke was implied when commentators invoked Israel's "right of self-defense," but denied that same right to Gazans. It was further implied when commentators delegitimized armed resistance in Gaza by arguing that Hamas should not have expended scarce resources on military infrastructure. And it was certainly implied when commentators rhetorically queried "what else was Israel supposed to do" as it leveled northern Gaza, displaced 1.9 million people, and killed

R. J. is an independent researcher and humanist living in the United States.

upward of 7,700 children, without ever once asking "what else was Gaza supposed to do" under much greater duress. Despite the bad faith that often accompanied it, however, the question why Gazans did not employ nonviolent means on October 7 to break Israel's unlawful siege was a good one. It has a simple answer: *they already tried that.*

In 2018, tens of thousands of Palestinians in Gaza embarked on a heroic campaign of mass, overwhelmingly nonviolent resistance along the perimeter fence. These forgotten people—abandoned to their fate in the "world's largest concentration camp"[1] after having endured three major massacres in under a decade—mustered the courage, the discipline, and the spiritual wherewithal to stage what they called a "Great March of Return" (GMR). By dramatizing their plight before the global public, they hoped to inspire enough international pressure to force Israel to respect their rights as refugees and to lift the "inhumane, illegal, and immoral blockade"[2] imposed on them. Israel responded by deploying a wall of snipers along its side of the fence. "It's not a barrage of fire," a journalist for *The Nation* reported. "It is methodical, patient, precise. A single shot rings out and someone falls. You wait a few minutes. The crosshairs settle on the next target. Another shot, another body drops. Again and again and again. It goes on for hours."[3]

Seeking "to leave as many young people as possible with permanent disabilities,"[4] Israeli marksmen systematically targeted the legs of Palestinian demonstrators. They fired high-velocity bullets at close range, resulting in "[p]ermanent, life-changing injuries."[5] One sharpshooter boasted that he "brought in seven-eight knees in one day."[6] In the first two months of protests, dozens of demonstrators were killed and more than 3,600 injured by live ammunition.[7] A Commission of Inquiry appointed by the United Nations (UN) found that Israeli forces deliberately shot children, medical workers, journalists, and persons with disabilities.[8] No participant in the Gaza protests would have been surprised by Israel's "systematic targeting of civilians."[9] Everyone in Gaza also knew that hospitals already "over capacity" would be "unable to treat all the wounded."[10] Yet day after day, for week after week, ordinary men, women, and children in Gaza assembled to chant, sit-in, and march for a fair chance at life. And day after day, for week after week, Israeli snipers in broad daylight "mowed'" them down.[11] The international community issued condemnations, and passed critical resolutions, but did not sanction Israel. The Great March of Return must surely rank among the most inspiring and humbling displays of nonviolent resistance in history. It did not just fail, but drowned in blood.

Why did the GMR falter? Nonviolent resistance works by publicizing injustice while provoking repression that pricks the conscience of onlookers and compels them to intervene. In the American South, during the Civil Rights Movement, images of peaceful demonstrators brutalized by white racists were transmitted to the north as well as abroad. "Nonviolent Black protest triggered violent segregationist resistance; which then aroused sympathetic white public opinion outside the South; which in turn compelled the federal government to stay the hand of local white armed power: that was the essential sequence, trajectory, and dynamic that averted a bloody defeat."[12] It follows that, to stand any chance of succeeding, civil disobedience requires "a sympathetic audience."[13] If relevant third parties are oblivious to the confrontation, or if they consider as illegitimate the means or objectives of those protesting, then unarmed demonstrators will simply be crushed. The unarmed Gazans who marched undefended toward Israel's wall of snipers put their lives in the world's hands. They gambled that, if they were gunned down, it would arouse sufficient public indignation as to compel influential states—above all the US—to restrain Israel.

The world did not redeem their faith: unarmed demonstrators in Gaza were left to the mercy of the Israel Defense Forces (IDF). Why did the GMR not resonate? One crucial factor was its systematic distortion by US media. Since international observers could not witness the protests firsthand, media representations of the GMR were decisive in the battle for international public opinion. Accordingly, this chapter analyzes how the most widely consumed US print[14] and television[15] news sources covered the GMR in the critical period between March 31 and May 28, 2018.[16] It finds that US media reproduced and reinforced three salient allegations by Israel. *First*, that Hamas was the principal organizer of the protests. *Second*, that Palestinian protesters who were killed or injured in Gaza posed a security threat to Israel. *Third*, that the IDF responded to the Gaza demonstrations in lawful self-defense. These contentions, separately and in combination, powerfully delegitimized the GMR and legitimized Israel's lethal repression. Yet not one of them bears scrutiny when juxtaposed against the consensus findings of human rights authorities.[17] They were falsehoods whose uncritical amplification in US media gave Israel the license to kill.

Myth One. Hamas organized the protests
Israeli spokespersons consistently alleged that Hamas had conceived, launched, and directed the Gaza protests. Israel's Ministry of Foreign Affairs asserted, for example, that the border demonstrators were "sen[t]" by "an organization that sanctifies murder and death" to participate in "this murderous spectacle."[18] Former defense minister Avigdor Lieberman purported that "[t]hose who are trying to challenge us at the border and breach it belong to Hamas's military wing," and added for

good measure that "there are no innocent people in the Gaza Strip."[19] Brigadier General Ronen Manelis, a former spokesman for the IDF, acknowledged that "hundreds of Gazans were injured . . . and several dozen died" at Israel's hands in Gaza—but explained that "most . . . were Hamas operatives" while "Hamas instigated and orchestrated" the violence deliberately as part of its "propaganda operation."[20] US media routinely reproduced Israel's depiction of the GMR as "Hamas-led" (*USA Today*), "led by Hamas" (Fox News), "largely . . . orchestrated by Hamas, the Islamic militant group that rules Gaza" (*New York Times*).[21] Even if the GMR was "original[ly]" organized by "nonviolent protesters," media outlets elsewhere allowed, Hamas had "hijacked it" (CNN)[22] to "launch violence" (MSNBC).[23]

Hamas was widely viewed in the US as a terrorist organization devoted to Israel's destruction. The GMR was therefore tarred by association. Yet in truth, the GMR was a broad-based popular mobilization from inception to fruition, emerging from "grassroots origins" to inspire "grassroots participation."[24] The GMR's organizing committee stipulated from the outset that "[p]articipants will be from all components of the Palestinian civil society and all political parties or factions that believe in peaceful public resistance."[25] The Palestinian Center for Human Rights in Gaza (PCHR) affirmed throughout that protesters did not attend on Hamas orders but were willing participants who formed a cross-section of Gazan society. The demonstrations comprised "hundreds of thousands of Palestinians" from across the "social and political spectrum," PCHR reported, including "children, women and elderlies."[26] PCHR fieldworkers specifically testified to the involvement of "entire families, including their children" who participated "with no influence from any political party encouraging them to do so."[27] These accounts were later validated by the UN Commission of Inquiry, which characterized the GMR leadership as follows:

> A higher national committee [HNC] and 12 subcommittees
> were . . . established to organize and oversee the planning of
> the march. Its members came from all sectors of Palestinian
> society, including civil society, cultural and social organiza-
> tions, student unions, women's groups, eminent persons and
> members of clans.[28]

This is not to say that Hamas was *not* involved in the GMR. "As
an HNC member," the UN Commission of Inquiry noted in its
detailed findings, "Hamas's and the de facto authorities' civilian
and political entities" provided demonstrators with "infrastructure, coordination, and technical and administrative support."[29] But Hamas neither initiated the protest campaign nor
compelled people to participate in it. As the UN Commission
found, "the thousands of people who responded to the calls to
demonstrate did not do so prompted by Hamas, which was
deeply unpopular at the time."[30]

It merits noting that, even if the protests *had* been orchestrated by Hamas, this would not have affected their civilian
character under international law.[31] Regardless of who organized the GMR, and irrespective of the party affiliation of its
participants, so long as the "demonstrations themselves" were
"not combative,"[32] Israel was obliged to apply "law enforcement
based on international human rights law" (IHRL) rather than
the more permissive framework of international humanitarian
law (IHL, or the "laws of war").[33] Under the more restrictive
IHRL framework, Israel's resort to lethal force was permissible only in response to "imminent threat of death or serious
injury"[34]—not the mere presence in a civilian demonstration
of Hamas members. But if conflating the GMR with Hamas
had no *legal* effect, the *political* consequences were devastating.
By following Israel in falsely attributing the GMR to Hamas,
US media outlets lent credibility to Israel's depiction of the

protests as a security threat requiring a military response. At the same time, this media distortion precluded any possibility that the nonviolent demonstrations in Gaza would resonate in US opinion—leaving civilian protesters in Gaza exposed before Israel's wall of snipers, denied the protective shield of sympathetic publicity.

Myth Two. Palestinian protesters posed a security threat
When pressed on the heavy civilian casualties inflicted at the fence, Israeli representatives claimed that Israel only targeted Palestinian "instigators" who presented a clear threat to Israel's security and sovereignty. This rationale assumed two main forms: that protesters targeted by Israel were *armed*—i.e., in possession of Molotov cocktails, grenades, improvised explosive devices (IEDs), and guns—and/or that they had *attempted to breach* the perimeter fence.

—Arms
US media relayed claims by Israel that "alleged terrorists"[35] in Gaza had staged "human wave attacks"[36] armed with guns,[37] "Molotov cocktails,"[38] and "hand grenades."[39] Israel figured in this reportage as the harsh protector, reluctantly responding to "terrorist" aggression. It was subtly implied that, even as Israel's response was unpleasant, it did not reflect any oppressive intent by Israel but, rather, the unenviable dilemma Palestinian infiltrators had thrust upon it. The human rights organizations, on the other hand, reached very different conclusions. They uniformly found that the only thing "overwhelming" about those targeted by the IDF in Gaza was that they were "overwhelmingly" *unarmed*. The documentation assembled by international, Palestinian, and Israeli human rights observers undermined every Israeli and, therefore, US media talking point:

- *Grenades*: The UN Commission of Inquiry affirmed that it "has not been able to verify claims, nor has it seen evidence that demonstrators carried or threw actual grenades at the demonstration sites during demonstration times."[40]
- *Guns*: The UN Commission of Inquiry concluded that there were two incidents, on May 14 and October 12, in which some Palestinians may have used arms, and where, as a result, Israel would have had a legitimate claim to use force. With the *sole exception* of these two incidents, "the use of live ammunition by Israeli security forces against demonstrators was unlawful."[41]
- *Stones and tires*: Al Mezan observed in May that, "even if some of the civilians threw stones or burned tires, it would not alter the categorization of the event as civilian."[42] In its 2019 annual report, PCHR concluded that "sometimes the young men approached the border fence to throw stones and [M]olotov cocktails and used slingshots . . . However, all those acts did not pose any imminent threat to the life of Israeli soldiers" and therefore did not render legitimate Israel's use of live ammunition in response.[43]

More generally, the PCHR consistently reported that "Israeli forces . . . use[d] force against Palestinian unarmed civilians and peaceful protesters in the Gaza Strip."[44] In June, HRW noted that the "vast majority of protesters were unarmed,"[45] Amnesty International reported that it had "not seen evidence of the use of firearms by Palestinians against Israeli soldiers during the protests,"[46] and Al-Haq observed that "Israeli occupying forces, despite overwhelming international condemnation, continued to use excessive, disproportionate, and unnecessary force against unarmed Palestinian protesters."[47] Recall that, by this point, Israeli soldiers had shot dead dozens of demonstrators and injured more than 3,600 with live ammunition.

As late as October 2018, Amnesty International observed that "Israel has repeatedly used lethal force unnecessarily and excessively against unarmed protesters in shameless violation of international law."[48] The following month, B'Tselem presented its conclusion that the "vast majority of casualties were unarmed."[49] In its concluding report, the UN Commission of Inquiry, while acknowledging that "not all demonstrators were peaceful," found "reasonable grounds to believe that the excessive use of force by Israeli security forces violated the rights of the thousands who were."[50]

—Breaching the fence

As well as posing an armed threat to Israeli soldiers, Palestinian protesters were also depicted as menacing Israel's sovereignty, as they attempted to "crash through,"[51] "breach,"[52] "cut,"[53] and "rush"[54] the Gaza fence. Two important messages were conveyed to Western audiences. The first was that Israel only shot those who were approaching the perimeter fence or damaging it. The second, which followed, was that Israel was merely protecting its borders from hostile infiltration. These claims would be difficult to sustain, however, if the majority of those shot by Israeli snipers were either distant from the fence or running away from it.

In April, Amnesty International reported that "Israeli soldiers shot unarmed protesters, bystanders, journalists and medical staff approximately 150–400m from the fence, where they did not pose any threat."[55] Al-Haq found that the IDF targeted "unarmed civilians standing hundreds of meters away from the fence with high velocity weaponry."[56] HRW, in a report released in June, stated that six of the witnesses they had interviewed were "200 to 300 meters from the two parallel fences" when "Israeli forces shot them or people close to them with live ammunition." The report also noted that "other witnesses said that soldiers shot them when they were between 30 and 40 meters from the fences."[57]

When it surveyed hundreds of protesters who had suffered live gunshot wounds, B'Tselem found that most reported being hit when they were "not in the immediate vicinity of the fence" while more than one-fifth reported being hit when they were over 150 meters from the fence.[58] The PCHR likewise found that many protesters "were killed while being hundreds of meters away from the border fence."[59] The UN Commission of Inquiry would eventually determine that "demonstrators who were hundreds of meters away from the Israeli forces and visibly engaged in civilian activities were intentionally shot."[60] In short, then, all of the human rights investigations found that the majority of those who were shot were neither near the fence nor attempting to break through it.[61]

Myth Three. Israel engaged in lawful self-defense

Once it was established—at any rate, to the satisfaction of US media—that Hamas had orchestrated the protests, that Palestinian demonstrators were violent, and that protesters were shot only when they attempted to breach Israel's "border," it was but a flea's hop to the conclusion that Israel's lethal repression was legitimate self-defense. This exculpatory verdict was typically attributed to the "Israeli military,"[62] "the IDF,"[63] and "Israeli officials"[64]—but audiences were given no reason to doubt it. Here again, however, the evidence marshaled by the human rights organizations completely undermined the claim. They found, overwhelmingly, that Israel deliberately targeted protesters who posed no threat whatsoever.

In March 2018, Al-Haq criticized the IDF for "deliberately and systematically" opening fire on unarmed Palestinian protesters.[65] HRW found that "Israeli soldiers were not merely using excessive force, but were apparently acting on orders" that resulted in the "foreseeable deaths and injuries" of unarmed protesters "who posed no imminent threat to life."[66] PCHR confirmed that "the Israeli soldiers deliberately" targeted protesters "in cold blood and deliberately inflicted casualties."[67] Amnesty International characterized the Israeli "response" as a "murderous assault."[68] In its final report, the UN Commission of Inquiry itemized the victims of this slaughter:

- *Children*: "Israeli security forces used lethal force against children who did not pose an imminent threat of death or serious injury to its soldiers"; "[there are] reasonable grounds to believe that Israeli snipers shot them *intentionally*, knowing that they were children."
- *Journalists*: "Israeli snipers shot journalists *intentionally*, despite seeing that they were clearly marked as such."
- *Disabled persons*: "Israeli snipers shot these [disabled] demonstrators *intentionally*, despite seeing that they had visible disabilities."
- *Health workers*: "Israeli snipers *intentionally* shot health workers, despite seeing that they were clearly marked as such."
- *Non-participants*: "[D]emonstrators who were hundreds of metres away from the Israeli forces and visibly engaged in civilian activities were intentionally shot."[69]

Israel falsely claimed it was exercising its right of self-defense as it put down a violent riot along its border, and US media coverage uncritically reinforced the propaganda. But human rights organizations reached a diametrically opposed conclusion. They unanimously found that Israel had been confronted with a protest in territory it was unlawfully blockading; that this protest was overwhelmingly unarmed; and that, in response, Israel carried out a "calculated" (HRW), "deliberate" (Adalah), "intentional" (UN Commission of Inquiry), "murderous assault" (Amnesty International) against civilians.

Gaza's Sharpeville
That the nonviolent character of the Great March of Return lasted as long as it did, in the face of overwhelming brutality, is a lasting testament to resilience, courage, and self-discipline. That US media betrayed this sacrifice is a lasting testament to cowardice. On March 21, 1960, the South African Police opened fire on thousands of unarmed protesters who were demonstrating against the racist pass laws. The incident, which left sixty-nine people dead and 180 injured, galvanized the international anti-apartheid movement and went down in history as the infamous "Sharpeville Massacre." On May 14, 2023, sixty Palestinians were killed in Gaza and *fully 1,359 were injured* with live ammunition. Yet that bloodletting, far from constituting a historic milestone in the long struggle for human rights, has already been forgotten.

To fully understand the events of October 7, 2023—why Hamas staged a violent prison break, and why the break took such vicious form—it must be acknowledged that alternative strategies had been tried, and tried again, without success. In 2018, when the people of Gaza embarked on mass nonviolent protest to draw attention to their plight, this effort was violently crushed. That does not justify the atrocities perpetrated by Hamas. But it does call for a more honest distribution of moral responsibility: culpability for the horrors of October 7 does not lie with Hamas *alone*, but *also* with the US and Israeli governments who strangled a nonviolent campaign for internationally recognized human rights, as well as the US media which—in abandoning objectivity, fairness, and truth—laid the groundwork for oppression, terrorism, and war.

PART II
CATACLYSM

"Burn Gaza now, nothing less!"

—Deputy Speaker of the Knesset
Nissim Vaturi MK

Targeting Civilians: Its Logic in Gaza and Israel

Yaniv Cogan

In a press briefing on October 7, while Hamas's unprecedented attack was still underway, US secretary of defense Lloyd Austin pledged "to ensure that Israel has what it needs to defend itself and protect civilians from indiscriminate violence and terrorism."[1] Hours later, Israeli prime minister Benjamin Netanyahu made his first public comment about the massacre. Referring to Gaza as "that city of evil," Netanyahu vowed to leave it in ruins, and issued a warning to the civilian population: "I'm telling the residents of Gaza: get out of there."[2]

Two months later, the fruits of Israel's US-backed mission to protect civilians from indiscriminate violence were as follows. According to the Government Media Office in Gaza, over 17,700 people in Gaza had been killed, overwhelmingly civilians. More than 7,700 children and 5,000 women were among the dead. Nearly 85 percent of the population had been displaced. Above 60 percent of housing units were damaged or destroyed.[3]

Yaniv Cogan studies computer science at Tel Aviv University.

Hospitals and clinics throughout Gaza had been systematically besieged and targeted by airstrikes, rendering the majority
of them inoperable and leading to a collapse of the healthcare
system.[4] A doctor working at the Indonesian Hospital in Beit
Lahiya testified about the conditions there: "We do surgeries
while the injuries are covered with flies. And we have worms
coming out of wounds, even after we do the surgery . . . The
whole hospital is full of blood and insects."[5] Other doctors
reported having to perform operations, including amputations,
without anesthesia due to lack of supplies, and having to dis-
infect wounds with vinegar and window cleaning products.[6]

Gaza's water infrastructure was decimated by aerial bombardment[7] and deprivation of fuel required to operate water
pumps and treatment plants.[8] This left streets in southern Gaza
overflowing with sewage.[9] Worsening sanitary conditions and
the healthcare collapse led to a spike in disease-related deaths,
especially among children. A spokesperson for the World
Health Organization (WHO) put it bluntly: "Basically, if you're
sick, if your child has diarrhoea, if you've got a respiratory infec-
tion, you're not going to get any [help]." She added that, unless
the healthcare system was reestablished, "we will see more people dying from disease than from bombardment."[10] Already in
November, Oxfam reported that "newborns up to three months
old are dying of diarrhoea, hypothermia, dehydration."[11] In
some cases observed by human rights groups, "children have
suffered from dehydration not only because there is no water,
but also because they refuse to drink."[12]

The north of Gaza had become "an uninhabitable moonscape," according to a report by the Associated Press, an assessment shared by Dr. Ghassan Abu-Sittah, a British-Palestinian
surgeon who warned, based on his experience working in several Gazan hospitals since the beginning of the assault, that the

Strip was being turned into "an uninhabitable death world." The *Economist* estimates it will remain so "for years."[13]

Yinon Magal, a right-wing Israeli pundit who fantasized about "dropping a bomb on Gaza that will erase 10,000 people,"[14] entered Gaza as an embedded reporter and was delighted by what he saw:

> [My] first impression—there is no Gaza. Everything is in ruins, everything is over, no roads, no houses, not a single undamaged home, everything has been destroyed. Our guys did a hell of a job here, and this is only the beginning.[15]

Israeli journalist Ron Ben-Yishai was also given a tour of the ruins. He noted with satisfaction the destruction wrought upon the place where "up until a week ago lived the mothers, wives, children, and parents of the sadistic murderers." Ben-Yishai continued: "Birds of prey are circling in the skies above us. In this area, on these days, there is a lot to stick a beak into. It is obvious that they got used to it. The firing of the cannons and mortars does not frighten them."[16]

Israel's means and ends

In the face of overwhelming evidence that the Israeli military (IDF) intentionally targeted civilians and civilian infrastructure in Gaza, the Biden administration did not waver from its position: "it is obvious" Israel seeks to minimize civilian casualties.[17] Indeed, Israeli officials did occasionally claim that their sole aim in Gaza was "destroying Hamas," and that, in pursuing this military objective, the IDF was attempting to prevent harm to civilians.[18] But that PR line was undercut by other statements from influential decision-makers in Israel's senior military and political echelons that were more consistent with Israel's manifest conduct in Gaza as well as with established information about its military doctrine.

Israeli officials typically explain attacks directed against civilian populations as an attempt to pressure civilians to turn against the "terror organizations." In 2004, then finance minister Netanyahu advocated "hitting infrastructure in Gaza in order to pressure the population to vomit out the Qassam launchers."[19] Two years later, after shrapnel from IDF shelling killed eight-year-old Hadeel Ghaban in Beit Lahia, IDF chief of staff Dan Halutz insisted that "the Palestinian population must understand that if it vomits out the rocket launchers, then it will be able to live in peace."[20] In 2018, a *Ha'aretz* military correspondent reported that "[t]he intention behind the latest batch of airstrikes [by Israel] is to put Hamas in a problematic position vis-á-vis the civilian population in the Strip."[21]

This philosophy is not limited to routine punishment of the civilian population. Israeli policymakers also apply it to the conduct of the IDF during major offensives. In such cases, the "price" the IDF seeks to inflict upon the civilian population inflates to barbaric proportions. Major General Gadi Eizenkot, who would later be appointed IDF chief of staff, is often credited with formalizing and promoting the approval of a military doctrine based on these principles, which he described in an October 2008 interview:

> I call it the a-Dahiya doctrine. What happened in the a-Dahiya district of Beirut in 2006 will happen in every village from which Israel is shot at. We will subject it to disproportionate force and cause enormous damage and destruction. We don't consider them to be civilian villages but military bases. . . . This is not a recommendation, this is the plan. And it has already been approved.[22]

The former head of Israel's National Security Council, Major General Giora Eiland, expanded upon Eizenkot's doctrine in a paper published by Israel's Institute for National Security Studies (INSS), concerning the application of these principles in the case of a third war in Lebanon. He argued that "the suffering of hundreds of thousands of people are the things that can have the most effect on the conduct of Hezbollah." On this basis, he recommended Israel make clear that "the next war will be between Israel and Lebanon, not Israel and Hezbollah," and that such a war "will bring about the elimination of the Lebanese military, destruction of infrastructure, and extreme suffering to the civilian population."[23] Eiland also laid out this vision in an opinion column for the Israeli news website *Ynet*:

> The only good thing that happened in the last war [i.e., the 2006 Lebanon War] was the relative damage caused to Lebanon's population. The destruction of thousands of homes of "innocents" preserved some of Israel's deterrent power. The only way to prevent another war is to make it clear that should one break out, Lebanon may be razed to the ground.[24]

Eiland's recommendation was adopted by the IDF and remained virtually unchanged over the last fifteen years, so much so that, in 2018, he was quoted almost verbatim by then head of the IDF's Northern Command, Major General Yoel Strick: "Our next war will be between Israel and Lebanon in its entirety, not Israel and Hezbollah."[25]

Two months after the publication of Eiland's INSS paper, Israel launched a major assault on Gaza, Operation Cast Lead, during which it implemented the Dahiya doctrine, leaving immense devastation in its wake. Eiland plainly laid out the pertinence of the doctrine to Israel's aims in Gaza:

[If our goal] is a real cease fire, with deterrence that will last for
a very long time, and sorting out additional issues including
prisoner exchanges, then this can be achieved relatively easily,
in a few days. The more pressure [we put] on Gaza, including
killing civilians, and the more the international community
gets mad at us, the better![26]

Commenting on the success of that offensive, Israeli officials
highlighted the restoration of Israel's "deterrence" not only
vis-á-vis Hamas but also—and primarily—in the eyes of other
regional actors. Major General Herzi Halevi dismissed the idea
that "we went too far":

It is true that there are streets [in Gaza] that look like [cities]
after the Second World War. Destruction and devastation that
even the pictures shown on TV don't adequately capture. Still,
the proportionality of our operation, given the location and
traps set by the enemy, was very appropriate. . . . The Iranians,
the Syrians, and Hezbollah looked at what happened here,
and got the message.[27]

Yoav Gallant, then commander of the IDF Southern Command,
similarly explained:

Operation Cast Lead came one and a half years after [the
2006 Lebanon War], and reeducated the entire region. It
was followed by Egypt, Syria, Iran, Hamas, Hezbollah.
They watched [the devastation in Gaza], and understood
that what the IDF did there, it could copy-and-paste [else-
where]. The significance of this to [our] deterrence towards
Lebanon is ten times greater than that of the [2006] Lebanon War, as unrelated as it may seem. It is very much
related.[28]

Netanyahu was the leader of the opposition during Cast Lead. But he agreed that blows should be inflicted on the civilian population in any one battlefield to enhance Israel's deterrence vis-à-vis regional actors in general. Thus, he boasted in 2006 that "during my tenure as Prime Minister no rockets or Qassams were launched [from Gaza], because whenever there was Katyusha fire [from Lebanon] we turned off the lights in Beirut."[29]

In the aftermath of Operation Cast Lead, Eizenkot's interview to the Israeli press was picked up by the UN Fact Finding Mission headed by Judge Richard Goldstone. Goldstone determined that the IDF had carried out in Gaza "a deliberately disproportionate attack designed to punish, humiliate, and terrorize a civilian population." He concluded that "the facts on the ground" demonstrate that "what [Eizenkot] prescribed as the best strategy appears to have been precisely what was put into practice."[30] After the publication of the UN report, Eizenkot was invited to speak at an event hosted by the Haifa University-affiliated National Security Studies Center (NSSC). He was preceded by the head of the NSSC, Professor Dan Schueftan. Schueftan urged that, in the next Lebanon war, "[g]round invasions" should inflict "devastation":

> Ground invasions should be carried out, perhaps under the banner of "harming enemy forces," but *their real significance is the devastation they leave behind them.* I don't mind that as a pretext we claim that there is some military objective, because that's required by all these International Law people, so we can bring in some lawyer to explain how to do it, but the main thing is that [we understand] very clearly [the real purpose]."[31]

Eizenkot appeared to agree with Schueftan, even as he was reluctant to say so explicitly:

I will not use the same words Dan allows himself to use, I did it once in a press interview some years ago, and I had to deal with it for many months afterwards, and also had my name appear in the Goldstone report. So I will use softer words: in case there is a conflict, we must inflict upon our enemy a severe blow that will create deterrence for years to come.[32]

Major General Benny Gantz, at the time the IDF's deputy chief of staff, also commented on the success of Cast Lead, and on the military doctrine Israel would rely upon in the event of a future war in Lebanon. "It will be painful for the Lebanese," he said. "It will be difficult, it will be ugly, and the State of Lebanon needs to understand that. . . . When the war reaches enemy territory . . . we will be unstoppable; a Wadi [valley] here, three villages there, until our government agrees to a ceasefire."[33]

By 2014, when Israel carried out yet another ferocious attack on Gaza, Gantz had been appointed IDF chief of staff. Debriefings after the assault indicated that, under his command, the IDF considered its most significant achievements to have been the "2,000 dead and 11,000 wounded, half a million refugees, [and] decades worth of destruction."[34] Most people killed were civilians. Gantz would go on to boast, in an election campaign video, that "parts of Gaza have been returned back to the Stone Age."[35] Gantz has since repeatedly threatened both Gaza and Lebanon with enormous devastation in line with the principles of the Dahiya Doctrine.[36]

During Israel's 2014 Gaza massacre, Yair Lapid was the finance minister and a member of the cabinet. He concluded approvingly that, "[w]hen the people of Gaza came out [of their houses], they saw destruction on a level they didn't know was possible. They saw Gaza flattened, and understood the scale of the disaster Hamas has brought upon them."[37]

Israel called its assault on Gaza after October 7, 2023, Operation Swords of Iron. The offensive was led by Prime Minister Netanyahu, Defense Minister Yoav Gallant, and IDF chief of staff Herzi Halevi—all three of whom were on record endorsing the intentional targeting of civilians as a core principle of Israel's military doctrine. Day-to-day operational decisions were made by an Emergency War Cabinet, which apart from Netanyahu and Gallant included Benny Gantz, another enthusiastic supporter of targeting civilians. Gadi Eizenkot, who formulated the Dahiya Doctrine, was one of two observing members of the War Cabinet. Defense Minister Gallant reportedly set up an independent "strategic thinking taskforce,"[38] which, alongside a PR consultant and experts on matters related to the management of the home front, included two advisors on military affairs: Giora Eiland and Yoel Strick. Both advocated targeting civilians, an approach also endorsed by the leader of the opposition, Yair Lapid.

The absolute consensus among Israeli war leaders that targeting civilians is both legitimate and necessary, together with the well-documented conduct of the IDF during the onslaught, leave no room for doubt that Israel's assault on Gaza's civilian population has been deliberate.

From containment to destruction

But the assault on Gaza after October 7 did not simply recapitulate the approach adopted in preceding "rounds."[39] In key respects, it marked a qualitative departure. During previous assaults Israel did not seek to depose Hamas from power; rather, as Gantz put it, Israel's strategy in Gaza entailed "[another] round of war, followed by another, and each such round will have worse consequences for the enemy than the previous one."[40] These "consequences," in the form of mass death and destruction, were supposed to compel the civilian population in

Gaza to apply pressure on Hamas, thus limiting its ability and willingness to attack Israel.

Following October 7, the top political and military echelons in Israel evinced a determination not just to contain Hamas, or degrade its capacity, but to annihilate its presence in Gaza. They held fast to this objective well past the point when its impracticality should have been apparent. Israel's strategy of inflicting massive damage upon the civilian population in Gaza could therefore no longer be explained on the basis of the conventional (Dahiya) doctrine. Instead, statements by Israeli officials indicated that a major component of current Israeli military doctrine is a genocidal aspiration to harm civilians for its own sake, either out of revenge for the October 7 attacks or to capitalize on the political opportunity those attacks created.[41]

In a letter to IDF soldiers, Prime Minister Netanyahu urged them to "'[r]emember what Amalek did to you' . . . This is a war between the sons of light and the sons of darkness."[42] This invoked the biblical injunction to carry out a war of annihilation against the people of Amalek, to "slay both man and woman, infant and suckling, ox and sheep, camel and ass."

At the outset of the assault, Defense Minister Gallant announced that Israel was "imposing a complete siege on the city of Gaza. There will be no electricity, no food, no water, no fuel, everything is closed. We are fighting animals," he explained, "and we are acting accordingly." Gallant elsewhere promised that Israel "will change the face of reality in the Gaza Strip for the coming 50 years." By attacking Israel, he vowed, Hamas leader "Yahya Sinwar . . . sealed the fate of Hamas and the fate of Gaza."[43]

Major General Giora Eiland declared that "our only way to bring back the hostages" held by Hamas "is to create a severe humanitarian crisis in Gaza."[44] He advised that Israel should not only cut Gaza's water supply but also put out of commission local water-related infrastructure, either by bombing wells and water treatment facilities, or by ensuring they can't operate due to lack of electricity.[45] And he urged that Israel maintain its resolve in the face of international pressure that would come when "the Palestinians show pictures of babies who died in their incubators due to blackouts resulting from the lack of fuel."[46] The end goal, Eiland said, is "to render Gaza an uninhabitable place, temporarily, or permanently," from which it followed that "Israel in this case cannot spare these civilians in Gaza."[47] In an article published six weeks into the assault, Eiland concluded:

> The international community warns us of a humanitarian disaster In Gaza and of severe epidemics. We must not shy away from it, as difficult as that may be. After all, severe epidemics in the south of the Gaza Strip will bring victory closer and reduce casualties among IDF soldiers. And no, this is not about cruelty for cruelty's sake, since we don't support the suffering of the other side as an end, but as a means.[48]

This aspect of Eiland's recommendations appears consistent with the policy implemented by the IDF in Gaza—both in general, as reviewed above, and in detail. In line with Eiland's warning that Israel would face international pressure once incubators in Gaza were rendered unusable for lack of electricity, the IDF spokesperson unit prepared a series of PR stunts to coincide with reports from Al-Shifa Hospital that premature babies had—exactly as foreseen—begun to perish.[49]

Discussion of major changes to the status quo in Gaza "the day after the war," and in particular hints by Israeli officials of a long-term Israeli military or civilian presence within Gaza, are significantly more commonplace than they were during previous ground invasions of the Strip. In 2014, then finance minister Yair Lapid's insistence that "[a]ll the options, including the reoccupation of Gaza, are on the table"[50] was relatively unusual. By contrast, after October 7, Israeli government ministers and military officials regularly suggested: reoccupying the entire Gaza Strip and reestablishing Israeli settlements there,[51] transferring the Gazan population to tent cities in the Sinai desert,[52] distributing Gazan refugees among the countries of the world,[53] installing a technocratic government to manage the civil affairs of the Strip backed by a UNIFIL-style international peacekeeping force,[54] transferring control over Gaza to the PA while maintaining Israel's ability to carry out ground invasions and airstrikes in the Strip whenever it wishes,[55] and marking a wide "kill-strip" along the perimeter fence to serve as a permanent buffer-zone.[56]

Former acting director of Israel's National Security Council, Ya'acov Nagel, explained that the "'day after' question, important as it may be, is secondary to the current war. . . . We must not let thinking about the 'day after' lead or influence our strategy during the fighting, or hinder the completion of our mission." Taken together with the relentless torrent of contradictory proposals put forward by Israeli officials, this statement might give the impression that the Israeli government is not actually pursuing long-term changes to the situation in Gaza and will eventually revert back to its comfort zone of permanent occupation via remote control. There are, however, initial signs that Israel is making logistical preparations for a long-term on-the-ground presence in Gaza,[57] and given the willingness of the US to go along with even the most outrageous Israeli initiatives,[58] there is a real possibility that the assault will end with the implementation of major changes to the mechanism of occupation and subjugation of the Strip.

The war in Israel
It is currently impossible to conclusively determine the rationale behind Hamas's October 7 operation and atrocities. Basic

details about how the attack was conceptualized in the minds of Hamas's leaders remain a mystery, with only sparse, unconvincing, and often contradictory pieces of evidence shedding any light on the operational plan.[59] More elusive still is the question of what Hamas hoped to gain from it. Even the most knowledgeable assessment of this question based on publicly available information is bound to be little more than guesswork, and it is reasonable to assume that different officials within the organization would offer radically different answers.

An examination of its record—both in words and in actions—might point to some aspects of Hamas's thinking behind October 7, even if there is no basis for confidently asserting knowledge of its intentions. Similarly, while there is no telling what trajectory history will take from this point on, looking back at the history of Israeli policy and social developments may illuminate some of the dynamics that are sure to play an important role in shaping conflict going forward.

Hamas has explained its previous reliance on ruthless violence against civilians, exemplified by the suicide bombings of the 1990s and 2000s, as attempts to encourage the emergence in Israel of a political force which is both aligned with the interests of Palestinians, and backed by the enthusiasm and commitment that characterize the pursuit of one's own pressing needs—as opposed to the existing solidarity-based pro-Palestinian left in Israel, which has been limited to a rather small and privileged section of the population, unwilling to make significant sacrifices in service of the cause. A lucid articulation of this approach was provided by Jamal Abu al-Hayjaa, a senior member of Hamas, in his explanation of the rationale behind attacks on Israeli soldiers and civilians during the second intifada:

> [We wanted] to change the perception of Israelis, who were under the impression they would be able to continue the

occupation forever. The diplomatic negotiations didn't bring any change. Our attacks, however, made Israelis feel the pain we have felt. We wanted them to pressure their government to halt its actions—and for us the [2005 Gaza] disengagement is proof of our ability to change the Israeli consciousness.[60]

This approach has enabled other regional actors to secure major concessions from Israel. The blow inflicted by Egypt's surprise attack in October 1973 forced Israel to abandon its rejectionist stance and negotiate a withdrawal from the occupied Sinai Peninsula. Similarly, it was Hezbollah's armed struggle that created the political conditions for the development of a popular pro-withdrawal camp in Israel, led by the Four Mothers movement.[61] That campaign quickly achieved what leftist movements in Israel, which had opposed the occupation of South Lebanon on principled grounds, failed to do for eighteen years.[62]

Palestinian armed groups which followed this line of thinking have had much more limited success so far; even the achievement cited by Abu al-Hayjaa—compelling Israel to evacuate its settlers from Gaza and redeploy the IDF along the perimeter—has proven to be, at best, a mixed bag.[63] In part, this failure reflects the fact that Israel's commitment to controlling Gaza and the West Bank has always been significantly greater than its commitment to controlling the Sinai Peninsula or South Lebanon. But this difference does not fully account for the failure of armed resistance to dislodge the occupation of the Palestinian territories.

Additional reasons for the underwhelming success of armed resistance to the occupation were pointed out early on by Sabri Jiryis, editor-at-large of *Shu'un Filastiniyya*, the journal of the PLO research center. Predicting from the outset that the largely nonviolent first intifada would fail, Jiryis harshly criticized the PLO leadership for "organizing international peace conferences and unending discussions of 'just peace'"[64] while demonstrating "clear incompetence" when it came to armed resistance:

> The Palestinians go out on demonstrations, throw stones, or carry out knife attacks—and the occupation forces respond by opening fire; and the martyrs fall one after another . . . the demonstrations and the stone throwing are an indisputable proof that organized armed resistance has failed. . . . There is no doubt this miserable showing does more harm than good: the resistance loses its credibility; the resistance doesn't play a part in convincing the enemy to change its views or pull it towards a more realistic and moderate position—instead it hardens their hearts, and—and here lies the danger—leads to Palestinian national aspirations not being taken seriously.

Jiryis, whose criticism was endorsed by other dissenting voices within the PLO, including poet Mahmoud Darwish and cartoonist Naji al-Ali,[65] likened armed struggle and diplomatic pressure in service of achievable goals to "two rails that make up a train track, both of which are required in order to reach the station." As he foresaw, the Palestinian national struggle soon derailed: the first intifada failed to compel Israel into conceding an inch toward the core demands of the Palestinians. Instead, the PLO became a de facto collaborator with the Israeli military occupation and an enabler of its apartheid regime.

If military incompetence previously limited the potential of Palestinian armed struggle, Hamas's October 7 assault and resilience in the face of Israeli retaliation indicates that this constraint has been overcome. Yet the goal of pulling the Israeli government "towards a more realistic and moderate position"—as Jiryis put it—or inducing Israelis to "pressure their government to [end the occupation]"—as Abu al-Hayjaa described Hamas's aim—still seems very far off.

The complexity inherent in any attempt to translate violent blows into lasting political gains can be usefully illustrated by examining a novel dimension of the current hostilities in Gaza: the large number of hostages taken by Hamas (as well as other Palestinian groups and private individuals) back into Gaza. This was an aspect of Hamas's assault that was undoubtedly part of its original plan, rather than a spur-of-the-moment development.

Almost 250 people were taken captive in southern Israel and brought to Gaza on October 7, the vast majority of them civilians.[66] The first protests calling on the government to prioritize returning hostages over destroying Hamas were organized by the marginalized Israeli left. They were met with a violent crackdown by police and right-wing hooligans.[67] The slogan "bring them back home" has remained prominent in anti-war protests,[68] even as direct opposition to the assault on Gaza—initially deemed both physically dangerous[69] and politically suicidal—became possible.

The Israeli government completely ignored these protests and instead elected to follow the policy outlined by Finance Minister Bezalel Smotrich: "Now we must be cruel, and not be overly concerned about the hostages."[70] The government has stuck to this policy even as Hamas began spreading claims that Israeli hostages had been killed by Israeli airstrikes in Gaza.[71] In polls conducted by the Israel Democracy Institute between October 15 and October 19, only around 17 percent of respondents supported an immediate ceasefire (a term which in Israeli discourse can be assumed to refer to a temporary pause) in order to facilitate the return of the hostages through negotiations with Hamas.[72]

It was within this seemingly inhospitable environment that a significant new political force emerged. A large number of families of the hostages formed "the HQ of the Families of the

Abducted," which soon became recognized as a representative organization of nearly all such families.[73] The HQ advocated an "all-for-all" prisoner exchange—that is, the release of all Palestinian prisoners in exchange for all the hostages held in Gaza[74]—and criticized the intensity of Israel's assault on Gaza, which put in jeopardy the lives of those held captive. In the initial days following October 7, these positions made the HQ a radical outlier in Israel's political landscape.

Crucially, the HQ was not part of the marginal Israeli Left, nor was it concerned with the well-being of Palestinians in Gaza. Although some speeches at their rallies highlighted the contradiction between bombarding Gaza and securing the return of hostages,[75] other speeches advocated a maximum pressure approach even more punishing than the one implemented by the IDF.

In an official statement posted on its Facebook page, the HQ bemoaned the entry of limited humanitarian aid into Gaza, accusing the government of "pampering the murderers and kidnappers with baklava and medicine."[76] Following statements by the Biden administration in favor of temporary humanitarian pauses, the HQ set up tents next to the Kirya military base, vowing not to leave without guarantees that "no ceasefire will be made without the return of all the hostages."[77]

The protests by families of the hostages soon grew to become the largest political demonstrations held in Israel since Hamas's attack. They culminated in a five-day march from Tel Aviv to Jerusalem, which reportedly drew over 25,000 participants.[78] The HQ was able to secure meetings with top Israeli officials including Prime Minister Netanyahu and Defense Minister Gallant, and forced officials from nearly the entire political spectrum to pay lip-service to their plight by repeatedly assuring the Israeli public that the safe return of hostages was guiding Israeli policy.[79]

By November 24, 49 percent of Israelis polled said the safe return of the hostages should be prioritized by the government over all other goals; only 32 percent of respondents said "destroying Hamas" was more important.[80] That same day, the Israeli government finally accepted a hostage exchange deal roughly in line with Qatari-mediated proposals that had reportedly been on the table almost immediately after October 7.[81] Notably, the government was compelled to accept the hostage exchange and accompanying ceasefire despite making very little progress toward its stated military objective of "destroying Hamas," or even the more limited aim of "denying Hamas its military capabilities."[82]

At a time when most expressions of dissent resulted in political marginalization, the HQ of the Families of the Abducted harshly criticized the government and yet remained well within the political mainstream. Eventually, the HQ forced the Israeli government to change its agenda and agree to a temporary ceasefire which afforded some relief to the people of Gaza. Could this development be considered a realization of Abu al-Hayjaa's hope that Israelis affected by Hamas's terror attacks will "pressure their government to halt its actions"? Perhaps, but if so, it also demonstrated the limits of this approach. Like the Four Mothers before it, the HQ of the Families of the Abducted was in no way committed to humanitarian principle; unlike the Four Mothers, it had not, at the time of writing, coalesced around a consistent political demand. As circumstances shift, it could become a reactionary force that will pressure the government to implement ever crueler measures in Gaza.

Yet the difficulties that have so far prevented the realization of Hamas's tactical aims—namely, forcing the release of all Palestinian prisoners while placing some limit on the ferocity of Israel's assault—pale in comparison to the seemingly insurmountable challenge Hamas faces when it comes to leveraging the blow it inflicted on Israel into a strategic achievement. Across virtually the entire Israeli political spectrum, Hamas has been completely written off as a partner for peace. Avi Dabush, executive director of the group "Rabbis for Human Rights," wrote: "Hamas . . . was revealed as ISIS, as a Nazi force, as absolute evil . . . Hamas, with which I called in the past to negotiate . . . in order to bring about a [peaceful] settlement, has lost its right to exist."[83] Representing the left-most edge of acceptable opinion, the communist Member of the Knesset Ofer Cassif (of the Hadash-Ta'al list) referred to the October 7 massacre as "monstrous, satanic carnage," described it as a "terror operation in the style of the Nazis," and characterized Hamas's Gaza-based leader Yahya Sinwar as "a vile fanatic . . . who aspires to commit genocide."[84] According to Cassif, Netanyahu has pursued a policy aimed at emboldening "the Hamas murderers" and weakening the Palestinian Authority,[85] a baseless myth which has its origins in the very same hawkish regime-change advocates who sabotaged Hamas's peace initiatives and set the foundations of Israeli policy in Gaza.[86]

This development presents a major problem for Hamas, which, unlike Hezbollah, cannot fulfill its main objective—an end to the occupation and the establishment of an independent Palestinian state—solely through unilateral action.

There is a stark contrast between the hawkish Israeli reaction to the blow inflicted by Hamas on October 7 and the equally severe surprise attack by Egyptian forces fifty years prior. During the 1973 War, major atrocities were committed by both sides.[87] Yet even before the fighting ceased, Israeli newspapers—alongside murderous calls to inflict suffering upon the Arab population[88]—were also graced by headlines preparing the ground for peace: "Sadat's Wife: 'I Have a Feeling We Are Standing on the Cusp of Peace'," "Instead of Stagnation—the Beginning of Progress Towards Peace?" By

the end of December, even long-time peace rejectionist Golda
Meir, the prime minister, had expressed "Support for Territorial
Concessions in Exchange for Peace."[89]

No such headlines have appeared in Israeli media since
October 7. The Hebrew press, without exception, ignored
comments made by Hamas leader Ismail Haniyeh in a tele-
vised speech on November 1, which reaffirmed Hamas's support for initiating negotiations on a two-state solution based
on internationally accepted principles.[90] The Israeli media
also quickly glossed over Israeli minister of health Aryeh
Deri's acknowledgment that Haniyeh's proposal (or one
very similar) was officially conveyed by Hamas to the Israeli
cabinet and immediately dismissed despite being deemed
serious.[91]

Nor has the Israeli media reported senior Hamas official
Mousa Abu Marzouk's comments on the October 7 attack:

> We said, "We want peace, but give us some of our rights"—
> but they didn't let us in . . . We tried *every* path. We didn't
> find one political path to take us out of this morass and free
> us from occupation.[92]

Israeli media outlets focused instead on bloodthirsty statements
made by Hamas officials Ghazi Hamad and Taher El-Nounou
in order to crush support for peace in Israel, while cheerleading
the carnage in Gaza. This approach is sure to wear out the seemingly unending willingness of the Palestinians to seek a political
solution.[93]

If any silver lining is to emerge from the horrors of October
7 and after, Hamas cannot be content with having momentar-
ily seized the reins of history but will have to take bold initiatives toward a just resolution of the conflict. If it does not do
so, and instead remains paralyzed by the absence of a political

strategy,[94] Israel's lasting response will end up being determined by a right-wing government and a warmongering media. It is unlikely that any progress toward peace will be made in this scenario. Instead, Israel and the US will continue to tighten the noose around Gaza, as Israel entrenches an increasingly vicious system of apartheid across the entirety of Palestine.

"Severe epidemics in the south of the Gaza Strip will bring victory closer"

—Advisor to the Defense Minister and former head of the National Security Council Giora Eiland

Just Like That: Life and Death in Gaza

Ahmed Alnaouq

I was born in 1994 in Deir al-Balah, Gaza. A small city, population around 80,000. It's not London or New York. There are few lights or towering buildings. But it's my home and I always loved it. The palm trees lift me. They are everywhere. If you climb to a high area in Deir al-Balah, it's all you see: hundreds of palm trees.

Most of the residents are farmers, or used to be. In Gaza, we joke that Deir al-Balah is the city where everyone goes to sleep at seven. Farmers can't lie in. My father was also born there. But like most in Gaza, my family hails from towns and cities that were destroyed or ethnically cleansed to make way for Israel.

My father's relatives lived in Yafa. The area is known today for the metropolis of Tel Aviv. My mother came from Beersheba. An Israeli city now. A few months before my father was born, in 1948, some 750,000 Palestinians were driven from their homes

---

Ahmed Alnaouq is a journalist from Gaza. He co-founded We Are Not Numbers, which helps young people in Gaza share their stories, and Border Gone, which publishes stories from Gaza in Hebrew. He works as an advocacy officer for the Euro-Med Human Rights Monitor.

in what is now Israel. My forebears fled to Gaza and our fate was sealed.

When my father was born, his grandfather went to the marketplace to fetch him a doctor. An Israeli airplane appeared from nowhere and bombed the market, killing 150 people, just like that. My great-grandfather was among them. You will search the records in vain for mention of this. Only a few Palestinians in Deir al-Balah still remember. Many such massacres have been erased from history. That's why the world is surprised when Palestinians, sometimes, fight back.

My father lived his whole life in Deir al-Balah. He was one of the smartest people I ever met. He had a photographic memory: at seventy-five years old, he could recite passages from textbooks he studied in elementary school. He spoke Hebrew, English, and Arabic, despite having been unable to attend university. Gaza didn't have one at the time, and anyway, he had family to support after his own father died.

When Israel occupied Gaza in 1967, it hollowed out the economy to make us dependent. Most Gazans could either work in Israel or not at all. I remember my father waking up at two in the morning to a catch a bus into Israel for work. He wouldn't return until seven in the evening. He did this every day, despite having to endure humiliations from his boss and from Israeli soldiers at the checkpoints.

There was no Hamas then. But the spirit which feeds it sprung from the degradation and physical abuse men like my father went through. Israeli soldiers would sometimes detain Palestinian laborers for hours, or order them to strip naked, just for their amusement. My mother was always worried for my father's safety. She spent her evenings by the window, awaiting his return.

My father shared a story when I was about five that I can never forget. His Israeli boss told him, "God created only Israelis as humans; the rest of the world were animals, created to serve them. But the early Israelis were disgusted with the animals, so they asked God to transform them into human-like beings. And that's how you all came to be." It seems many in Israel still don't view Palestinians as fully human. In October 2023, Israel's defense minister Yoav Gallant ordered a "complete siege" on Gaza: "no electricity, no food, no water, no fuel." "We are fighting human animals," he said, "and we are acting accordingly."

The second intifada erupted in 2000, when I was six. Israel stopped allowing Palestinians to cross from Gaza to find work. Just like that, my father lost his job, so he bought a car and found work as a taxi driver. Another joke in Gaza: everyone is a taxi driver, because there are no other jobs around. Like every Palestinian revolt, the second intifada was a reaction to Israel's suffocating restrictions. People from abroad should try to understand: when you are forced to live under military occupation, when you are constricted, confined, and controlled, with no end in sight, you will push back, and may even, at times, lash out.

The second intifada period was formative for me. I began to understand what was going on, what I had been born into. On my walks to school, I saw protests, and funerals. I remember an Israeli tank invading Deir al-Balah, my city, and killing people in its tracks. Apache helicopters and M-16s supplied the soundtrack. Of course, my friends and I played, too. But our dominant memories are of violence.

One day my older brother, Ayman, came back more scared than usual. He was trembling. "Ayman, what happened?" He had been walking in the street when, just like that, a tank killed six of his friends, all thirteen or fourteen years old. "Why?" All he could say was that the tank shot everyone in its path.

This memory is joined by others. Muhammad al-Durrah, from the Buraij refugee camp in Gaza, was killed by Israeli bullets while his father tried to shield him with a hug. We saw it on TV. And there was Iman Hajjo, three months old, from my city. An Israeli tank fired, and Iman was killed in the arms of her mother. Just like that. One day my brother went missing, and my mother was beside herself. A neighbor told her, "We saw an Israeli man killing your son." Fortunately, this was untrue. We survived.

The intifada ended and Israel withdrew its settlers from Gaza. We could now move more freely. But when Hamas won elections in 2006, Israel put Gaza under a blockade. Israel always claims it does not target civilians. But who is hurt when food, water, gas, and electricity are limited?

I was twelve when the borders were sealed. I remember my father collecting firewood every morning so he could make food for us. The siege sent us back hundreds of years. But we still had television, to remind us how others lived. Almost all the factories in Gaza closed. Farmers stopped working for lack of fuel, fertilizer, and spare parts. My father, still driving his taxi to support us, resorted to vegetable oil for gas. Israeli technicians calculated the minimum number of calories we needed to survive, and only that much food was allowed in.

On December 27, 2008, Israel launched its first major assault on Gaza. I was in the ninth grade, waiting nervously for an exam. I had not studied much and was worried about how it would go. Suddenly, I heard loud explosions outside the school. My first thought was, *It's Yawm al-Qiyamah.* Judgment Day. I heard screams and saw fire and smoke in the sky. I had never been so close to a bombing. As I ran home, I saw corpses in the streets, blood everywhere.

In the end, 1,400 Palestinians were killed in that war. 5,000 more were injured. And 60,000 homes were damaged or destroyed. When the bombardment ceased, after three weeks, we tried to pick up the pieces of our lives. But then, in 2012, another war. About a hundred people killed in just over a week. And in 2014, they came again. This one lasted fifty-one days. The bombing was everywhere and did not stop. This time, my family did not escape.

My brother was killed, along with six of my friends. He was my closest companion. We grew up together, and now I was nineteen, and he was gone. Just like that. My last memory of him is his face covered in blood. As for my friends, they were buried under the rubble for eight days. When their bodies were eventually retrieved, during a "humanitarian pause," they had already begun to decompose.

I was never the same after that war. I spent my days beside my brother's grave. When an American friend, Pam, reached out to me on Facebook, I told her "I'm fine." She insisted, "No, tell me something real." And my feelings poured out. She encouraged me to write about Ayman, to celebrate his life. With her coaching, I wrote my first story in English—about my brother—and she published it.

That was a turning point for me. My story was read by many people, some of whom reached out to learn more about Palestine and offer support. I realized the power of words to educate people abroad, to show that we are more than mere statistics. Pam and I set up a platform, We Are Not Numbers, pairing young people in Gaza with writing mentors from around the world.

*

In 2023, Gaza entered its seventeenth year under Israeli blockade. There was no hope of relief. Then Hamas launched an attack that reportedly killed 1,200 Israelis, and Israel retaliated with its most devastating assault on Gaza yet. I had settled in London after studying in the UK on a scholarship, but was on holiday in Turkey when the bombing started. Unlike in 2008,

2012, and 2014, I was away from my family during a war. I worried about them constantly.

Most of my relatives gathered at my father's place in Deir al-Balah. It was in a residential neighborhood, with no military installations or warehouses nearby. If anywhere was safe, we thought, it's there. I called them every day, asking how they were. "We're fine, we're OK." They were running out of food and water, though. "The situation is very difficult," they admitted—"but we're together. Together, we'll be OK."

They were asleep when, on October 22, at five in the morning, some Israeli pilot dropped a bomb on our house. Just like that. My family wiped out.

My father, Nasri Alnaouq, aged seventy-five.

My sister Walaa, thirty-six, and her children: Raghd, thirteen; Eslam, twelve; Sara, nine; and Abdullah, six.

My sister Alaa, thirty-five, and her children: Eslam, thirteen; Dima, twelve; Tala, eight; Noor, four; and Nasmah, two.

My sister Aya, thirty-three, and her children: Malak, twelve; Mohammed, nine; and Tamim, six.

My oldest brother, Muhammad, thirty-five, and his children: Bakr, eleven, and Basema, nine.

And Mahmoud, twenty-five, a human rights activist who had just been admitted to a master's program in Australia. My little brother.

Why was my family eliminated? There was no reason. Were militants there? No. Were rockets there? No. They turned my home into ash and vaporized the life from those people because they were Palestinian. Because the occupation decreed that a decent life is not for us, and if we demand it, then life is not for us.

Many of my relatives were left for days under the rubble. One family member went to my home to recover the pieces. He put these remains that were once my nieces and nephews, brothers and sisters in a trash bag and gave it to my sister. Just like that. For me, and my surviving family, this is an epic tragedy. It is also an epic tragedy for the world. Because what the world let happen to Gaza, in 2023 and before 2023, is a stain that can never be removed.

"The children in Gaza have brought this upon themselves"

—Meirav Ben-Ari MK, Yesh Atid, opposition

Nothing Fails Like Success: Hamas and the Gaza Explosion

Khaled Hroub

What did Hamas hope to achieve by its attack of October 7, 2023? Why did it select that date? How far did events unfold according to plan, and in particular, to what extent was the targeting of civilians in southern Israel premeditated? The evidence pertaining to such questions currently ranges from suggestive to non-existent. It seems that Hamas launched the operation without notifying its main allies, Hezbollah and Iran. Even the external leadership of Hamas was apparently kept in the dark. It would have been reckless to provoke a massive Israeli offensive without preparing the ground for covering interventions from other fronts. Failure to coordinate with the "resistance axis" therefore indicates that the blow inflicted by Hamas on October 7 exceeded what its architects had designed.

One plausible interpretation is that Operation Al-Aqsa Deluge was an attempt by Hamas to repeat its Operation Jerusalem Sword of May 2021. That confrontation began after

Khaled Hroub is professor of Middle Eastern studies at Northwestern University/Qatar and the author of two books on Hamas.

Hamas demanded that Israel halt evictions in the East Jerusalem neighborhood of Sheikh Jarrah as well as encroachments by far-right Jewish nationalists on the Al-Aqsa Mosque. When Israel failed to comply, Hamas and the Palestinian Islamic Jihad fired hundreds of rockets from Gaza. The conflict which ensued ended with a ceasefire after eleven days. Hamas launched Jerusalem Sword in part to answer criticisms that, since its military takeover of the Gaza Strip in 2007, it had become absorbed by local problems at the expense of the broader national agenda. The operation was a political triumph as, almost immediately, large demonstrations erupted in the West Bank, the Arab world, and among Palestinian citizens of Israel. This concerted effort was celebrated by Palestinians whose struggle had been hobbled for so long by geographic and political fragmentation. National unity had been realized in resistance.

Hamas might have conceived Operation Al-Aqsa Deluge as an attempt to recreate this "unity of the battlefields" on a larger scale. In a speech on October 12, Hamas spokesman Abu Obeida declared that the "current battle has started where Operation Jerusalem Sword left off."[1] There are notable parallels between the two initiatives. In both 2021 and 2023, unlike previous confrontations, Hamas struck first. In both cases, too, Hamas presented its attack as a response to national challenges rather than grievances specific to Gaza. As the leader of Hamas's military wing, Mohammed Deif, stated on October 7, 2023:

> The incursions of the occupation troops into Al-Aqsa increased, and they desecrated the holiness of the Mosque, dragged praying women, the elderly, the children and the youth and prevented them from arriving to the mosque . . . At the same time, the occupation authorities still imprison thousands of our heroes and practice against them the most brutal methods of humiliation and torture. There are hundreds of

our prisoners who spent more than twenty years in prison, and dozens of them, males and females, whose bodies were eaten by cancer and illnesses, and many of them died because of lack of medical treatment, and a deliberate slow death. All our offers to undertake exchange of prisoners based on human reasons were met by rejection and stubbornness.[2]

Synonymous with Jerusalem, Al-Aqsa is a national reference point as well as the primary symbol through which the Palestinian struggle resonates with Muslim constituencies around the world. Hamas's decision to spotlight it pointed to a political rationale for the attack: enhancing Hamas's stature in Palestinian as well as regional politics, bridging across divided Palestinian constituencies, and returning the Palestinian cause to international and Arab agendas. The frequent references by Hamas to Palestinian prisoners also fell within a broad national agenda, as these prisoners come from various parts of Palestine, and at the same time indicated the operation's practical objective: capturing Israelis to secure the release of more than six thousand Palestinians detained by Israel.

Beyond these preliminary conclusions, no definitive answers can yet be given. But if the precise details of the October 7 eruption could not be foreseen, and remain mysterious, that Gaza would explode *somehow* was widely predicted.[3] To understand why, it is necessary to recognize with UN secretary-general António Guterres that "the attacks by Hamas did not happen in a vacuum," and attend to what Amnesty International termed "the root causes of these repeated cycles of violence."[4] It is commonly said that "nothing succeeds like success." But if Hamas resorted to the violent incursion of October 7, it was because the movement had repeatedly failed to translate short-term triumphs into lasting political gains. Hamas's persistent efforts to participate in a unified Palestinian political system and to acquire international legitimacy were unable to overcome the unyielding intransigence of Israel, the United States, and the rival Palestinian faction Fatah. Meanwhile, if Israel suffered the devastating blow of October 7, this was because its achievements—annexing the Occupied Palestinian Territory (OPT) and sealing off the Gaza concentration camp while simultaneously side-lining the Palestine Question abroad—finally pushed Hamas, and the people of Gaza in general, beyond what they could bear.

Hamas and the "peace process"

In 1987, Palestinians in the West Bank, including East Jerusalem, and Gaza undertook a mass civil revolt against Israel's occupation. In the 1990s, exiled Palestine Liberation Organization (PLO) leaders entered diplomatic talks to capitalize on the uprising. They secured permission to establish a Palestinian Authority (PA) in the OPT. In return, the PLO unilaterally recognized Israel, disavowed armed struggle, and agreed to administer the OPT pending a final settlement of the conflict. These concessions were formalized in the interim 1993 and 1995 Oslo Accords, which did not require Israel to end its colonization of the OPT or commit to Palestinian statehood. Whereas Palestinians expected the Oslo process to culminate in Palestinian independence, it actually gave Israel political cover to further entrench the occupation while conscripting the PA as its functionary. When the Oslo process finally collapsed in 2000, Palestinian disappointment curdled into rage, and a second intifada broke out. What began as another popular uprising rapidly militarized in response to Israel's lethal repression. By 2005 the revolt was quelled.

Hamas—an Islamist nationalist movement comprising an armed wing, a political party, and a social welfare infrastructure—was founded during the first intifada. It generally cooperated with other factions during the uprising. But it rejected the Oslo agreements that followed as a capitulation that abandoned Palestinian rights to their homeland. In the 1990s, Hamas led an anti-Oslo coalition, known as "The Ten Faction," that included the Islamic Jihad movement as well as the main left-wing groups of the PLO. This represented a new phase in Hamas's political trajectory: by combining Islamist, Marxist, and nationalist factions, the alliance prioritized a common political program over ideological conformity. On the ground, Hamas was harshly repressed by the newly installed PA, which hoped thereby to appease its US-Israeli interlocutors and prevent Hamas resistance from derailing negotiations.

The collapse of Oslo and the intifada that ensued gave Hamas room to breathe. The uprising was initially led by Fatah,[5] but the easing of PA repression gave Hamas and the Islamic Jihad a green light to join in. As the violence escalated, Fatah and the PLO factions competed with Hamas over who could fight Israel more ferociously. Fatah even resorted to suicide bombings, a tactic Hamas had employed in the mid-1990s. The resumption of armed struggle by the PLO factions appeared to vindicate the military approach of Hamas and Islamic Jihad. Yet Israel's superior might eventually prevailed while its indiscriminate repression took a severe toll on the PA, all armed factions, and Palestinian society in general.

In 2005, amidst a post-intifada impasse, Hamas took stock and reconsidered its approach.[6] It made three consequential decisions. *First*, to unilaterally end the suicide attacks, which had tarred its image and led not only Israel and the US but also many European states to proscribe Hamas as a terrorist organization.[7] *Second*, to seek membership of the PLO. *Third*, to participate in any municipal or national elections held in Palestine. Taken together, these new policies amounted to a strategic transformation: from the consummate outsider, Hamas would henceforth try desperately to become part of the formal and internationally recognized Palestinian political system.

Frozen out

Hamas's new political strategy yielded short-term successes. But the movement's adversaries—Israel, the US, the PA, and certain Arab governments—undertook a concerted effort to prevent the movement from translating those achievements into lasting gains. Hamas was unable to overcome this opposition and eventually concluded that the political strategy was a dead end.

In January 2006, Hamas contested national elections for the Palestinian Legislative Council. Hamas had for many years opposed Palestinian elections on the grounds that they would be conducted within the framework of the Oslo Accords, which Hamas considered illegitimate. It changed this stance for two main reasons. First, it hoped to circumvent the targeting of the movement by the US. The George W. Bush administration had declared a "global war on terror" and included Hamas in its gallery of evildoers. The PA had signed up for this "war" under US-Israeli pressure, which created a risk of factional conflict with Hamas. In order to legitimize its aggressive policy, the Bush administration simultaneously trumpeted its commitment to "democracy promotion," institutionalized regionally in the Middle East Partnership Initiative. In this context, Hamas participated in Palestinian elections to promote its reconceptualization by the US as a legitimate political party rather than a terrorist group. It hoped to use US "democracy promotion" as a shield against the US "war on terror." Second, Hamas judged that it had sufficient support to win many seats, even as it did not want a full victory.[8] Running in the election would therefore allow it to influence Palestinian decision-making as an opposition party without having to assume the burden of executive authority.

To everyone's surprise, including its own, Hamas won the election.[9] This put the group in an uncomfortable position: a militant resistance force suddenly became the ruling party of an institution that functioned within a framework (the Oslo Accord) it vehemently rejected. Unprepared for this outcome, and lacking administrative experience, Hamas sought to convince other Palestinian factions to join in a coalition government. When Fatah refused and encouraged others to do the same, Hamas reluctantly formed a Hamas-exclusive cabinet in March 2006. Seeking regional and international legitimacy, the Hamas government issued a manifesto whose language hovered around "ending the occupation," well-understood code for accepting the two-state solution.[10] That gesture fell on deaf ears. Israel together with the US and EU imposed economic sanctions on the Hamas government while Israel undertook major military offensives against it. Hamas remained isolated.

Even after Hamas assumed power, the PA security forces remained under the control of the Fatah-aligned President Mahmoud Abbas. This effectively created a dual power structure. The US then collaborated with certain PA security officials to paralyze the Hamas government and ultimately foment a coup against it.[11] In June 2007, Hamas pre-emptively attacked the Fatah-aligned paramilitaries that were causing most of the trouble. Hamas's immediate objective was narrow: to "punish" and constrain the PA's security apparatus.[12] But to its surprise, Hamas fighters found that the PA security forces offered little to no effective resistance and were easily overrun. This tempted Hamas to expand its operation across the entire Gaza Strip, culminating in the dismissal of all PA security forces and the imposition of Hamas's sole military control. Hamas fighters triumphed—but the chalice was poisoned.

When Hamas launched its anticipatory strike, it no more expected to end up in sole command of Gaza than it had foreseen, prior to January 2006, that it would form the next Palestinian government. Once again, a short-term, tactical move wound up having strategic significance. And once again, Hamas was unable to translate its unexpected success into lasting political gain, due primarily to the unbending refusal of international and other Palestinian actors to engage with it. Immediately after Hamas's electoral victory, and even before it formed a government, the US and Israel mobilized Western and other states to boycott any Hamas-led administration. To achieve this, the Middle East "Quartet"—comprising the US, EU, UN, and Russia—issued three conditions that any Hamas government would need to meet in order to qualify for diplomatic engagement.[13] These stipulated that Hamas should renounce "terrorism," abide by all agreements reached between Israel and the PLO, and recognize Israel. Hamas had hoped that its decisions to unilaterally end suicide attacks, run for elections, and attempt to join the PLO would be received positively as progress toward international expectations. That didn't work, and the cage door began to swing shut.

The Hamas takeover of Gaza in June 2007 triggered further factional warfare that culminated in the PA seizing complete control of the West Bank. The geographical separation Israel had engineered between Gaza and the West Bank was now reinforced by a corresponding political divide. Israel immediately intensified its blockade of Gaza, cutting off access by land, sea, and air. International and regional powers refused to recognize the Hamas authority in Gaza but dealt with it indirectly via UN agencies and NGOs. The movement found itself the de facto ruler of a besieged enclave, isolated from most of the world, committed to resisting the occupation, yet also responsible for delivering services and security to more than two million Palestinians.

Under siege

Notwithstanding these difficulties, the movement managed to consolidate its rule in Gaza. It was especially effective in the realm of internal security. Following Israel's disengagement in 2005, the residents of Gaza had been plagued by criminal and clan violence. The PA's multiple and overlapping security forces were unable to address the problem, but after June 2007, Hamas enforced order.[14] Hamas was also credited with running a more efficient, less corrupt civil bureaucracy than the PA, despite the hardships attending Israel's blockade.[15]

Israel's closure regime nevertheless remained as the overriding factor that determined and constricted possibilities in Gaza. The siege did not only preclude meaningful development; it extinguished the economy, with the inevitable and intended consequence that humanitarian conditions in the Gaza prison camp relentlessly deteriorated. Israel's objective was to turn public opinion in Gaza against Hamas.

To this end, it did not rest content with suffocating the population economically, but also periodically "mowed the lawn"—massacring civilians and flattening civilian infrastructure to weaken Hamas, maintain the population in its state of destitution, and deter other regional actors from challenging Israeli domination. Those devastating assaults—in 2008–9, 2012, 2014, 2018, 2021, 2022, and mid-2023—killed thousands of Palestinians, wounded many thousands more, and, together with the blockade, rendered Gaza "unlivable."[16] The people of Gaza blamed Israel more than Hamas for their worsening plight. Nonetheless, they did look to the Hamas authorities for effective relief, and when this was not provided, support for Hamas declined.

Hounded, hamstrung, and hemmed in, Hamas's survival strategy combined military deterrence with political outreach. By developing its military capabilities and engaging in low-intensity operations along the perimeter fence, Hamas sought to maintain its credibility as a resistance force while deterring Israel from deploying its ground forces in urban areas. This strategy scored limited successes—prisoner exchanges, temporary easings of the blockade—but never came close to breaking the siege. Meanwhile, the firing of projectiles argu-ably helped legitimize Israel's regular resort to overwhelming force that exhausted the population and fomented criticism of Hamas.[17] In an attempt to appease public opinion in Gaza, Hamas gradually relaxed its grip on Fatah and other groups in the Strip, became more tolerant of public criticism, and abandoned early attempts to impose its conservative religious mores on women.[18] The Hamas administration was not free of corruption, and engaged in authoritarian impositions, but its performance in key aspects of governance still received higher approval ratings than the PA in the West Bank, even as the latter enjoyed international benefaction and was not under siege.[19]

At the same time, Hamas sought to overcome its political isolation by extending conciliatory overtures internally, toward the PA, and abroad, to the US and European Union (EU). Internally, Hamas repeatedly albeit unsuccessfully engaged in efforts to reconcile with Fatah. Both factions were severely crit-icized, by each other and in public opinion at large, for prior-itizing their particular interests over the national struggle. In 2017, during reconciliation talks with Fatah and other factions in Cairo, Hamas made landmark concessions that would have seen the administration of Gaza transferred to the PA and the establishment of a unity government across the West Bank and Gaza.[20] In 2021, Hamas offered another major concession when it agreed to participate in "engineered elections" structured to guarantee that Hamas would not win a majority, as a prelimi-nary to the formation of a national unity government after the vote.[21] But three weeks before polling day, Abbas canceled the vote, fearing poor results in light of "fragmentation and lack of discipline within the [Fatah] movement."[22] Hamas denounced the move but, once again, remained caged in the Strip. Without absolving either Hamas or the PA from culpability for the factional divide which continues to paralyze Palestinian politics, they have not been the principal obstacles to reconciliation. The unity government of 2007 was sabotaged by Israel and the US, and those actors have effectively vetoed Palestinian unity ever since. The PA knows that integration with Hamas will put in jeopardy the aid it receives from the US and EU as well as the tax revenues controlled by Israel, without which the PA would collapse.

Externally, Hamas attempted to prize a political opening by formally revising its political program. In May 2017, the movement published a "Document of General Principles and Policies"[23] to replace its (in practice, long defunct) 1988 charter. The main element of the new document was the reaffirmation of Hamas's acceptance of a Palestinian state on the 1967 borders:

> Hamas considers the establishment of a fully sovereign and independent Palestinian state, with Jerusalem as its capital along the lines of the 4th of June 1967, with the return of the refugees and the displaced to their homes from which they were expelled, to be a formula of national consensus.

Measured against Hamas's early insistence on the liberation of Palestine from the River Jordan to the Mediterranean Sea, the formalization of this revised rhetoric marked a major milestone in Hamas's trajectory toward the PLO's terms for resolving the conflict. It also paved the way for factional reconciliation based on shared political objectives. Israel's response was categorical rejection, with Prime Minister Benjamin Netanyahu theatrically tossing a copy of the document into a trashcan.[24] This response was hardly unexpected given that Israel was refusing to engage in negotiations even with the PA, whose preparedness to compromise well beyond the international consensus two-state settlement was a matter of unambiguous record. Hamas saw President Abbas humiliated and the PA rendered irrelevant, except in its capacity as Israel's enforcer, and it understood that compromising further—for instance, by unilaterally recognizing Israel—would destroy its own political credibility without yielding anything in return.[25] Hamas's integrationist political strategy had reached a dead end.

Pyrrhic victories

The path from there to the explosion of October 7, 2023, was short and direct. Even Israeli intelligence could connect the dots. In 2016, Israel's military intelligence chief observed that the "humanitarian condition in Gaza is progressively deteriorating" and warned that "if it blows up, it'll be in Israel's direction."[26] In 2018, when tens of thousands of people in Gaza embarked on mass nonviolent demonstrations along the perimeter, Netanyahu had little difficulty identifying the cause. "They're suffocating economically, and therefore, they decided to crash the fence."[27]

As living conditions degenerated, political horizons were comprehensively foreclosed. Israel declared its intention to annex the OPT, accomplished this in practice, pledged never to permit the establishment of a Palestinian state, and relentlessly expanded the illegal settlements that materially precluded Palestinian self-determination. Israelis voted into power far-right parties whose program gave Palestinians just three options: resign themselves to permanent subjugation in an apartheid regime, or leave, or be put down.[28] Worse still, these developments did not incur any political price from those international actors that remained at least formally committed to a two-state settlement. On the contrary, Israel's lurch to the ultra-nationalist far-right coincided with increased US hostility to the PA, the Trump administration's abandonment of even the pre-text of support for Palestinian independence, and the signing of normalization agreements between Israel and several Arab states. The implication for Palestinians in Gaza, and Hamas as their government, was clear. No political concession would be rewarded, resistance in any form would be crushed, and the Palestinian cause was dead, as the world moved on. One million children were fated to rot in Gaza prison camp, with death their only deliverance. And so, on October 7, Hamas rolled the dice.

As with its 2006 electoral victory and 2007 takeover of Gaza, it is unlikely that Hamas expected to achieve what it did on October 7. The question now is whether, unlike those previous episodes, Hamas will be able to translate a short-term success into lasting political gain. No answer can yet be given, as it remains unclear at the time of writing how Israel's assault on Gaza will end. Thus far, the US and Israel have responded to October 7 by doubling down on their demonization of Hamas and refusal to engage it in any political process. This approach either seeks to eliminate the Palestinian people by expulsion and/or genocide, or it considers repeated massacres (including of Israelis) an acceptable price to pay for maintaining Israeli rule in the OPT, or it is delusional in its refusal to learn from the history surveyed above. So long as Israel offers Palestinians under its boot nothing but permanent subjugation, the conditions will remain for another explosion, and another, whether at the hands of Hamas or some other group. Hamas does not have a monopoly on Pyrrhic victories.

"Gaza will become a
place where no human
being can exist"

—Advisor to the Defense Minister and
former head of the National Security
Council Giora Eiland

8

The Quiet Front: Reflections From the West Bank

Musa Abuhashhash

These lines were written as the war in Gaza, which began on October 7, was still underway. They do not offer definitive answers as any conclusions and predictions will be directly affected by the outcomes of the war. But they pose questions that Palestinians themselves have raised since the war began and they identify historical as well as political factors that will shape the possibilities going forward.

The first question raised since the first day of the war was: *Will the West Bank rise up and form a supportive front for Gaza?* Similar questions were asked of Hezbollah, Iran, and other players in the region. There were reasons to think they would intervene. Hezbollah, Hamas, and their allies had promoted the "unification of the fronts" while it was immediately evident that this conflict represented a qualitative escalation from previous confrontations. More importantly, the Gaza war marked a turning point in Palestinian and global awareness of the Israel-Palestinian conflict. In the immediate aftermath of the

Musa Abuhashhash worked for many years as Hebron field researcher for B'Tselem, the Israeli Information Center for Human Rights in the Occupied Territories. He grew up in Fawwar refugee camp.

October 7 attack, some even considered the extent of Israel's security and intelligence failures to mark the beginning of the end for its existence as a state.

Hamas's surprise attack left the Israeli government and its military leadership in a state of astonishment and confusion, prompting them to retaliate with excessive and overwhelming force that resulted in widespread massacres. At the time of writing, more than 17,000 Palestinian citizens, mostly civilians, had fallen victim. More than half were children and women. Hundreds of medical personnel and employees of the United Nations refugee agency (UNRWA) have been killed. Tens of thousands of homes, schools, universities, hospitals, and even churches have been destroyed.

All this unfolded before the lenses of international cameras. Livestreams broadcast across the world ignited public anger against Israel. For the first time, a wave of sympathy for the Palestinians and their cause even reached to staff inside the White House. Unfortunately, this did not prompt commensurate action from Palestinians in the West Bank, Jerusalem, the diaspora, or even the Arab nations closest to the Palestinian cause. When the Arab League met in Riyadh on November 11, Palestinians did not take this embarrassment seriously but greeted it with scorn and anger. The summit revealed the falseness of Palestinian expectations and hopes pinned on their Arab brothers, especially Egypt and Jordan, the only geographical outlets for Palestinian communication with the outside world. Numerous chants heard during the limited and dwindling protests in the West Bank and Arab countries accused the Palestinian Authority (PA) and some Arab regimes of being silent, complicit, and conspiring against the Palestinian cause. But Palestinians themselves also did not rise to the occasion.

Missing in action

More than forty days into Israel's genocidal war in Gaza, Palestinians in the West Bank had still failed to form a unified emergency command that would organize the people, direct their efforts, and strengthen their steadfastness. This was primarily due to the opposition of the PA as well as the largest faction of the Fatah movement. The PA was virtually silent after October 7, while popular demonstrations were limited to spontaneous and random reactions—much less than the mobilizations seen in Europe.

Why did Palestinians in the West Bank fail to act in large numbers to support their brethren in Gaza?

One factor is that, from the first day of the war, the Israeli army preemptively implemented an unprecedented policy of suppression and terrorism. Its aim was to neutralize Palestinians and prevent any attempt to open a second front in support of Gaza. Israel imposed a comprehensive and strict siege on cities, towns, and camps in the West Bank, as well as on the roads. The Israeli army carried out extensive raids on Palestinian gatherings. More than 2,500 people were arrested and more than 200 were killed, with hundreds more injured. This campaign was reminiscent of the "iron fist" deployed by Israeli prime minister Yitzhak Rabin during the first intifada, except this time, without any uprising to put down. On top of the movement restrictions and military repression, some 170,000 Palestinians were prevented from accessing their jobs in Israel. This inflicted serious damage on the Palestinian economy, which is closely linked to the economy of Israel.

A second factor is the way in which Israel has managed to artificially insulate many Palestinians in the West Bank from the reality of Israeli occupation. As a result of the 1993 and 1995 Oslo Accords, Palestinians in the West Bank are managed by a Palestinian Authority which operates on Israel's permission and functions as Israel's security contractor. The PA has helped Israel to hollow out the Palestinian cause and establish a tolerable equilibrium under Israel's overall control. Both Israel and the PA work to preserve this arrangement through security and political cooperation. Many residents of the West Bank have accused the PA of corruption and incompetence. The PA is also discredited in the eyes of the political elite—except for Fatah, which benefits from the status quo. But the reality is that many Palestinians in the West Bank have acquired a material stake in stability under Israeli occupation. They observe their brothers in Gaza living under Israeli siege and strict Hamas administration and feel comfortable by comparison.

Even as Israel's occupation deepened, the construction industry flourished and individual living standards in the West Bank improved. The economy developed in an unnatural way that took advantage of the imposed calm. More than 150,000 employees work directly for the PA, with over 70,000 in the security forces. The role of the latter is limited to maintaining internal order and preventing confrontations with the Israeli occupation that would expose the PA and West Bank residents to sanctions. In addition, a class of Palestinian investors and merchants has been granted permits to import goods and commodities from Israel and through Israeli ports. These are marketed to a growing Palestinian consumer society, whose purchases are fueled by the incomes of Palestinian workers employed in Israel. These workers receive relatively high wages compared to the salaries available not only in Gaza but also in most Arab countries, excluding the Gulf States. This contradictory situation is evident in cities like Ramallah, which boasts a flourishing real estate market as well as hundreds of restaurants and cafés that would not feel out of place in Europe.

Across the West Bank, one also finds that many Palestinians have taken out long-term bank loans with high interest rates, to fund consumer purchases such as apartments and cars as well as commercial ventures. According to recent statistics, the number of borrowers exceeded 220,000 by the end of 2022, most of whom were people on low incomes. The total amount borrowed has reached $10 billion. But it is not only their incomes and their liabilities that have bound Palestinians in the West Bank. A psychological stability has been constructed and, however artificial it is, many fear losing it. Anyone who tries to fundamentally change this reality will face resistance.

The groups most likely to oppose such efforts are employees of the PA, the major traders, and the workers in Israel who have built enviable lives based on their higher incomes. These conservative elements comprise a majority of the West Bank population and also reside in all Palestinian areas, from booming cities to the most impoverished camps. It is worth noting that what appears to be a recent uprising against the status quo, marked by the emergence of armed resistance in the northern West Bank, specifically in Jenin, Nablus, and Tulkarm, does not necessarily represent a significant departure from the picture described above. Many observers believe that this phenomenon amounts to little more than small-scale protests against internal shortcomings within Palestinian organizations. Young members of those groups felt neglected and unfairly excluded from jobs and privileges, and therefore rebelled by setting up their own armed brigades. These included many militants who have troubled the Israeli army and even the PA, leading to the expulsion, killing, and arrest of dozens of them in their own communities.

A third factor impeding popular mobilization in the West Bank is the continued political division between the Fatah and Hamas movements. All attempts since 2007 have failed to end the split and unite the Palestinian people behind a common national program that would guide their struggle, strengthen their steadfastness, supply a clear political vision, and provide a basis for responding effectively to unforeseen developments, as occurred on October 7. Hamas hoped that the people in the West Bank would launch a massive intifada, including armed operations against Israeli soldiers and settler paramilitaries, that would relieve Gaza by creating a second front. But in the absence of a unified leadership, or any common national program, few believed that their sacrifice would contribute toward victory.

What next?
The absence of a West Bank front was not just a failure of national commitment. It also betrayed an unwarranted complacency in the face of Israeli plans. Since October 7, Israeli settlers armed themselves and escalated attacks on Palestinians, with tolerance and cover from the Israeli army. The army imposed a strict siege on Palestinian cities, towns, and camps, while the common roads were restricted for use by the settlers. This aggression was accompanied by fascist declarations threatening to expel the Palestinians to Jordan in a repeat of the 1948 Nakba. Already, the economic impact of Israel's closures has threatened the legitimacy of the PA. If Israeli violence in the West Bank escalates, and the genocidal war in Gaza continues for an extended period, the PA will face a serious risk of collapse. This could create a crisis that would allow Israel to solve its demographic "problem" once and for all.

Palestinians in the West Bank are aware that Israel's actions in Gaza exceed its declared goals of exacting revenge on Hamas and eliminating its military infrastructure. Some have speculated that Israel intends to expel the Palestinians from Gaza first, then from the West Bank, and finally from population centers in Jerusalem and the interior. Some residents of the West Bank would like the PA leadership, backed by Fatah, to break its silence, define a new vision for the next phase, and prepare for the worst-case scenario, which threatens Palestinian existence not only in Gaza but also in the West Bank. At minimum, they believe, the PA should end its security coordination with Israel, provide basic protection for the besieged Palestinian people, and confront the terrorism of Israeli soldiers and settlers.

But even now, many Palestinians in the West Bank, the PA, and the Fatah leadership are preparing a return to the old delusions of betting on the international community to deliver justice and statehood for the Palestinian people. Even now, they draw comfort from the fantasy that Israel will suddenly halt its genocidal war and things will return to "normal," as if this were just another "round" in the Israel-Palestine conflict and not its bloody conclusion. Those Palestinians who look at Gaza, and are grateful not to be there, are avoiding the harsh reality. As they observe the neighborhoods reduced to rubble, the hundreds of thousands displaced, the hospitals and schools destroyed, the question West Bank Palestinians should be asking is this: Once Israel has annihilated the people in Gaza, who will it go after next?

Very sad is the condition of the Palestinians in the West Bank who sit in front of television sets, watching the news, hoping for a ceasefire announcement that will not come soon, taking to the streets and squares in ever smaller numbers, but otherwise waiting for the unknown, with a mixture of fears, hopes, and prayers that things will not deteriorate further. When the bombing ceases, and the snow melts, many, including the Palestinians in the West Bank, will understand that their hesitation and timid sympathy was not enough, that the time to act has passed, and that their fate was linked to the fate of their brothers in Gaza from the second day of the outbreak of the war.

"One goal: Nakba!"

—Ariel Kallner MK, Likud, governing

9

All Shook Up: Regional Dynamics of the Gaza War

Mouin Rabbani

In the wake of the devastating attacks launched by Hamas and other Palestinian organizations against Israel on October 7, 2023, observers and analysts began seeking a motive for these actions, particularly one that might help explain their timing.

A consensus soon emerged that the prospect of a normalization agreement between Israel and the Kingdom of Saudi Arabia (KSA) was a key factor in Hamas's calculations. The Palestinians, so the argument went, felt increasingly isolated and marginalized by the series of Arab-Israeli normalization agreements engineered by the United States during the final months of the Donald Trump administration, the grandiosely named Abraham Accords. In this context a Saudi-Israeli sequel was considered a particularly heavy if not mortal blow in view of KSA's leadership position in both the Arab and broader Islamic worlds. If Riyadh normalized, the floodgates would open and numerous other states would follow suit.

Mouin Rabbani is co-editor of *Jadaliyya* and host of its *Connections* podcast.

Whereas the United Arab Emirates (UAE) and Bahrain had been condemned and shunned by the formal Palestinian leadership of Mahmoud Abbas after their embrace of Israel, in KSA's case Abbas negotiated with Riyadh to ensure that any deal incorporated Palestinian interests, or at least enhanced funding for the Palestinian Authority (PA). In other words, the Palestinian leadership believed it was not in a position to ostracize KSA as it had attempted to do with respect to the UAE and had previously succeeded with Egypt after its 1979 peace treaty with Israel.

The identification of KSA-Israeli normalization as an important motivating factor for Hamas in launching the October 7 offensive is, however, problematic in multiple respects. These include, prominently, the slim prospects of such an agreement materializing, let alone imminently. This is because rather than consisting of a pact negotiated bilaterally between Israel and KSA, it is in the first instance an American initiative and one in which US rather than Israeli or Saudi commitments are decisive. In other words, KSA was primarily seeking to extract benefits from Washington rather than Israel.

The key commitments KSA sought to obtain from the US were a formal security guarantee, which would obligate the US military to defend the Kingdom from foreign attack, and a nuclear reactor with uranium enrichment capability. Neither of these can be provided without approval by the US Congress, and given the hostility to either KSA, the Biden administration, or both among many of its members, as well as the vilification of KSA's de facto leader, Crown Prince Muhammad bin Salman (MBS), such an endorsement is extremely unlikely.

Secondly, the deal as proposed by Washington would include a number of Israeli gestures toward the Palestinians. These would be largely cosmetic in nature, intended to strengthen the PA and to improve Palestinian economic prospects under occupation rather than end Israeli rule. Even so, they would be a non-starter for key members of Israel's governing coalition, and not only its most extreme elements. There are indications that the Biden administration hoped to use this obstacle to cajole Israeli prime minister Benjamin Netanyahu into abandoning his most fanatical coalition partners and form a different government. But this would have jeopardized Netanyahu's legislative agenda and the prospects of overhauling Israel's judiciary, which remains a key political and personal objective of his. Furthermore, the most likely alternative partner, opposition leader Yair Lapid, has repeatedly proclaimed his refusal to endorse any agreement that provides KSA with a nuclear reactor. Additionally, KSA may be an absolute monarchy but its rulers cannot simply ignore public opinion. And Saudi public opinion is considerably more engaged than that in the UAE. In other words, Riyadh may have felt the need for more and more substantive Israeli gestures than Washington is prepared to offer.

Were one to conclude that despite the above an agreement was nevertheless likely, Hamas would have had little reason to believe it could successfully sabotage its consummation through war with Israel. There is no previous instance of an Arab state renouncing normalization with Israel on account of the Palestinians. Thus Egypt's 1979 peace treaty handily survived Israel's 1982 invasion of Lebanon and the Sabra-Shatila massacres; Egypt and Jordan went no further than a temporary recall of their ambassadors from Israel in response to the collapse of Israeli-Palestinian negotiations in 2000 and the eruption of the second intifada; and none of Israel's newer Arab friends felt the need to punish Israel for its actions during the 2021 Unity Uprising, including extensive bombing of the Gaza Strip, or the current Netanyahu government's explicitly annexationist agenda. If an agreement was indeed awaiting signature, the most the Palestinians could have hoped to achieve would have been to postpone the inevitable by a decent interval after the guns fell silent and corpses retrieved from under the rubble were properly buried.

Regional considerations did play an important role in Palestinian assessments, but in a fundamentally different way than posited by the many instant specialists migrating from commentary on the war in Ukraine and expertise in epidemiology. After the Palestinians renounced the use of force and recognized Israeli sovereignty over 78 percent of Mandatory Palestine in the context of the 1993 Oslo Accord, their perceived veto power over Arab-Israeli normalization remained as their final source of strategic leverage. Palestinian leaders in fact enunciated the belief that Israel entered negotiations with the PLO not primarily to achieve peace with the Palestinians, but because it perceived such a peace as the price of admission for normalized relations with the Arab world. In this perception, the Palestinians formed the bridge Israel would need to cross to enter the Arab world, and the PLO controlled access to it, determined to extend Israel passage only in exchange for an end to the occupation and establishment of a Palestinian state.

The problem for the Palestinians was that their own normalization of relations with Israel during the 1990s legitimized Arab relations with the Jewish state. Such relations of course preceded Oslo by decades, but after 1993 they expanded rapidly in size and scope. Unlike the Egyptian-Israeli peace treaty, which transformed a relationship previously characterized by war and enmity, the Israel-UAE normalization agreement primarily formalized an existing web of relations and allowed for their further expansion.

A further development was that since 2000 Israel, with few exceptions, abandoned the model of resolving its conflict with the Palestinians through bilateral negotiations conducted under

US auspices. Instead, acting with the active support of the US and passive acquiescence of the Europeans, Israel reverted to unilateralism, seeking to determine core issues by force, exclusively on the basis of its own interests and without reference to Palestinian rights or reaching agreements with them. Israel's 2005 "disengagement" from the Gaza Strip was not only conducted unilaterally, but deliberately rejected coordination with the PA or an orderly handover of the territory to it. It would also prove to be a key turning point in the fortunes of Hamas.

By 2020 the new reality was indisputable. The US issued its latest diplomatic initiative, *From Peace to Prosperity*, which essentially dealt with the Palestinians as an inconvenient afterthought. About a third of the West Bank was slated for formal Israeli annexation, the Palestinian refugee question pronounced non-existent, and Palestinian statehood both severely circumscribed and postponed to the hereafter. Later that same year the UAE-Israel normalization agreement was dressed up to suggest that, on its account, Israel at the last moment aborted plans to formally annex West Bank territory pursuant to the US initiative. In reality, Israel had already reconsidered its plans to do so on account of a number of domestic and foreign policy considerations. The subsequent Bahrain-Israel agreement by contrast left the Palestinians entirely unmentioned, and that between Morocco and Israel did little better.

Thus, rather than the Palestinians leveraging the prospect of Arab-Israeli normalization to achieve statehood, Israel was successfully forming relationships with Arab states to further marginalize and isolate the Palestinians, and obtaining halal certificates for Greater Israel from key regional actors. It is this perception of abandonment by not only the West and the international community, but also what Palestinians had always considered their natural hinterland, that helped Hamas decide it was time to act and irrevocably shatter the status quo. It is difficult to assess the extent to which this sense of isolation and abandonment played a role, but reasonable to assume that local factors, such as conditions in the Gaza Strip, East Jerusalem and the Haram Al-Sharif, the Jordan Valley, and Israeli prisons, were more prominent factors than regional realities. Simply stated, Israel had gone too far, for too long. That the world and increasingly the region as well shrugged its shoulders and looked the other way formed a contributing more than causative factor.

A different regional dynamic relevant to understanding the current crisis concerns the self-styled Axis of Resistance, a coalition of states and movements opposed to US-Israeli hegemony in the region. Composed of a combination of states, movements, and militias, most prominently Iran and Hezbollah in Lebanon, Hamas has always had a somewhat ambivalent relationship with this coalition. Most notably, it in 2012 broke with Damascus, where it had maintained its headquarters for the previous decade, relocated to Qatar, and aligned with the Syrian opposition. This in turn led to a rupture between Hamas and Iran.

Under the leadership of Yahya Sinwar things began to change. After his 2011 release from several decades in Israel's prisons in that year's exchange with Israel, Sinwar was elected head of Hamas's Gaza branch and quickly became the movement's dominant personality. His approach was that Hamas's relations with regional states should reflect the movement's interests rather than preferences. Whereas Qatar and Turkey offered financial support and safe haven, Egypt is the only Arab state bordering the Gaza Strip, while the Axis of Resistance was vital for military assistance. Relations with Cairo, which had deteriorated almost to the point of armed hostilities after the 2013 coup that brought Abdel Fattah El-Sisi to power, were normalized, as were those with Tehran and more recently Syria.

The repaired relations with the Axis of Resistance were central to Hamas's ability to successfully confront Israel's military and intelligence services on October 7. But the attacks also demonstrated that the coalition's individual members operate according to their own priorities rather than, as often portrayed, as proxies beholden to Iran. Thus, it is now widely accepted that Hamas neither coordinated its attacks with its coalition partners nor provided them with advance warning. This secrecy appears to have extended even to the Palestinian Islamic Jihad (PIJ) until the very last moment.

Hamas's unilateralism also helps explains why its coalition partners didn't fully throw their weight into the conflict. Like the Palestinian movement, they too have priorities of their own. But Hamas also confronted them with a dilemma. If they remained on the sidelines while Palestinians were slaughtered by the thousand, the Axis of Resistance would be exposed as a toothless illusion. And if they followed Hamas into open confrontation with Israel, they would be ceding control over their agenda and decision-making to a member of the coalition that failed to coordinate its actions with them or take their views into account.

The response was one of controlled escalation. Thus Hezbollah in Lebanon entered the fray virtually from the outset, conducting more intensive exchanges as time progressed and permitting Palestinian organizations based in Lebanon to launch attacks of their own, but without engaging in all-out war. Subsequently militias in Iraq began targeting US bases in Iraq and Syria, and the Houthis in addition to launching strikes against Israel used their strategic location astride Bab al-Mandab to prohibit shipping—first ships owned or operated by Israel, and from December ships of any nationality docking in Israel. More than any other party, the Yemenis transformed Israel's war on the Gaza Strip from a regional to an international crisis. All this was done "in support of the Palestinians," sending the message that calm would be restored once the US called a halt to Israel's war on the Gaza Strip.

If Hamas acted on the basis that the scale of its October 7 attacks would embolden its allies to throw caution to the wind and seek to match its efforts, they miscalculated. If their assumption was that Israel would unleash an orgy of violence that would shame its partners into coming to Gaza's defense, they succeeded but only partially. Yet in doing so the Axis of Resistance sent daily reminders to Israel's sponsors in the West that the region in its entirety could erupt in flames at any moment, and was more likely to do so as the conflict was prolonged. This may yet prove to be the trigger that forces a halt to Israel's onslaught.

Notably, Hezbollah leader Hassan Nasrallah has publicly expressed a requirement for this war to end with a "victory for the [Palestinian] resistance," and of Hamas in particular, as well as his confidence in this outcome. It's a somewhat ambiguous statement that could either mean he wishes Hamas the best of luck in its confrontation with Israel, or that Hezbollah will not allow its Palestinian coalition partners to be defeated. Given that Israeli leaders have stated an intention to take on Hezbollah and settle accounts with the Lebanese organization when the time is right, it would appear unlikely that Nasrallah will sit idly by if Israel appears to be achieving a decisive outcome in the Gaza Strip. This may also help explain the intensification of Israeli-Lebanese confrontations after the temporary Israeli-Palestinian truce collapsed on December 1.

Less clear is what if any expectations Hamas may have had regarding the regional response. Given the unprecedented intensity of Israel's onslaught on the Gaza Strip, the response of Arab governments was essentially one of all talk and no action. The Arab League did not convene a summit on the crisis until

November 11. At the last minute, the Saudi hosts combined it with an Organization of Islamic Cooperation conclave to make it a joint meeting; the latter's considerably larger and more diverse membership ensured it would conclude with weaker decisions, particularly concerning relations with the United States. Its resolution to ignore the siege and ensure the delivery of humanitarian aid to the Gaza Strip was essentially stillborn. The delegation of foreign ministers dispatched to foreign capitals similarly did not rush off to Washington, which has real and direct influence on Israeli policy, but rather sauntered to Beijing, Moscow, and other destinations before finally meeting with US secretary of state Antony Blinken at Foggy Bottom in December.

Arab governments did, however, play a decisive role early in the crisis. As Israel began the most intensive bombing campaign in the history of the Middle East, its leaders openly spoke of removing the population of the Gaza Strip to Egypt's Sinai Peninsula. The proposal was also embraced by the US, as Blinken on his first visit to the Middle East convened with pro-Western Arab governments and sought to sell them on the idea. His efforts were met with determined and unanimous rejection.

By way of background, Israel has aspired to reduce the population of the Gaza Strip, and particularly of its refugees, since the early 1950s, and has formulated and even tried to implement a variety of initiatives to this end over the decades. More recently, Israel has on several occasions offered to relinquish control over the Gaza Strip to Egypt, which borders the territory and ruled it from 1948–1967 (but unlike Jordan in the West Bank staked no territorial claim). Cairo has energetically rejected such offers, refusing to transform an Israeli challenge into an Egyptian national security problem. In fact, refusing to relieve Israel of responsibility for the Gaza Strip has been among the most consistent Egyptian national security principles since

President Anwar Sadat initiated relations with Israel in 1977. Blinken, seemingly ignorant of this reality, nevertheless tried to market it to his various Arab hosts.

Jordan, which lives in perennial fear of being transformed by Israel into an alternative Palestinian homeland, was similarly opposed, on the grounds that the ethnic cleansing of Gaza could set a precedent for the West Bank, and because once displaced to Egypt it was likely that a significant number of uprooted Palestinians would make their way to Jordan, which already has a substantial population of Gaza Palestinians displaced in 1967.

The Arab states further indicated that they would neither participate in an Arab peacekeeping force nor bear responsibility for reconstruction costs, roles that were assigned to them by the US and Israel. Scenario planning for the "day after" commenced almost as soon as the first bombs were launched into the Gaza Strip, and ever more ambitious plans have been emerging from the Washington echo chamber.

Some have suggested that once the dust settles, Arab governments can be persuaded to participate in such plans. Yet the prospects are unlikely. To begin with, all such plans are predicated on the successful eradication of Hamas, which repeatedly indicated that it views any participant in them as doing Israel's bidding and therefore an enemy. Secondly, given the widespread and intense rage in the region at Israel's genocidal onslaught, such governments will be careful about further inflaming public opinion.

Israel's response was to say that it received many private words of encouragement from Arab governments. Given widespread opposition to Hamas and the Muslim Brotherhood that spawned it, this was a not entirely implausible contention. At the same time, for Israel to claim, against the available evidence, that its war had unanimous backing, because it was supported either openly and vocally by its allies, or quietly and informally by others, smacked suspiciously of propaganda. Here again Egypt is instructive: Sisi's Cairo detests Hamas, not least because of its organic relationship with the Muslim Brotherhood and vocal opposition to Sisi's coup. Yet Egypt thereafter also concluded that its sentiments about Hamas notwithstanding, the PA was incapable of administering the Gaza Strip, and the alternative to Hamas was either a power vacuum and chaos, or a new regime aligned with jihadi movements rather than one focused on the Palestinian arena. Claims that Sisi has been salivating over the prospects of Hamas being removed from power should therefore be taken with some skepticism.

Arab states could potentially accept a role in post-war planning if offered a clear pathway to a political resolution in the form of a two-state settlement. This would, however, require a US willingness to compel Israel to end its occupation of not only the Gaza Strip but also the West Bank. Washington has made clear its political horizon is a revival of the Oslo process, which has over three decades resulted in the consolidation of occupation rather than a Palestinian statehood which was not incorporated into its terms, and even this is strenuously rejected by Israel.

The war on the Gaza Strip has once again exposed the impotence of the formal Arab state system, and its inability to function in coherent and purposeful fashion. Yet it has also revealed significant weaknesses in Israel, that in the coming years are likely to embolden Arabs now convinced that the Jewish state can be not only effectively challenged but also defeated. How these countervailing pressures may play out is too early to determine, but it is already clear they will be in tension for years to come.

"Gaza has become a graveyard for children"

—UNICEF

10

Into the Abyss

Nathan J. Brown

Hamas's dramatic and unexpected offensive on October 7 thrust Israel-Palestine rapidly forward—but less toward a clear outcome and more toward deepening conflict. The immediate effect on each individual actor was to retreat back into a bubble. Hamas showed that it could dominate the public sphere among Palestinians; it could also capture global attention but at the cost of exposing Palestinians to unprecedented levels of violence and isolation. Israelis endorsed any actions that responded harshly and abandoned efforts to link short-term tactics to a dispassionate calculation of long-term consequences. If each actor fell backward, however, the effect on the inhabitants of Israel-Palestine was to shove them onward into an abyss in which—to paraphrase Jean-Paul Sartre's *No Exit*—hell is other peoples.

Israelis and Palestinians rushed ahead not merely impulsively but with moral blindness as well. The moral blindness should be easy to see—except that blindness is about not being

Nathan J. Brown is professor of political science and international affairs at George Washington University and nonresident senior fellow at the Carnegie Endowment for International Peace. He wrote this while a visiting fellow at the Hamburg Institute for Advanced Study in Germany.

able to see. Hamas's tactical brilliance was harnessed to a set of atrocities directed against civilians that were collectively far bloodier than Deir Yassin. For others, the immense cruelty of the Israeli closure of Gaza had long dropped from view—a closure whose origin predates Hamas's control of the territory and was clearly far more effective at impoverishing two million people than making Hamas militarily incapable.

I make these observations not in an effort to draw up moral balance sheets or assign culpability, but simply to observe that very few observers and none of the participants are able to keep more than one party's sins in view. No sense of shared humanity has driven either understanding or action. And indeed, it seems that nobody is driving events now—or rather that those driving events have no realistic path to follow that will deliver a better world to anyone.

Hamas: seizing the initiative

For Hamas's part, its brutal campaign showed less solid long-term thinking than the United States' invasion of Iraq in 2003. And indeed, that may have been the point. The extent of despair and powerlessness among Palestinians had grown so profound that the ground was open to anyone who seized any kind of initiative. With apartheid-like conditions entrenched by harsh security measures, settler violence, diplomatic inertia, and political decay, Hamas's leaders seem to have been driven by a grim determination that upending arrangements was bound to have a positive outcome. But if they had a plan for following up on their success with anything more substantial than hostage negotiations, this was kept even more secret than the initial attack.

Hamas's decision-making has often been linked to the regional situation (the desire to energize the "resistance camp" or disrupt Saudi-Israeli normalization). If regional politics was indeed the driver, Hamas may have miscalculated. But the October 7 attack was far more likely geared first and foremost to the Palestinian arena, where there is pressure to engage in resistance and where the national leadership is bankrupt. There was also a long-held understanding within Hamas that its truncated and blockaded republic of Gaza was not a tolerable outcome. This led some leaders within the movement to drag the rest of Hamas into uncharted waters.

And in some ways that effort paid off short-term. Hamas showed Palestinian and international actors that it could not be ignored, it thrust the Palestinian cause on to the agenda of the leaders of the most powerful states in the world, it showed the bankruptcy of Israeli tactics and dragged Israel into a costly (and perhaps unwinnable) military conflict, and it forced Israel as well as other global actors to negotiate (over hostages, though, not Palestinian rights). The historic national leadership in Ramallah reacted to events with a deafening silence born of impotence. Many Palestinians who had waited for someone to do something rallied around Hamas's boldness.

But if it came to dominate Palestinian politics, Hamas showed no ability to construct any framework for unified action or to translate its propaganda victories into practical ones. Tactics seemed to be connected to a prayer rather than a strategy or a plan.

Israel: A ferocious response in support of an endless war
Hamas's October 7 offensive meant that Israel's central goal of maintaining the status quo in Gaza collapsed. So Israel invaded Gaza, killed enormous numbers of fighters but many, many more civilians, decimated Gazan civilian life still further—with great immediate impact but unknowable long-term effects. Deeply divided Israelis will give their leaders a blank check for any harsh measures, without abandoning an impulse toward

recrimination (much of it justified) based on the warring camp in Israel to which they belong.

Initial reactions to Hamas's bloody attack on Israelis and Israel's declaration of war focused on the short term: how strongly would Israel react and what would its objectives be? When Israel finally spelled out war aims, they were very ambitious: to oust Hamas from governance and to destroy its military capability. Some, including Prime Minister Benjamin Netanyahu, went further: the goal was to kill every member of Hamas whether inside Gaza or not. While few international actors echoed the bloodthirsty rhetoric of Israeli leaders, the goal of eliminating Hamas politically and militarily was widely embraced without thinking by US and European leaders who only asked what would come next—and showed an inability to hear the Israeli answer that there would not be anything next. There would be no "day after."

It rapidly became clear that the Israeli military operation was killing many civilians and destroying part of Gaza, including housing, infrastructure, and critical aspects of civilian life. What outsiders were slow to realize was that this was not simply collateral damage; it was also related to a new security regime. Israeli leaders hinted and then spoke more openly about imposing significant military buffer zones within Gaza that would be inaccessible to Palestinians for a while, if not indefinitely. The Israeli military operation seemed designed to force a significant number of people to leave Gaza into the Sinai Peninsula, but that possibility was hampered as a result of external pressure and very sharp Egyptian resistance. Population shifts within the Gaza Strip, however, were profound. As they flattened neighborhoods and forced hundreds of thousands to move, Israeli officials were steadfastly silent on any possibility that displaced people would be allowed to return to their (often no longer standing) homes. And they made clear that, even when fighting died down, the ongoing Israeli military stance in Gaza would tighten the border and increase security forces' capacity to conduct incursions into populated areas.

Israel will not seek to dominate Gaza to the same degree as the West Bank, because without settlements in Gaza, that level of control is not necessary. (Israel will likely not reintroduce settlers into Gaza, though the idea is discussed.) Future military moves might include setting up military installations within Gaza. Parts of the north of Gaza might be effectively annexed—at least in security terms—and turned into a closed Israeli military zone.

And governance? Israel made clear that was not its problem.

No good options

The United States played a dramatic role in the war's initial stages, hardwiring the American and Israeli decision-making processes together in an unprecedented way. European states have followed their general pattern of tailing the United States while advocating a bit more publicly for civilian lives and longer-term diplomacy. The result may be that the United States gains real leverage with Israel, but it is unclear whether the US would know what to do with it.

The United States immediately pressed Israel for its post-war plans and observers rushed out one unrealistic proposal after another. But there was no sign of consensus, and even the most detailed authoritative statements lacked clarity. US secretary of state Antony Blinken's comments on October 31 were the most specific offered, but they only suggested that the United States and other countries were looking at "a variety of possible permutations." He mused that an "effective and revitalized Palestinian Authority" (PA) should ultimately govern Gaza but offered no clues on how to make the PA effective or overcome Israeli opposition. He only suggested vaguely that, in the meantime, "there are other temporary arrangements that may involve a number of other countries in the region. It may involve international agencies that would help provide for both security and governance." The nominees floated for this interim role include Arab states and the United Nations (UN), supported by other governmental and nongovernmental international organizations.

After 2007, the Hamas government could not provide for all its people's needs, and so international bodies stepped in. For example, a desalination plant was managed by the UN Children's Fund, a power plant managed by the Palestinian Energy and Natural Resources Authority, some schools managed by the UN's Relief and Works Agency for Palestine Refugees in the Near East (UNRWA), and salaries of hospital staff paid by Ramallah. This setup was necessary to avoid essential services being cut off when the international community boycotted Hamas and to facilitate vital cooperation with Israel in running these services.

Most of the ideas about the "day after" that assume Hamas will soon be gone are based on expanding these ad hoc international arrangements with less involvement (or none at all) by formerly Hamas-led structures. But multilateral institutions have been far more adept at service provision and humanitarian aid than governance. Misleading comparisons to Kosovo or Iraq obscure the far more hostile context: UNRWA alone has already seen more than 130 of its workers killed, Israeli officials have heaped vituperation on senior UN officials, and internal security has dissolved in Gaza. For the UN to establish a political or peacekeeping mission, a high degree of consensus would have to be possible in the UN Security Council, which is already deeply divided on many global issues.

Regional management seems even less plausible. Why would countries in the region want to take responsibility for administering Gaza under the military control of Israel? And why would

Israel want regional actors to have military control of Gaza? Arab states never wished to be made responsible for Gaza and that preference has likely been strengthened. Nor are they likely to band together to manage a problem they feel was caused by the recklessness of others. The few experiences of multilateral involvement by Arab states in "peacekeeping" or security arrangements do not provide positive models. In short, Arab states are unlikely to accept a role. And in the unlikely event they were persuaded to step in, such involvement would likely be ineffective in providing administration, much less security.

The PA is unlikely to restore its pre-2007 institutional and legal framework. First, Israel's long-standing policy to disconnect Gaza from the West Bank and to treat Gaza as a nonentity in political and governing terms would have to be completely reversed, and that seems unlikely. Second, the PA lacks popular support to begin with; to be seen as the agent of Israeli invasion and US complicity—which is how most Palestinians would see it—might be close to suicidal. The PA is clear on this point; its prime minister has said that

> [t]o have the Palestinian Authority go to Gaza and run the affairs of Gaza without a political solution for the West Bank, as if this Palestinian Authority is going aboard an F-16 or an Israeli tank? I don't accept it. Our president [Mahmoud Abbas] does not accept it. None of us will accept it.

And the PA's stubbornly passive behavior has been consistent with this stance: PA officials launched an initiative to participate in a humanitarian response in Gaza but did not engage in strategic communication to promote a ceasefire. There has been no political dialogue with Hamas nor other Palestinian factions. On top of that, the potential PA administration would be under Israel's complete security control, similar to the West

Bank's Area C. This complete control would likely exacerbate the image of the PA as an Israeli "contractor." A "revitalized" PA capable of undertaking administration and providing security in Gaza would seem to require both elections and a very muscular diplomatic process within an acceptable horizon. Neither is likely; those now calling for a "revitalized" PA are precisely the same actors who have resisted such steps for many years.

Evolving actors
Changes within each actor are likely to complicate matters further.

Israel's future posture is unknown even to most Israelis. Over the short term, there is unity behind a military effort, but the underlying fissures in Israeli society seem more deferred than resolved. The religious nationalist camp has lost its centrality with the expansion of Israel's governing coalition, but it retains key ministries for now, and its citizens' violent activities against Palestinians in the West Bank have stepped up. Its vision for annexing the land but denying rights to non-Jewish inhabitants has already advanced very far. The country's military and security leaders are both leading much of the country's response, but they are also taking blame for missing the signs that Hamas would strike out; the tensions between the leadership and rightist politicians seem to be just below the surface. Leading Israeli political and security figures are divided about whether the PA in Ramallah is annoying, hostile, or a potential partner, but the idea that Palestinians are a national community that should be treated as such is accepted only in pockets of the Israeli political spectrum. The political configuration in Israel is volatile, and the stance and composition of the country's leadership a year from now are difficult to foresee.

Meanwhile, Hamas is not likely to be destroyed, though it will undoubtedly suffer tremendous losses. It may be that the movement's political wing—since it operates above-ground—is a softer target than the military wing, which is both hardened and already partially underground. There is a significant possibility that the military wing will actually increase its hold on the organization—and that it will identify any postwar governance that targets the movement as collaboration with Israeli efforts to eliminate it.

So how will Gaza be governed? Maybe it won't be

The question is not whether Israel will "reoccupy" Gaza. The most onerous aspects of Israel's occupation never ended: what ended with the Oslo Accords was Israel's post-1967 strong role in overseeing administration and internal security outside of settlements; what changed in 2005 was the withdrawal of Israel's settlements and the attendant military presence. Now that Israel has moved back inside Gaza, rearranged its population, and disrupted all aspects of civilian life, it seems quite content to let matters rest there until something better comes along. And maybe nothing will.

Rather than a "day after," what seems more likely is a shift from intensive to low-level combat that has no clear resolution. There will be efforts to devise arrangements, to be sure. But the most notable diplomatic fallout from the fighting might be that diplomacy becomes even more difficult. The coordination necessary to make any arrangements for governance functions may be extremely hard to achieve.

Gazans will live in the surviving buildings and makeshift structures for a while. Any rebuilding will exclude significant portions of Gaza. Commerce, manufacturing, agriculture, and other businesses will be effectively destroyed, rendering Gazans completely dependent on humanitarian aid. Once a "besieged enclave," Gaza will be reduced to a "supercamp" of internally displaced persons.

For the foreseeable future, there will be no central government for Gaza. Not only will no force be able to supply security in terms of public security and basic law and order, but also, continuous Israeli raids or Hamas attacks on perceived collaborators may be ongoing.

In that context, law and order on the streets will likely be handled—if they are handled at all—by camp committees and self-appointed gangs. And this deterioration at the level of governance, security, and public order will likely be deepened by the absence of a political horizon, diplomatic process, or future prospects. Gazans will be offered a dispiriting present and a future of statelessness and denial of dignity, national rights, and individual rights.

This seems less like the day after a conflict than a long twilight of disintegration and despair.

And when the dust settles, the people of Israel-Palestine will be left facing each other with more bitterness, but with no more tools to craft a less violent future.

PART III
SOLIDARITIES

"All of our missiles . . . it's all from the US. The minute they turn off the tap, you can't keep fighting"

—Israel Defense Forces Major General (Ret.) Yitzhak Brick

Breakthroughs and Backlash in the Belly of the Beast

Mitchell Plitnick

On November 19, 2023, the latest in a long line of polls came out demonstrating that US president Joe Biden was losing votes in key sectors due to his support for Israel's massive assault on the Gaza Strip.[1] Since October 7, when the Palestinian group Hamas launched a bloody attack that killed some 1,200 Israelis, injured thousands more, and kidnapped some 250 others, Israel had been relentlessly bombing Gaza, and its troops were, at that point, in the middle of a bloody invasion. As of November 17, Gazan authorities reported that more than 11,000 people had been killed, mostly women and children, and another 27,490 had been injured.[2]

Biden's response included mobilizing two massive aircraft carriers, threatening other states against helping the Gazans militarily, and asking Congress to approve $14.3 billion in military

Mitchell Plitnick is president of ReThinking Foreign Policy and co-author, with Marc Lamont Hill, of *Except for Palestine: The Limits of Progressive Politics*. His earlier positions included co-director of Jewish Voice for Peace and founding director of the US office of B'Tselem, the Israeli Information Center for Human Rights in the Occupied Territories.

aid for Israel on top of its annual allotment of $3.8 billion. This policy was controversial, particularly within the president's own Democratic Party. Many wanted a ceasefire, were uncomfortable with Biden's full-throated support for Israel, and appalled at his apparent disregard for the massive destruction Israel was inflicting. Yet the president persisted.

In the United States, it is often said that Israel is a domestic issue. While few Americans are particularly well-informed about the conflict—and many who believe they are only know what they get from a very narrow range of sources—it tends to generate very strong opinions. Due to the outsized influence the US has on Palestine and Israel, those opinions matter, as do the collective social and cultural responses to events in Palestine and Israel. They influence United States policy in the region and are also important signals to actors in the Middle East.

When Hamas attacked Israel on October 7, there was an enormous outpouring of emotion all around the world, and the US was certainly no exception. A few voices were immediately raised in justifying Hamas's attack, but the overwhelming message—from opponents of Israel's policies toward the Palestinians as well as supporters—was one of outrage at the atrocities and sympathy for those killed, injured, and kidnapped, along with their families.

That sympathy started to splinter, however, once Israel began its relentless assault on Gaza. The split widened the longer Israel's bombing campaign, and then ground offensive, continued. As Israel inflicted unprecedented death and destruction, administration spokespeople and Biden himself took public stands that helped legitimize Israel's offensive. Notably, Biden called into question the reliability of casualty statistics from the Ministry of Health in Gaza, telling reporters on October 25 that "I have no notion that the Palestinians are telling the truth about how many people are killed." He said this even as the

Ministry of Health's numbers had been routinely relied on for years by international humanitarian organizations, the United Nations, and even the US Department of State.[3]

Biden's lockstep support for Israel despite concerns about the massive civilian casualty figures and widespread devastation of Gaza helped polarize public opinion. Passionate debate raged on college campuses, in public spaces, in Congress, in the media, and within the Jewish community. Whereas before October 7, 2023, the issue of the Israeli occupation and denial of Palestinian rights had long seemed to be fading from the public agenda, its salience in public debate has been firmly reestablished.

October 7 in context

The situation in both the West Bank and Gaza had been deteriorating for years and gotten considerably worse since Biden took office. In 2022, Israelis elected their most right-wing government ever. Meanwhile, the Biden administration preferred to ignore the Palestinian issue in favor of building on President Donald Trump's success in brokering normalization agreements between Israel and the countries of Bahrain, Morocco, Sudan, and the United Arab Emirates. This combination magnified the feelings of hopelessness among Palestinians and impunity among Israelis. While Israeli settlers attacked Palestinian villages, Israelis within the internationally recognized borders of the state felt a relative comfort, despite occasional attacks, most carried out by rogue Palestinians operating alone or consisting of largely ineffective rockets that typically caused no damage.

Just eight days before Hamas launched its attack, US national security advisor Jake Sullivan declared that "[t]he Middle East region is quieter today than it has been in two decades."[4] Sullivan's boast reflected the Biden administration's indifference to both the worsening humanitarian crisis in Gaza and the escalating attacks by Israeli settlers and soldiers in the West Bank. According to United Nations (UN) data, 237 Palestinians had been killed in the seven months leading up to October 7. Twenty-nine Israelis had been killed, all but four in the West Bank.[5]

Those figures were both the highest in years. But with no major clashes, Sullivan's statement reflected a general mood in the United States that the Israeli occupation was being effectively "managed."[6] Hamas destroyed that illusion with its attack.

US diplomacy on Palestine had been virtually non-existent for a decade. After talks broke down in 2013, President Barack Obama turned his focus to Iran. Trump, Obama's successor, did not take a serious approach to the issue and made numerous moves that deeply alienated the Palestinians, particularly his decision to relocate the US embassy from Tel Aviv to Jerusalem. Biden, for his part, has preferred to maintain the status quo. In fact, the major battleground over Israel's occupation and its denial of Palestinian rights in the United States just before October 7 was a contested definition of antisemitism, which encompassed criticism of Israel, effectively collapsing antisemitism and anti-Zionism; and the attempt to label the movement for boycott, divestment, and sanctions (BDS) against Israel an expression of antisemitism.

The International Holocaust Remembrance Alliance (IHRA) definition of antisemitism came with several examples of purported antisemitism that consisted of nothing more than criticisms of Israel.[7] It was adopted in 2016 and the debate around it grew steadily over time. Though championed by large Jewish organizations, such as the Anti-Defamation League and American Jewish Committee, it met with significant opposition from other Jewish groups as well as Palestinians and those in solidarity with them.

That debate, often heated, was linked to ongoing tensions over the BDS movement. Launched in 2005, BDS calls for equality for all Israelis and Palestinians, including Palestinian refugees. It has been besieged for years by Israel and its supporters worldwide. Rather than accept that Palestinians had found a nonviolent method of fighting for their liberation after the second intifada, pro-Israel forces delegitimized the movement as antisemitic and primarily interested not in Palestinian liberation but in harming, or even annihilating, Jews.

With little diplomacy to influence, the contest over Palestinian rights in the United States had thus been largely relegated to a battle over the very legitimacy of support for those rights. In the courts, the streets, even in the halls of Congress, the question of whether support for Palestinian rights was inherently antisemitic was the subject. Naturally, this was not explicit; defenders of Israeli policies claimed that Palestinians should be free, but that security concerns forced Israel's hand. Nonetheless, they responded to nearly every criticism of Israel with accusations of antisemitism and the claim that the criticisms were being leveled not to defend human rights but to "delegitimize" Israel. Criticism of the far-right government headed by Benjamin Netanyahu was fair game only because there was such massive protest against it in Israel and because the major legacy Jewish organizations saw a threat to their ability to defend Israel in the extremist government. The fact that the Israeli protest movement intensely resisted any connection to Israel's ongoing occupation of the West Bank and siege of Gaza allowed for this exception.

The controversies over IHRA and BDS did little to change the minds of people involved in or observing the debates. But they put the idea in the minds of Americans—who, for the most part, were not deeply involved in or concerned with the

question of Palestine and Israel—that criticizing Israel at least
ran the risk of antisemitism, and often was thought to be inherently antisemitic. This fed, in turn, into a broader atmosphere
of Islamophobia in the United States. As Professor Sahar Aziz
and I observed:

> Islamophobia is juxtaposed against antisemitism, portraying
> Muslims globally and domestically as agents of antisemitism;
> attempting to create a competition, or even a zero-sum sce-
> nario between Muslims and Jews . . . As a result, legitimate
> efforts to combat antisemitism are disingenuously co-opted
> to undermine Palestinian aspirations for self-determination
> and human rights, as well as to defame Muslim and Arab
> human rights defenders as inherently antisemitic. Palestin-
> ian aspirations are often portrayed by the media and Zion-
> ist organizations as a cover for a uniquely Arab and Muslim
> antisemitism.[8]

This was the American atmosphere that the Hamas attack of
October 7 appeared in.

The killing begins

Any student of history knows that one of the most fundamental choices one must make, when trying to convey a historical
subject, is where to start. For most Americans, and certainly
for the overwhelming majority of American leaders and media,
the history of what Hamas called Operation Al-Aqsa Deluge
and Israel called Operation Swords of Iron began on October
7, 2023. In the days after Hamas's attack and the beginning of
Israel's response, it seemed almost de rigueur that the Hamas
attack be described as "unprovoked." This was not the usual
skirmish over semantics. As Yousef Munayyer, Senior Fellow at
the Arab Center, Washington DC, wrote,

> [t]o call this "unprovoked" . . . is to ignore the daily and con-
> stant Israeli violence and war crimes against Palestinians which
> has only escalated in recent years. It is language that erases Pal-
> estinians and enables continued violence against them.[9]

Indeed, the presumption that the attack was unprovoked provided the basis for the common narrative in the United States
that Hamas was uninterested in Palestinian liberation but only
wanted to kill Jews. It allowed for the equating of Hamas—
undoubtedly as violent and militant a group as any, but also
a political entity with a distinctively nationalist ideology—to
groups like al-Qaeda or ISIS, which are motivated by zealous
visions of global jihad that Hamas does not share.[10]

The twin ideas that Hamas was motivated by murderous antisemitism and that they were a carbon copy of ISIS stretched the
tolerance of much of the American public and allowed both the
president and Congress to support what was sure to be an unprecedented Israeli reaction to an unprecedented Palestinian strike.

When UN secretary-general António Guterres stated, cor-
rectly, that the Hamas attack didn't happen in a vacuum—a
reference to the ongoing conflict, the occupation since 1967,
and the blockade of Gaza since 2006, as well as the increas-
ing Israeli violence against Palestinians and provocations on the
Temple Mount in Jerusalem since Israel's far-right government
came to power in 2022—the response from Israel was to call
for his resignation. While American leaders largely kept quiet
about this demand, they were quite vocal on the matter of a
ceasefire. White House press secretary Karin Jean-Pierre, when
asked about the very few members of Congress who were calling almost immediately for a ceasefire, responded:

> I've seen some of those statements this weekend. And we're
> gonna continue to be very clear. We believe they're wrong.

We believe they're repugnant and we believe they're disgraceful . . . There are not two sides here. There are not two sides.[11]

In fact, whereas many Hamas members doubtless harbor little love for Jews, Hamas did not attack anyone because they
were Jewish on October 7. It murdered and brutalized people
because they were Israeli. This crucial difference in no way mitigates, much less justifies, Hamas's criminal and bloody actions.
But understanding what happened and why is important if we
want to stop the suffering, stop the killing, and make sure that
Israelis and Palestinians can all live with the rights that all humans are entitled to.

Nor should we underestimate the magnitude of Hamas's
crime and the shock it caused Israelis and anyone, this author
included, who has friends and relatives in Israel. This was an
unprecedented attack in the history of a state which has seen
many of them in its relatively brief existence. The rage and grief
it produced, regardless of the circumstances, were enormous, as
befits a crime of that magnitude. The response from Israel was
universally expected to be extreme. But the massive toll on civilians and the brazen declarations from Israeli leaders of disregard
for those civilian casualties led to a sharpened split in American
attitudes. While some saw an overriding need to eliminate
Gaza, others saw the casualties and destruction in Gaza as far
too high a price to pay, whatever their feelings about Hamas.

Dividing opinions
These ideological divisions often play out most visibly on college campuses, and this time was no exception. Reporting of
those conflicts frequently focused on discomfort felt by Jewish
students and encapsulated some of the factors that distort
thinking in the US about the conflict.

On the macro level, the dependence of the American university system on wealthy donors was again exposed for the harm this can cause to academic freedom and liberty of speech. As students on campuses came out in support of either Israel or the Palestinians, those donors—naturally disposed to right-wing and conservative views due to their position of wealth and power and motivated by an equally radical and right-wing support for Israel—came out overwhelmingly in support of Israel. More to the point, they pressured universities to take action against students who were protesting Israel's massive bombardment of Gaza.

On November 10, Columbia University, which has been a site of some of the fiercest campus battles over Israel, Palestine, and academic freedom, suspended two student groups—Students for Justice in Palestine (SJP) and Jewish Voice for Peace (JVP)—claiming safety concerns.[12] This was the clearest example of an atmosphere of tension, even fear, among university administrations, created by a large wave of donors cutting off their support to both private and public educational institutions.[13] Columbia's suspension of JVP and SJP was indicative of the panic this phenomenon caused.

Media of all kinds discussed the massive spike in reported antisemitic, Islamophobic, and anti-Arab incidents across the United States since October 7. Some news items focused on one or the other and some on both. In all cases, we saw reports of assaults, vandalism, threats, harassment, and other kinds of intolerable abuse. But the coverage of Jewish students also brought forward complaints about their comfort level that highlighted the difficulties in conversations about Israel and Palestine.

One *New York Times* article, headlined "After Antisemitic Attacks, Colleges Debate What Kind of Speech Is Out of Bounds," typified this problem.[14] While the article cited some very disturbing examples of antisemitism, its focus was on the discomfort of Jewish students at expressions of a Palestinian narrative that is valid, fact-based, and worthy of respect. The article opened with the example of Max Strozenberg, a Jewish student at Northwestern University. Mr. Strozenberg was upset because he saw a poster in a public area in his dorm that referred to Gaza as a "modern-day concentration camp" and later heard protesters on campus chanting, "Hey, Schill, what do you say, how many kids did you kill today?"—referring to Northwestern's president Michael Schill, who is Jewish, and to ongoing efforts by student activists to get Northwestern to divest from Israel.[15]

According to the *Times*, these incidents prompted Mr. Strozenberg to say that he feels unsafe and that the mood on his campus "is not pro-Palestinian, it's antisemitic." The focus of the *Times* piece was on the question of what is and is not "acceptable language" of protest. Yet consider what Mr. Strozenberg is presented as reacting to. Nothing about either incident is specific to Jews. While "concentration camps" are obviously associated deeply with the Holocaust, it is not unique to that act of genocide. It's a distinct term that long predates World War II and has been applied in many other cases.

That doesn't diminish Mr. Strozenberg's visceral reaction. But Gaza is commonly referred to as an open-air prison, even as the Strip's dense population and the problems that brings with it are not fully encompassed by that term. It isn't unreasonable to choose "concentration camp" as a closer reflection of life in Gaza before October 7, as prominent Israeli officials as well as commentators have done.

Similarly, while the chant that disturbed Mr. Strozenberg might have been directed at a person who happened to be Jewish, it was not the Jewishness of the man in question, but rather his position as president of the university, that made him the target. The chant itself is a very familiar one that has been heard at American protests since the 1960s and has nothing in it that can reasonably be interpreted as expressing any comment at all about Jews. And if it was the accusation of children being killed that discomforted, that was simply a factual aspect of Israel's campaign in Gaza, which killed thousands of Palestinian children in a small area of land, half of whose population are under the age of eighteen.

This too does not minimize Mr. Strozenberg's reaction, nor that of other Jewish students made uncomfortable by these words and the protests themselves. But what made them uncomfortable, exactly? They feel there is antisemitism here, but the only way this can be interpreted as antisemitism, given the very real circumstances of Israel's actions in Gaza, is by branding any criticism of Israel antisemitic by definition.

Mr. Strozenberg was not alone. On CNN, Jake Tapper interviewed a young Jewish woman, Talia Kahn, on a similar topic. Ms. Kahn is a student at the Massachusetts Institute of Technology (MIT). When Tapper asked her why she feels unsafe, she responded that the campus and local "anti-Israel groups" had staged protests at the entrance of the campus and the student center. As Tapper tried to get some concrete example of a reason to fear for her safety, Ms. Kahn could only point to language that supported Palestinian resistance to Israeli oppression and the fact that the groups tried to enter specific offices that promoted partnership with Israel.

Ms. Kahn also relayed that, during the protests, the university administration advised parents to pick up their children from the university day care center because they were "worried that it would get violent." But no such thing happened.[16]

These students were doubtless experiencing real fear. But that fear was not grounded in the experience of actual violence. They were, to be sure, being confronted with significant anger by Palestinian students and their supporters, but those feelings were at least as legitimate as those of the Jewish students, especially under the circumstances of week after week of massive Palestinian death tolls.

The fear Jewish students experienced, though an authentic emotion, was also at least in part a product of the Islamophobic dynamics of American society, culture, and politics. These dynamics are particularly strong with regard to Palestinians, who are routinely associated in the American mind with violence.[17] The Bridge Initiative at Georgetown University explains:

> One of the most common tropes about Muslims is that they have a unique penchant for violence or that their religion encourages it. This narrative is often reinforced by media coverage which primarily reports on Muslims in the context of violence and terrorism. Bound up with this narrative is the idea that the more religious a person becomes the more violent he/she is likely to become.[18]

In an atmosphere informed by this trope, it is unsurprising if protests led by Muslims, Arabs, or their supporters, and using the phraseology of Palestinian resistance, produces visceral fear reactions. But for Jewish students whose identity is strongly connected to Israel it is even more powerful.

As a Jew who grew up in a radically pro-Israel environment, I can attest to the propaganda that is constantly thrust at many young Jews. Many of my own contemporaries have told similar stories and, while subsequent generations have experienced this differently and often with more nuance, the wall of propaganda around Israel remains steadfast. Indeed, it is this wall of false perception, reinforced by a fantastical version of both Israel and the Palestinians put forth by American political leaders,[19] that challenges young Jews, as it is relentlessly contradicted by the reality of Palestinian experience. Most American Jews, especially younger Jews, hold to liberal values. While supporters of Palestinian rights may sometimes be glib about the ability of American liberals—Jewish and not—to suspend their principles as they make an exception for Palestine, it is important to recognize that this apparent double standard, based on a version of Israel and the Palestinians that is largely detached from reality, is what allows many Jews, young and old, to avoid having to truly choose between their liberal values and their identification with the Jewish state.

In that context, we can better understand why protest for Palestinian rights evokes a visceral reaction for Jews. That reaction is perhaps most acute for the young, who are also being exposed every day at university to sharp, and often angry, support for Palestinians. But it is very real for all Jews who associate their Jewish identity strongly with Israel.

It is this visceral reaction that the push to adopt the IHRA definition of antisemitism and the demonization of BDS seeks to exploit. By construing all criticism of Israel as antisemitism, those who support the IHRA definition and demonize BDS play on deep anxieties harbored by many Jews attempting to reconcile Israeli behavior with their values. Understandably, then, many people feel nervous, as the *Times* and CNN reported, whenever support for Palestinians is expressed, particularly when expressed in Palestinian terms.

Yet these attempted conflations fail badly to account for the deep divisions among American Jews on Israel generally and on the assault on Gaza in particular. The major American Jewish institutions have historically dominated the policy conversation on Israel, giving the impression of uniformity, if not on all policies, then at least on the basic question of Zionism. Long before October 7, 2023, that impression was being challenged by anti-Zionist groups like Jewish Voice for Peace or groups that were noncommittal on that issue such as IfNotNow (INN).

With the Hamas attack and the subsequent Israeli onslaught on Gaza, JVP and INN took on much greater prominence, leading dramatic demonstrations all over the country and making clear that Jewish support for Israel's campaign of total destruction of Gaza was far from absolute. Perhaps most dramatically, JVP led protests that shut down business in the Hart Senate office building and disrupted a meeting of the Democratic National Committee in Washington[20] as well as Grand Central Station in New York.[21]

A pro-war demonstration was organized by the larger and better-funded Jewish organizations, which descended into controversy when Pastor John Hagee—a so-called "Christian Zionist" leader who once claimed that Hitler was sent by God to force the Jews to settle in Palestine—was invited to speak.[22] The bloodthirstiness of the gathering was made clear when one speaker, the liberal CNN commentator Van Jones, was shouted down with chants of "no ceasefire" when he dared say that he wanted to see bombs and rockets stop falling on both sides.[23]

That single rally, though, had little impact when compared to the many anti-war demonstrations held all over the United States throughout October and November 2023.[24] On November 4 alone, some 300,000 people reportedly gathered in Washington to support the Palestinians—by far the largest such gathering ever in the United States.[25] This matched the estimate organizers reported for the far better-funded pro-war march.[26]

Censuring "from the river to the sea"
These dynamics played out as well in the distortion of the common Palestinian slogan, "From the river to the sea, Palestine

will be free." That phrase, in one form or another, has been used for many years by Palestinians, while some Israelis also use "from the river to the sea" to designate all of Israel, the West Bank, and Gaza. But after October 7, especially, the slogan's use by Palestine solidarity activists was labeled anti-semitic by pro-Israel forces. They argued that it called for the elimination of Israel and of Jews from the Jordan River to the Mediterranean Sea, the bodies of water on either side of Israel and Palestine.

As Professor Maha Nassar of the University of Arizona explains, "[t]he majority of Palestinians who use this phrase do so because they believe that, in 10 short words, it sums up their personal ties, their national rights, and their vision for the land they call Palestine." As a popular Palestinian phrase, it is hardly surprising that Hamas would also use it. And it absolutely is connected with the contention that Zionism is incompatible with true democracy or political, cultural, and social equality in the state. That is its own debate, but as Professor Nassar elaborates, "[m]ost Palestinians using this chant do not see it as advocating for a specific political platform or as belonging to a specific political group. Rather, the majority of people using the phrase see it as a principled vision of freedom and coexistence."[27]

Bad faith actors have arbitrarily translated the slogan as calling for a Palestine "free of Jews,"[28] but Professor Nassar notes that the phrase in the original Arabic, "*Filastin hurra,* means liberated Palestine. 'Free from' would be a different Arabic word altogether." So while the phrase is contentious, no reasonable person could conclude that it can only be said with antisemitic intent.

Yet it was uttering that phrase that led Rep. Rashida Tlaib—the only Palestinian-American in Congress and one of only three Muslims—to be censured, a highly unusual practice in the House of Representatives that has only occurred twenty-six

times in the chamber's 234-year history. In recent years, there
have been several incidents of censure along party lines, but in
Rep. Tlaib's case, twenty-two members of her *own* party voted
to censure her, a remarkable feature of this episode.

The censure resolution,[29] which contained numerous errors
of fact and some outright false accusations, specifically cited
Tlaib's use of the phrase "from the river to the sea" among the
charges. Yet no official objections were raised to the words of
Rep. Brian Mast, during a speech he made on the floor of the
House of Representatives. "I would encourage the other side
to not so lightly throw around the idea of innocent Palestinian
civilians," Mast admonished during debate on an amendment
to a bill whose purpose was to reduce aid to civilians in Gaza. "I
don't think we would so lightly throw around the term 'innocent
Nazi civilians' during World War II. It is not a far stretch to say
there are very few innocent Palestinian civilians."[30]

The comparison of Palestinians to Nazis was bad enough,
but the legal implication of stating that there are few Palestinian
civilians in Gaza ran dangerously close to endorsing the indiscriminate killing of Palestinians. One Democrat, Rep. Sara
Jacobs, filed a motion to censure Mast, but when she tried
to force a vote on the measure, the bill was pulled from consideration by Democratic minority leader Hakeem Jeffries.
Whereas nearly two dozen Democrats voted to censure Tlaib,
no Democrat would agree to cosponsor Jacobs's resolution
against Mast, and those who spoke, even when critical of Mast,
expressed no support for censure.[31]

The two incidents exemplify the overwhelming, biparti-
san support in Congress for Israel's assault on the Gaza Strip.
But they obscure the views of the American public, which
supported a truce in Gaza and Israel soon after October 7,
even as it sympathized with Israel. An October 20 poll by
Data for Progress found that fully 66 percent of respondents

supported a ceasefire.[32] A November 15 poll by Reuters/
Ipsos found that 68 percent of Americans wanted the United
States to call for a ceasefire and negotiate a settlement between
Israel and the Palestinians.[33] That remarkably consistent result
demonstrated the disconnect between American opinion and
congressional views.

As of November 18, only thirty-six members of the House
of Representatives and one senator had called for a ceasefire.
Though the list was growing, it was doing so slowly. The
foot-dragging in Washington was, however, far from unanimous.

Dissent in the establishment

Less than two weeks into Israel's bombing campaign against
Gaza, stories began appearing about problems at the State
Department. These internal rifts were so severe, they were
described by one State Department staffer as a brewing "mutiny."[34] In early November, more reports surfaced of "dissent
memos" sent by State staffers to the top of the agency, including
Secretary Antony Blinken.[35]

The complaints included a letter from employees of USAID,
the State Department's international development agency. Their
communication, signed by over a thousand staffers, informed
the secretary that they were "alarmed and disheartened at the
numerous violations of international law; laws which aim
to protect civilians, medical and media personnel, as well as
schools, hospitals, and places of worship."[36]

Indeed, it was apparent from the outset, and became clearer
as the days wore on and the death toll mounted, that US policy
on Israel's actions was being made by a small, insular group at
the very top and was not drawing on the expertise available
among White House and State Department staff. Essentially,
the president was deciding these matters alone, with his closest
advisors there to support his decisions.[37]

It was so bad that an eleven-year veteran director at State, Josh Paul, resigned from his position handling arms sales to foreign countries, a role he acknowledged often came with difficult moral compromises. "I have had my fair share of debates and discussions and efforts to shift policy on controversial arms sales," he explained. "It was clear that there's no arguing with this one. Given that I couldn't shift anything, I resigned."[38]

Finally, on November 14, Blinken felt he had to address his critics. His reported response condescended to the diplomats in his department by suggesting they were letting their sympathy for the suffering of Palestinians in Gaza trump their policy judgment. He acknowledged that they had disagreements about policy and simply offered dissatisfied officials a forum where they could be "heard." This did little to still the dissenting voices.

The disconnect between establishment leadership and staff was reflected in US media as well, as mainstream outlets such as the *New York Times* and CNN came under withering attack for their biased coverage of Israel's onslaught. A letter signed by over 1,200 professional journalists on November 9 sharply criticized mainstream news coverage.[39] The *Los Angeles Times* informed its reporters and staffers who signed the letter that they were barred from covering the Gaza war.[40]

Accusations of media bias have long been a focal point of contention for supporters of both Israel and Palestine. This time, however, we saw a significant number of journalists willing to put their professional futures at risk to speak out against anti-Palestinian bias in American media.

An overdue awakening
Given the forces of politics, media bias, and Islamophobia, it is remarkable that Americans were so consistent in preferring a

ceasefire to maintaining Israel's ability to wage a war that had no defined endpoint. It is even more telling that this opinion held even though there was no evidence that people had forgotten the bloody events of October 7 or that their outrage over Hamas's brutality had diminished. Rather, the message one got from the zeitgeist in the United States was a simple yearning for the atrocities to end.

There was also a deep disappointment evident from significant sectors of the US public in the administration of Joe Biden. While Biden had the enthusiastic support of the pro-Israel community, key sectors that Biden counts on for support were alienated by his policy of full support of Israel regardless of the level of death and destruction Israel visited on Palestinian civilians.

Democratic activist and Arab-American leader Jim Zogby spoke about the plummeting support among Arab and Muslim Americans for Biden's re-election campaign. He shared that White House staff dismissed these concerns, saying those communities "are not going to vote for Donald Trump, because they don't want [to return to] what he was doing during his four years, and so they'll come around in a year."[41]

This smug attitude, Zogby said, was "insulting and dismissive," and the voices of Muslim and Arab Americans, as well as their allies, echoed that sentiment. The National Muslim Democratic Council pledged "to mobilize Muslim, Arab, and allied voters to withhold endorsement, support, or votes for any candidate who did not advocate for a ceasefire and endorse[d] the Israeli offensive against the Palestinian people."[42] Muslim voters are key in some of the most contested states in presidential elections.

Has Biden doomed his 2024 reelection bid by insisting on blind support for Israel? Only time will tell, and the specter of another Donald Trump presidency may yet be enough to compel voters to support Biden despite the blood on his hands.

But he has clearly gone against the wishes of the American public, not least his own voters, as 80 percent of Democrats attested in the polls cited above. In another poll at the end of November, not only did 77 percent of Democrats back a ceasefire, but so did 58 percent of Republicans and 60 percent of unaffiliated voters.[43] Among young voters—a Biden demographic—fully 70 percent said they disapproved of Biden's policy in Gaza, while Biden's overall approval rating among that group fell to 31 percent in mid-November.[44] Democrats generally rely on younger voters turning out to win elections.

This level of public criticism is unlike what has come before. While many Palestine solidarity groups reported increases in membership and support during previous Israeli assaults on Gaza, polling numbers never shifted this dramatically. For example, a January 2009 survey taken at the height of Israel's massive bombing campaign dubbed Operation Cast Lead showed little change in either American support for Israel or desire for greater US action.[45] The rifts Gaza has aggravated in American society over the entire Israel-Palestine question will no longer be so easily shunted aside as a topic of conversation best avoided.

It is crucial that it not be. Americans, due to our tax dollars and our government's strong support for Israel on the world stage, cannot be neutral, much less silent, on this issue. Nor can the issue be placed on the backburner. Biden tried to do that, and the result was unconditional support for what could turn out to be a genocide in Gaza, and one that may not stop there. Americans clearly don't want that. But if we are to be responsible for our own democratic power, we will have to press harder on our elected officials to reflect the will of the majority of Americans, not the few who support Israel with no limits.

"Starvation is being used as a weapon of war against Gaza civilians"

—Oxfam

Palestine Solidarity in Britain

Talal Hangari

The Palestine solidarity movement in Britain put forward two
demands to stop the massacre in Gaza: *ceasefire now* and *lift the
siege*. These positions aligned with those adopted by most UN
member states as well as the consensus among human rights
organizations.[1] They also enjoyed broad public support.[2] Yet
Britain's ruling Conservative and opposition Labour parties
united behind Israel's devastating offensive—despite repeated
calls to end British complicity in Israel's crimes—while popular
solidarity with Palestinians under fire was subjected to unprecedented delegitimization. This chapter reviews the continuities
and changes in British responses to the Gaza catastrophe, the
obstacles confronting the solidarity movement here, and the
opportunities now available to it.

Government policy
Britain opposed Palestinian self-determination after the First
World War and in 1936 brutally suppressed a Palestinian in-
dependence revolt. "I do not agree," future prime minister
Winston Churchill explained the following year, "that the

Talal Hangari is a socialist who lives in London and has written for several
left-wing publications. His website is talalhangari.com.

dog in a manger has the final right to the manger even though he may have lain there for a very long time."[3] After the 1967 Arab-Israel War, successive British administrations colluded in Israel's refusal to resolve its conflict with the Palestinians on the terms prescribed by international law.[4] When Palestinians under occupation elected Hamas in 2006, Britain "tacitly or openly supported" Israel's "policy of protracted collective punishment" which, for the past seventeen years, has been primarily responsible for the hopeless situation in Gaza.[5] And when Israeli foreign minister Tzipi Livni was threatened with prosecution after boasting that Israel had gone "wild" in Gaza during Operation Cast Lead,[6] the British government helped shield her from accountability under the law.[7] Britain's response to the Gaza massacre of 2023 added another chapter to this shameful record.

In the weeks after October 7, as Gaza was being pummeled and pulverized, Prime Minister Rishi Sunak expressed his "absolute" support for "Israel's right to defend itself, to go after Hamas and take back the hostages, to deter further incursions, and to strengthen its security for the long term."[8] Sunak refused to call for a ceasefire while Israel was "still facing rocket fire," apparently misunderstanding the concept.[9] During an official visit "to demonstrate British backing for the Israeli government," Sunak personally informed Israel's prime minister that "we . . . want you to win."[10] By this point, Israel had killed nearly 3,500 people in Gaza, including more than 850 children, and damaged or destroyed one out of every four homes.[11]

Sunak did enter the rider that Israel's retaliation "must be done in line with international humanitarian law." But this qualification was itself immediately qualified as Sunak alleged that Israel "face[d] a vicious enemy that embeds itself behind civilians."[12] The caveat was emptied of meaning entirely when Sunak announced that Israel was already "taking every precaution to avoid harming civilians."[13] He issued this all-clear on

October 19—long after human rights observers had warned that Israel was inflicting the "war crime" of "collective punishment" (Human Rights Watch) as part of a "criminal policy of revenge" (B'Tselem) and one day before Amnesty International published documentation of "unlawful Israeli attacks, including indiscriminate attacks, which caused mass civilian casualties."[14] Whereas human rights organizations uniformly condemned Israel's evacuation order to the entire population of northern Gaza as "not compatible with international humanitarian law" (Red Cross), Sunak commended it as "absolutely right."[15]

British complicity in Israel's massacre extended beyond verbal support. In the United Nations (UN) Security Council, Britain abstained on a resolution for "humanitarian pauses" in Gaza and vetoed another that demanded an immediate ceasefire.[16] At the military level, the Conservative government has authorized the sale of more than £470 million worth of arms to Israel since 2015, including components for F-35 stealth combat aircraft reportedly deployed by Israel in Gaza.[17] After October 7, the Royal Air Force was sent to conduct regional surveillance patrols, the Royal Navy was dispatched to the Eastern Mediterranean, and British forces in the region were strengthened "to prevent escalation and further threats against Israel."[18] The government presented this military "package" as "a significant demonstration of the UK's support for Israel's right to self-defense."[19] Calls by leading human rights groups for Britain to "suspend military assistance and arms sales to Israel so long as its forces commit . . . war crimes" were not reported in the British press.[20]

In sum, the British government extended its unconditional support as Israel unleashed one of "the most intense aerial bombardment[s] this century" upon an occupied and besieged civilian population.[21] This depravity was compounded by deceit as the government promulgated a sequence of lies designed to obscure its complicity in a terror bombing. First, the government asserted, quite fantastically, that it wanted to "revive the long-term prospects for a two-state solution,"[22] notwithstanding the total expiry of the "peace process" and Israel's admitted opposition to Palestinian statehood.[23] In March 2023, Britain and Israel agreed on a "roadmap" establishing the "mutual priorities" that would steer their "strategic partnership" until 2030. This document did not mention a two-state solution.[24]

Second, the government repeatedly misrepresented the unfolding catastrophe to the British public. When parliamentarians raised the prospect of a ceasefire, James Cleverly, the foreign secretary, alleged that "Hamas have no interest in a ceasefire" and "have never attempted to engage in a two-state solution."[25] He added: "I have seen nothing—nothing—that leads me to believe that Hamas would respect calls for a ceasefire."[26] Yet Hamas had already expressed its openness to a ceasefire on October 9, more than a week before Cleverly's statement;[27] Hamas has a more impressive record of upholding ceasefires than Israel;[28] and Hamas has repeatedly indicated a willingness to negotiate a resolution of the conflict.[29] Cleverly deceived his listeners on all these points, and further deceived them by omitting Israel's opposition to a ceasefire and steadfast rejection of a Palestinian state.

To excuse the soaring civilian casualties in Gaza, Cleverly incessantly repeated that Hamas uses "human shields," the implication being that Israel could not exercise its "right to defend itself" except by inflicting large civilian casualties. But human rights investigations did not sustain "human shields" allegations against Hamas in previous hostilities, whereas they did find credible evidence that Israeli forces used Palestinians as human shields.[30] Cleverly also cast doubt on the casualty figures provided by the Gaza health ministry: Hamas "abuse the figures they put in the public domain. We must be highly skeptical of any information coming out of Hamas."[31] Yet reputable human rights organizations and international agencies judged these figures reliable.[32]

These aspects of British policy—facilitating while lying about Israeli war crimes—are consistent with Britain's long record on Palestine, as noted above. This should not surprise as they are rooted in entrenched institutions. Foremost among these is Britain's international position as a subordinate member of a US-led alliance. British policy on Palestine has largely tracked that of the United States since the 1970s, when British planners recognized "the need for association with the United States over Middle East issues" to avoid "injury to the general Anglo-US relationship."[33]

Recent developments have only exacerbated Britain's dependence on its former colony. Britain previously sought to position its Palestine policy between the US, the European Union (EU), and the oil-producing Gulf States—though always much closer to the US than the others. But the Donald Trump administration shifted US policy further toward uncritical support for the most overtly annexationist government in Israel's history, while President Joe Biden did not effect a substantive course correction. At the same time, Brexit likely diminished the EU's influence over British foreign policy, while normalization between Israel and leading Arab states meant that the latter no longer acted as an effective counterweight to pro-Israel pressures. This helps to explain the wildly unbalanced "roadmap" agreed to by Britain and Israel, which proposed to deepen their "extensive defense and security cooperation" irrespective of any commitment or progress by Israel toward ceasing its violations of Palestinian rights.[34]

In 2006, Britain imposed sanctions on the elected Hamas government in coordination with the Middle East "Quartet." That body nominally comprised the UN, US, EU, and Russia,

but was in fact dominated by the US.[35] The same is doubtless true of the "Quintet," a Western grouping—including
Britain—that on October 10, 2023, declared its "united support" for Israel.[36] In short: the US approved Israel's massacre
in Gaza, therefore, the British government approved it also.
Britain's former defense secretary, Michael Portillo, accordingly
praised the opposition leader Sir Keir Starmer for resisting
grassroots pressure to support a ceasefire. This was "important," Portillo explained, "because the United States, for example, would want to know whether a Labour government was
going to deviate from the alliance with the United States."[37]
Guardian columnist Polly Toynbee sounded the same note: "as
he [Starmer] expects to be prime minister next year, breaking
ranks with all Britain's allies would be frivolous."[38] Labour MPs
themselves were reportedly informed that "party policy on Gaza
will simply follow the White House."[39]

Within the overall context of British subordination to
American power, pro-Israel advocacy groups also shape government policy in significant ways. Israel's supporters are effi-
ciently organized, well-funded, and in some cases receive assistance from the Israeli government.[40] In recent decades they have
had influence at the highest official levels, especially, though
not exclusively, in the Conservative Party.[41] It was reported
in November 2023 that fully thirteen of thirty-one Labour
shadow cabinet members had received money from pro-Israel
donors while Starmer's 2019 Labour leadership campaign had
been secretly funded by a prominent pro-Israel lobbyist.[42] The
diligence of the Israel lobby, the resources at its disposal, and
the overlap between its demands and the interests of British
elites committed to the US alliance, make it a formidable political force. Prominent pro-Israel organizations rallied in support
of Israel's previous offensives in Gaza and they reprised this role
after October 7.[43] The Board of Deputies of British Jews, for

example, produced guidance explaining that Israel's attack on Gaza "is a legitimate military action to prevent future acts of terror and to prevent civilian casualties."[44] Labour Friends of Israel claimed that "Israel is fighting Hamas, not the Palestinian people," albeit with the usual *pro forma* mention of Israel's legal responsibilities.[45] And the Campaign Against Antisemitism convened a rally in London that depicted Palestine solidarity protests as antisemitic and expressed solidarity with Israel.[46]

Alongside support for Israel's criminal assault, and public deceptions to justify this, the final plank of the government's policy was to delegitimize Palestine solidarity activism. In a letter to police leadership, Suella Braverman, the home secretary,[47] warned that "whenever Israel is attacked, Islamists and other racists, seek to use legitimate Israeli defensive measures as a pretext to stir up hatred against British Jews." Braverman reminded the police that Hamas is a proscribed terrorist organization and that support for it is a criminal offence; she asked them "to consider whether chants such as 'From the river to the sea, Palestine will be free' should be understood as an expression of a violent desire to see Israel erased from the world, and whether its use in certain contexts may amount to a racially aggravated . . . public order offence"; she suggested that "[b]ehaviors that are legitimate in some circumstances, for example the waving of a Palestinian flag, may not be legitimate . . . when intended to glorify acts of terrorism"; and she encouraged "a strong police presence" at demonstrations."[48] The letter was sent the day after the first major Palestine solidarity demonstration outside the Israeli embassy. After a 150,000 strong protest march on October 14, which called for an end to the violence and to Israel's apartheid system, Braverman fulminated that "an intimidating mob" had "marched through London."[49] She alleged that the slogan "[f]rom the river to the sea" was "a staple of an antisemitic discourse" and threatened that "[t]hose who promote hate on Britain's streets should real-ize that our tolerance has limits."[50]

The government's policy of delegitimizing solidarity was aided by the hysterical denunciation of pro-Palestine protest-ers in the media. The commissioner for countering extremism wrote in the *Times* that protest chants supporting resistance and Palestinian freedom after October 7 in fact meant "death to Jews, and the erasure of Israel from the map." With their wily tactics, he warned, "the overwhelming majority" of pro-testers were careful to conduct themselves "just below the legal threshold for hate crime, glorification of terror, or public order offences." In other words, "the overwhelming majority" of pro-testers behaved lawfully. In doing so, he charged, the protest-ers were "exploiting . . . freedom of expression, to pursue a shameful extremist agenda."[51] In other words, they exercised their lawful right to free expression. Abandoning any pretense of fairness, the commissioner did not consider the possibil-ity that any extremism had emanated from pro-Israel groups or individuals.

Worst of all were calls for the elimination of hard-won lib-erties on the false premise that Palestine solidarity protests were violent and hateful. The alt-right commentator Douglas Murray, responding to demonstrations scheduled for the Armistice Day weekend on November 11, declared: "This is the tipping point. If such a march goes ahead then the people of Britain must come out and stop these barbarians."[52] Other right-wing fig-ures and parties also called for the marches to be banned,[53] reversing their otherwise well-publicized opposition to "cancel culture" and support for "free speech." The Campaign Against Antisemitism petitioned the police to ask that marches be pre-vented and replaced by "static protests of no more than 20,000 people" instead.[54]

Government officials voiced indignation that Palestine solidarity activists had planned a demonstration on Armistice Day,
with the odd implication that calls for a ceasefire violated the
spirit of peace and remembrance.[55] Sunak charged that the rally
was "provocative and disrespectful" and alleged there was "a clear
and present risk that the Cenotaph and other war memorials
could be desecrated."[56] But the organizers of the pro-Palestine
demonstration had "no intention of marching on or near
Whitehall, in order not to disrupt events at the Cenotaph."[57]
Braverman condemned the "hate marchers" and suggested that
"pro-Palestinian mobs" had been generously treated by the
police in comparison to "[r]ight-wing and nationalist protesters."[58] Emboldened, a number of far-right protesters gathered
in Whitehall, near the Cenotaph, and fought with police on
Armistice Day.[59]

The reality is that the solidarity protests were overwhelmingly peaceful. After demonstrations in London on November
4, a police commander noted that, although there were pockets
of disorder, "the vast majority of people demonstrated peacefully."[60] A statement by the Metropolitan Police acknowledged
"the positive work of organizers who have supported tens of
thousands of people to protest peacefully and lawfully since 7
October."[61] The number of arrests was minuscule in proportion
to the number of people demonstrating, with estimates ranging
between 100,000 and 800,000 marching in London alongside
thousands more in other parts of the country.[62]

This intensified delegitimization of Palestine solidarity activism cannot be explained simply in terms of the long-standing
structural features of British policy described above. Two novel
developments also played a role. First, Israel has been forced
on the back foot in public debate; there is now a broad consensus among reputable human rights organizations that Israel
is committing crimes against humanity and this consensus has

increasingly percolated into public knowledge. When argument is difficult, censorship presents a straightforward alternative. Indeed, it is a longstanding practice of liberal democracies to revoke civil liberties precisely when they are most needed for dissenting from the government.

Second, the Conservatives have adopted a repressive posture in general since they were elected in 2019. Amid economic stagnation, a degeneration in public services, and escalating labor struggles, the government used attacks on refugees, left-wing protesters, strikes, and climate measures as props. Beyond legislation that constrained protest and strengthened police powers in general, Palestine solidarity activism has faced specially targeted repressive measures. In 2020, the government pressured universities to adopt the International Holocaust Remembrance Alliance (IHRA) Working Definition of Antisemitism, including its associated "examples" that conflate legitimate, accurate criticism of Israel with antisemitism.[63] The education secretary, Gavin Williamson, went so far as to threaten the funding of universities that refused to comply.[64] In June 2023, the government introduced a bill to ban public bodies—including local authorities—from boycotting, divesting from, and sanctioning Israel.[65]

These measures to restrict speech went hand-in-hand with the passage of a "freedom of speech" bill and the appointment of England's first "free speech tsar" to promote liberty of expression in the academy. In practice, the government's championing of free speech has been restricted to its preferred targets of criticism, namely transgender people, Muslims, and refugees, as well as other "culture war" items on its agenda. When it comes to forthright criticism of Israel, however, "legitimate opinion" transmogrifies into abhorrent "antisemitism" that must be stigmatized or suppressed. By virtue of its "roadmap" agreement with Israel, the government is formally committed to "fighting all forms of antisemitism including in its modern form of de-legitimization of the State of Israel, as elaborated in the IHRA definition."[66]

Loyal opposition
The Labour Party's response to developments beginning October 7 could scarcely be distinguished from government policy. After Israel began its onslaught on Gaza, Starmer proclaimed that "Labour stands with Israel. Britain stands with Israel . . . Israel has the right to bring her people home, to defend herself and to keep her people safe."[67] But he was mistaken. The British labor movement was historically pro-Zionist. But first left-wing and then liberal support for Israel progressively eroded after the 1982 Lebanon War, 1987 intifada, and 2006 Lebanon War, reaching a seemingly irreversible nadir following Israel's 2008–2009 massacre in Gaza. As of 2023, contra Starmer, most Labour Party members were more sympathetic to Palestine than they were with Israel. This was dramatized in 2018, when hundreds of members unfurled Palestinian flags at Labour's annual conference, and in 2021, when Labour's conference passed a motion condemning Israel's apartheid and ethnic cleansing of Palestinians, despite opposition from the party's Blairite wing.[68] Polling data shows that the public at large is also more supportive of Palestine than Israel—especially Labour voters, 62 percent of whom view Israel unfavorably.[69] This chasm between Labour's official position, and the opinions of most party members as well as much of the population, represents an opportunity for the solidarity movement.

Starmer also agreed with the government that "responsibility for this crisis lies with Hamas" and ignored any Israeli responsibility.[70] But he did not stop there. In an interview on October 11, Starmer explicitly endorsed Israel's "right" to collectively punish Palestinians in Gaza:

PRESENTER: A siege is appropriate? Cutting off power, cutting off water, Sir Keir?

STARMER: I think that Israel does have that right. It is an ongoing situation. Obviously everything should be done within international law, but I don't want to step away from the core principles that Israel has a right to defend herself and Hamas bears responsibility for these terrorist acts.[71]

How the collective punishment of two million people can be reconciled with international law is a mystery that only the most nimble—or degenerate—legal minds can grasp. In an interview on October 12, Labour's shadow foreign secretary, Emily Thornberry, refused to answer whether cutting off essential supplies to Gaza was consistent with international law; instead she affirmed Israel's right to defend itself.[72] Labour also strongly advised its MPs not to attend events in solidarity with Gaza; local council leaders were told "they must not, under any circumstance" participate in such events.[73]

The policy of supporting the government, opposing the opinions of the majority of Labour members and voters, and endorsing Israel's "right" to inflict collective punishment "within international law" came with a political price. Dozens of local councilors resigned from the party. MPs defied orders by speaking at protests. Several trade unions backed Palestine solidarity demonstrations. Muslim support for Labour dropped significantly. And dozens of MPs, along with a few prominent local politicians, including the mayor of London and the leader of Scottish Labour, called for a ceasefire, explicitly opposing Labour's official policy.[74]

Starmer was not wholly unresponsive to such pressure. His support for Israel's illegal siege provoked such outrage that, in his typical manner, he simply lied about statements he had made in public on national radio: "I was saying that Israel has the right to self-defense . . . I was not saying that Israel had the right to cut off water, food, fuel or medicines."[75] But if that were the case, it would be astonishing that Starmer waited for more than a week to clarify his immediately controversial remarks; this lag is evidence that his change of position was a concession to political pressure.

Nevertheless, Starmer maintained his opposition to a cease-fire, instead supporting "humanitarian pauses" in line with US and British government policy.[76] Starmer thereby staked out a position in favor of continued violence, in opposition to the vast majority of the British public as well as much of his own shadow cabinet.[77] By way of compensation, Starmer did express gentle opposition to certain Israeli policies: "[t]he sup-ply of basic utilities like water, medicines, electricity and . . . fuel to civilians in Gaza," he admonished, "cannot be blocked by Israel." The harshest adjectives he applied to Israel's con-duct were "unacceptable"—referring to Israel's refusal to lift the "siege conditions" in Gaza—and "unlawful"—referring to its West Bank settlements.[78] But when asked by a journalist whether he thought Israel's actions against Gaza were lawful, Starmer responded thus: "it's unwise for politicians . . . [to] pronounce day by day which acts may or may not be in accord-ance with international law . . . I think it's not the role of poli-ticians." He added that it often takes weeks or months to judge whether the law has been broken.[79] Yet Starmer did not hesitate to accuse Russia of committing war crimes in the course of its "illegal" invasion of Ukraine: he is content to make such judge-ments when they pose no political difficulty.[80]

Labour's internal conflict came to a head on November 15, when MPs had to decide whether to call for a ceasefire in par-liament. The Scottish National Party submitted an amendment supporting an immediate ceasefire whereas Labour remained officially committed to humanitarian pauses. Starmer warned that shadow ministers who supported a ceasefire would be sacked; even so, the Labour leadership faced a significant rebellion. A total of 56 Labour MPs—above one-quarter of the parliamentary party—voted for an immediate ceasefire, including ten members of the shadow front bench.[81] The amendment was supported by 125 MPs in total, but they were greatly outnumbered by the 294 MPs who voted against it,[82] thereby giving Israel a green light to continue its massacre. It is probable that the scale of the Labour rebellion was influenced by the fear of electoral consequences as well as growing public indignation at Israel's conduct; the solidarity movement made an impact. On the day of the ceasefire vote, a large crowd rallied outside parliament to support Palestinians under siege.

During the New Labour period, and in particular under the leadership of former prime minister Tony Blair, the Labour Party had staunchly supported Israel. It was unsurprising that Starmer, who has associated himself with Blair and surrounded himself with Blairite advisors, should follow suit. But the extent of Labour's support for Israel after October 7, and its willingness to punish critics of Israel inside the party, still marked a departure. The suspension of Andy McDonald MP from the parliamentary party was an indication of how hair-trigger the leadership's pro-Israel censoriousness had become. McDonald, speaking at a pro-Palestine rally, said: "We won't rest until we have justice. Until all people, Israelis and Palestinians, between the river and the sea, can live in peaceful liberty." According to the Labour Party, these remarks were "deeply offensive, particularly at a time of rising antisemitism which has left Jewish people fearful for their safety."[83] The charge is too ludicrous to merit comment.

To understand this escalation of censorship, we must remember that the election of the far-left Jeremy Corbyn MP as Labour leader in 2015 terrified the British ruling class, as well as pro-Israel groups who feared that Corbyn would reverse longstanding British policy by genuinely supporting a two-state solution and attempting to hold Israel accountable for its international law violations. The result was a four-year campaign, as frenzied as it was evidence-free, accusing Corbyn personally and the party at large of antisemitism. Much of Starmer's leadership has been defined by the repudiation of Corbynism: Labour's reputation as a ruling class party has been re-established with the enthusiasm typical of a counter-revolution. The symbol of Labour's return to its historical role as a reliable alternate for the Conservatives has been the reaffirmation of its support for Israel. Starmer has greatly intensified the purge of left-wing members from the Labour Party, including by suspending Corbyn himself from the parliamentary party and confirming his ineligibility to stand as a Labour candidate at the next election. In this way the dominance of the Labour Right has been cemented and wealthy donors who abandoned Labour because of Corbyn have been won back.

Possibilities

As Israel pounded Gaza, large numbers in Britain turned out week after week to express their indignation. These demonstrations were striking for their stamina as well as size: the Armistice Day rally took place several weeks into Israel's onslaught, and was probably the largest seen in Britain since the 2003 mobilizations against the Iraq War. A report by two Jewish attendees captured its spirit:

> The mood was exhilarating. Rightfully outraged at Israel's genocidal bombing and starving of Gaza; furious at the cowardice of our mainstream politicians clinging to the US's coat tails who seem to have lost all sense of their humanity; and

warm, supportive and solidaristic towards all participating
and all those caring about what is happening to Palestinians,
in Gaza especially but also to those in the West Bank as the
settlers use the war as an opportunity to run wild there.[84]

In addition to the enormous protests in London, there were
sit-ins at major train stations across Britain; more than 150 activists and trade unionists blockaded an arms factory in Kent to
oppose arms exports to Israel; school children in Manchester,
Bristol, and London went on strike for a ceasefire; and somber
vigils commemorated lives lost.

What comes next? The immediate demands highlighted
above strike this author as correct. But the prospect of these
positions being adopted by any British government is slim
unless the US agrees. In order to influence policy going forward, the solidarity movement will have to consider ways to
institutionalize a coalition of sufficient breadth and organization that any administration will have to reckon with it. Indeed,
the Palestine issue points to a long-held tenet of the socialist
Left that domestic policy and foreign policy cannot be separated from each other. The dominant class interests that make
Britain a deeply unequal society are the same class interests that
favor subordination to American power, with complicity in war
crimes the inevitable corollary.

In challenging the oppression of Palestinians, the solidarity movement confronts American hegemony, Britain's ruling class, and the entrenched constitutional order. These are
formidable obstacles for any campaign to overcome. Yet it is
precisely because the struggle for justice in Palestine engages
these broader inequities that the Palestine Question resonates
beyond its core precincts. What is required, therefore, is not
just a movement that attempts to wrest local concessions from
the powerful—though that work is crucial, and there are some

possibilities—but also the sustained work of constructing an alternative to the present system. The Left should organize to democratize the country.

British governments of all stripes have supported Israel's repressive policies for decades. What changed in 2023 was the intensity; the delegitimization of Palestine solidarity was harsher, the apologies for Israel's abuses less apologetic. This reflected broader tendencies: the widening gulf between public and ruling class opinion; economic stagnation that has provoked a right-populist response; and the left-populist insurgency of 2015–2019, during which Palestine solidarity became a symbol for radical opposition to an unjust order. The opportunities for the solidarity movement at this juncture are clear. It must continue to press for a ceasefire and a lifting of the siege and, longer term, promote a reconstitution of the British Left as a fearless oppositional force, rather than one that is cowed by censorship.

"The whole hospital is full of blood and insects"

—Doctor at the Indonesian Hospital in Beit Lahiya

13

Sins of Commission: How Europe Was Bounced into Supporting Israel's War Crimes in Gaza

Clare Daly MEP

On the morning of Saturday October 7, as reports emerged about attacks in southern Israel, European Commission president Ursula von der Leyen took to Twitter to make an announcement:

> I unequivocally condemn the attack carried out by Hamas terrorists against Israel. It is terrorism in its most despicable form. Israel has the right to defend itself against such heinous attacks.

Clare Daly MEP is an Irish politician, currently serving as a member of the European Parliament, representing the constituency of Dublin. Elected as an independent socialist, she is affiliated to the Left in the European Parliament, and works across a range of policy areas, including migration and human rights, data protection, home affairs, transport, and defense. She is a vocal advocate for peace and a critic of EU foreign policy.

She would repeat this message throughout the day, including at an event in Bordeaux, where she announced that *"L'UE se tient aux côtés d'Israël"* ("The EU stands with Israel"), and in a further tweet, which reiterated that "Israel has the right to self-defense" and affirmed that "[t]he EU . . . stands by Israel today and in the next weeks."

Her statements were wrong on several levels. To begin with, she mangled the law. Israel—like any sovereign state—has a right in international law to self-defense pursuant to Article 51 of the United Nations Charter. But as the International Court of Justice confirmed in 2004, that right only applies to armed attacks by one state against another state.[1] Gaza is not a sovereign state but rather a territory occupied by Israel. It follows that Israel cannot invoke Article 51 in response to an attack by armed groups in Gaza. Israel's right of self-defense simply does not apply to the events of October 7.

This is not to say Israel has no right in law to guarantee its internal security or the safety of its population, for instance, through a police response. But Israel always invokes the "right to self-defense" because it is effective propaganda. It is considered unacceptable for a state to respond to an internal security situation as Israel always does, by unleashing its armed forces on a civilian population for whose welfare it is responsible. But if Israel can hoodwink international public opinion into viewing this situation as a conventional war rather than the policing of an occupation, then Israel's onslaught will seem less out of place, and the standards to which Israel is held will be lowered. By parroting this Israeli propaganda lie, von der Leyen propped up the false "war" narrative, enabling what was to come.

Morally, the statements by von der Leyen were clearly abhorrent. Anyone familiar with the history of Israel's occupation knew, on the morning of October 7, what Israel was going to do. Colonial powers, when they encounter violence from a colonized people, usually respond with revenge, and out of all proportion. They draw the conclusion that it is not their own colonial terror and domination that has provoked the violence, but only that there hasn't been enough of it. They visit the same violence on that population, but tenfold. They go on a rampage. This pattern is repeated across history. Whenever the occupied strike back, the occupiers, drunk on power and sick with wrath, exact a terrible price in blood.

Israel is no stranger to the tradition of colonial sadism. Its vicious military assaults on Gaza have never halted before an astronomical ratio of Palestinian to Israeli casualties has been achieved. In what is called the "Israel-Palestine conflict," between 2005 and 2014, according to figures collected by the Israeli human rights organization B'Tselem, twenty-three Palestinians were killed for every one Israeli.[2] Despite lie after lie from Israeli spokespeople, these campaigns have always involved indiscriminate attacks on civilians, blatant to any honest observer, and which afterward have been independently confirmed to have been in flagrant violation of international law.

Ursula von der Leyen therefore cannot credibly claim she didn't know how Israel was going to respond. When she made her initial statements, she could have limited herself to deploring attacks on civilians, expressing sympathy for the victims, and calling for peace and calm. Instead, she announced that the EU stood by Israel "today and in the next weeks," without any qualification or caveat, knowing full well what those weeks would bring. In public view, she willfully and unconditionally endorsed what she knew would be a massacre of unprecedented proportions, on behalf of the European Union (EU) and its 448 million citizens.

Even by the end of that first day, events had shown the recklessness of her position. Israel had retaliated with airstrikes on Gaza, which according to the Gaza Health Ministry had killed at least 230 Palestinians, wounding 1,610. Israeli prime minister Benjamin Netanyahu that evening vowed a "mighty vengeance" and pledged that Israel would "turn into ruins" all of the places that "Hamas hides in," which in traditional Israeli government parlance means the entirety of Gaza. "Get out of there now," he warned a civilian population that could not comply, because it has been imprisoned there for sixteen years by Israel, for most of that time under his premiership.

None of this gave Ursula von der Leyen any pause. At a minute past midnight, she tweeted a photograph of the Berlaymont building on Schumann roundabout in Brussels, the European Commission headquarters where she has a private residence on the thirteenth floor. Onto its side was projected a giant image of the Israeli flag. "Israel has the right to defend itself—today and in the days to come," she wrote. "The European Union stands with Israel." Throughout the next day, while Israel formally declared war and the death toll mounted, posts to the same effect continued, standing "strong with Israel" and showing Commission buildings draped with Israeli flags. On the evening of Sunday 8, at which point the count in deaths from relentless Israeli airstrikes in Gaza was nearing 413, von der Leyen again tweeted the Berlaymont image, declaring "We stand with 🇮🇱."

These statements by von der Leyen were not just legally and morally unsound. They also flew in the face of the facts. To start with, the people of the European Union—which represents itself as a democratic polity—had not been consulted on where they stood. They soon made their views known. Within a week, the most significant sequence of mass mobilizations since the 2003 Iraq War had begun in cities all over Europe (despite preemptive bans placed on public displays of solidarity with Palestine in many countries). Contrary to von der Leyen's assertions, it was clear that a very large number of Europeans did *not* "stand with Israel" as it bombarded an occupied and besieged prison camp.

On top of that, von der Leyen's statements departed from standing EU policy concerning Israel and Palestine. For certain, the EU maintains with Israel one of the closest partnerships it has with any third country, allegedly founded on "shared democratic values" and "the rule of law." Total trade volume between Israel and the EU amounted to €46.8 billion in 2022.[3] In the decade preceding 2020, almost 30 percent of international transfers of major conventional weaponry to Israel were from EU member states, worth €4.1 billion.[4] Israel is given privileged access to EU research financing, with €1.28 billion of public funds going to Israeli applicants, many of which are universities and companies with key positions in Israel's arms industry and its occupation.[5]

The legal basis for this cozy relationship is the 1995 EU-Israel Association Agreement. Although "respect for human rights and democratic principles" are stipulated as an "essential" basis for the Agreement, Israeli atrocities have never led to its suspension. When Israel demolishes educational facilities built with EU funds,[6] or when Israeli spyware is implicated in European political scandals,[7] pro-Israel conservative factions in EU politics stonewall to shield Israel from real accountability. German supporters of Israel and the Hungarian far-right promote disinformation and campaign relentlessly to block EU aid to Palestine in the EU budget.[8] The EU officially opposes Israeli settlement expansion,[9] but Israel's friends in Europe ensure there are never any material consequences.

The balance of EU politics is therefore objectively pro-Israel. But on paper, at least, the EU has always hidden behind a liberal internationalist facade. Rarely much of a champion of Palestinian rights, the EU has nonetheless tried to avoid explicit, one-sided, and unconditional support for Israel. It practices ambiguity, trumpeting itself as the largest international donor to the Occupied Territories—even as much of this aid effectively doubles as a subsidy for Israel's occupation; advocating for a two-state solution—while doing little to bring it about; and professing a commitment to upholding international law—only to sit on its hands while Israel flouts it. But von der Leyen's interventions left no room for such equivocation. Even at the rhetorical level, none of the EU's traditional commitments were compatible with extending unconditional support to Israel as it perpetrated international crimes against the people and territory it occupied.

In short, then, Ursula von der Leyen's claims that the EU stood with Israel as it targeted a civilian population were legally wrong, because they invoked Israel's right of self-defense even as this did not apply; morally wrong, because they gave Israel a warrant to commit war crimes; and factually wrong, because many Europeans opposed Israel's military assault, while existing EU policy was incompatible with green lighting the devastation of Gaza. But it's not just that von der Leyen's statements were ill-informed, appalling, and destructive. It's also that she had no standing to make them. It was not her place to say those things.

Playing president

That Ursula von der Leyen spoke out of turn is not obvious to a lot of people. This is how she gets away with it, so it bears explaining. Von der Leyen is a "president," which sounds very important. She is also seen doing presidential things, like holding press conferences and traveling to war zones to pose for photos. So when this seemingly very important and visible person stands in front of cameras and says "the EU stands with Israel," many take her word for it. Surely, they reason, this person would not be allowed to do that, and the cameras would not be rolling, if she wasn't in charge. Even if we radically disagree with her statements on behalf of the EU, we must assume she is exercising some legitimate democratic authority when she makes them. Right?

Wrong. Von der Leyen has precisely zero authority to speak on behalf of the EU in matters relating to foreign affairs. The international press, fond of shorthand and disinterested in the internal workings of the EU, has developed a habit of treating her as a counterpart to the president of the United States—the holder of the "EU's top job." But this is untrue. In the EU, the twenty-seven member states are in charge. They make decisions collectively, in a body called the Council. The Commission, headed by von der Leyen, is delegated certain powers in certain policy areas. *Foreign policy is not one of them.* Each member state pursues its own foreign policy. When they wish, the member states come together in the Council and negotiate a "common position" by consensus, with each member state holding the power of veto. That is how EU foreign policy is made. The president of the Commission has nothing to do with it.

After October 7, the Council was singing a different tune. The EU official responsible for expressing the Council's common foreign policy—i.e., the formal EU position—is the High Representative for Foreign Affairs, Josep Borrell, a Spanish social democrat. From the outset, his pronouncements were more restrained than those of von der Leyen. On October 7, in line with a statement agreed among the member states and posted on the official Council website that morning,[10] Borrell tweeted that the EU deplored the loss of lives and recalled "the importance of working towards a lasting and sustainable peace." This statement was clearly an effort at squaring the circle between longstanding EU policy, the hard line emerging from Washington, pro-Israel member states such as Germany and Czechia, and those member states who were sticking up for Palestinian rights such as Ireland, Spain, and Slovenia. The

Council stood "in solidarity with" Israel, rather than *standing with* Israel. On behalf of the EU, Borrell qualified Israel's "right to defend itself" with the critical caveat, *"in line with international law."*

This meant that, as the corpses piled up in Gaza, there were not one but two apparent EU foreign policies on the developing crisis. A legitimate one, emanating from the Council, tried to strike some semblance of balance and acknowledged the binding obligations imposed by international law on all parties. Meanwhile, a freelance position, formulated on the fly by someone masquerading as the leader of the EU, unequivocally backed Israel and placed no constraints on its conduct whatsoever. Von der Leyen was aware of the Council position, and if she continued to proclaim the EU's unconditional support for Israel regardless, this was no accident. She was purposefully signaling a different line to the press, the public, and the world—and daring the Council to stop her. It was the Council's failure to reassert its authority, its failure to offer even a verbal rebuke of her usurpations, that emboldened von der Leyen and other figures in EU politics to push further, and pour yet more fuel on the Gaza inferno.

On Monday, October 9, Israel's "war" entered a new phase. While spokespeople continued to feed Western media the usual lines about Israel going to unique lengths to avoid civilian harm, these were undermined by a torrent of genocidal statements from Israeli politicians. "Nakba to the enemy now!" tweeted Ariel Kallner, a Likud Member of the Knesset. "The war is not against Hamas but against the state of Gaza," said May Golan, a government minister. "Erase Gaza," demanded a deputy speaker of the Knesset, Nissim Vaturi. "Nothing else will satisfy us!" Whatever the propagandists were saying, the punishment of all Gazans for the actions of a few was evidently a mainstream position in Israel. It now became declared military policy. The

Israeli minister of defense, Yoav Gallant, announced that he had ordered "a complete siege on the Gaza Strip," an explicit strategy of collective punishment. "There will be no electricity, no food, no water, no fuel, everything is closed," he said. "We are fighting human animals and we are acting accordingly."

From this point on, for the weeks of slaughter that followed, a confined population of two million people, under relentless bombardment from the air, would also face starvation, dehydration, and the denial of electricity for critical facilities such as hospitals. The policy was condemned by international organizations as a war crime. It was past time for the EU to course correct, distance itself from Israel, and demand respect for international law. Instead, into the breach stepped a key von der Leyen ally, the far-right, notoriously pro-Israel Hungarian commissioner Oliver Varhelyi, who seized the chance to do something he had been trying to do for years: cancel EU aid to Palestine. "The scale of terror and brutality against #Israel and its people is a turning point . . . There can be no business as usual," he tweeted, announcing a "review" of the EU's development aid to Palestine, worth €691 million. "All payments immediately suspended," he said, suggesting that even humanitarian aid was now blocked.

This decision would have been appalling in any context. But following Israel's imposition of an illegal siege earlier that day, it was positively diabolical. Much EU aid is dispensed to the Palestinian Authority, which holds sway in the West Bank, not Gaza. By declaring a freeze on aid even to this rival Palestinian administration, which had no presence in the theater of combat and no involvement in the October 7 attack, Varhelyi was committing the EU to a truly extreme policy of collective punishment. The announcement was immediately condemned by international civil society and aroused the concern of the secretariat of the United Nations. At this point, finally, the Council

found its voice. "[T]here is no legal basis for a unilateral decision of this kind by an individual commissioner," the Irish
Department of Foreign Affairs informed the press. "[W]e do not
support a suspension of aid."[11] Similar statements issued from
other capitals, as well as from Borrell himself. Within hours, the
Commission was forced to backtrack. A review would proceed,
the Commission said, but there would be no suspension of payments. Varhelyi had acted alone, the press concluded.[12]

At an emergency Council meeting the following day,
Tuesday, October 10, an "overwhelming majority of ministers"
affirmed that "EU funds should not be discontinued." The
Council statement also called for "the protection of civilians,"
"for allowing access to food, water and medicines to Gaza," and
again qualified Israel's "right to self-defense" with the need for
the "full respect of international humanitarian law."[13] Once
again, though, the Council did not directly rebuke von der
Leyen or her parallel foreign policy. The Council had shot down
Varhelyi, but as the Hungarian commissioner from the party
of liberal Europe's favorite bogeyman, Prime Minister Viktor
Orbán, he was an easy target. Routinely enabled and shielded
from accountability by von der Leyen, he was nothing more
than a symptom. The source of the rot was the Commission
president herself. By singling him out, the Council gave her a
fall guy—and a blank check for all that followed.

At this stage, Palestinian deaths from indiscriminate Israeli
bombing were climbing toward 900, with over a quarter of a
million people internally displaced. "Human beasts are dealt
with accordingly," Israel's coordinator for humanitarian aid in
Gaza had said, in a video posted online that day. "No electricity,
no water, just damage. You wanted hell—you will get hell." Sky
News reported an Israeli defense official vowing that "Gaza will
eventually turn into a city of tents. There will be no buildings."

It was becoming increasingly clear to world public opinion that Israel was in the throes of a genocidal frenzy. A deluge of online posts, images, and videos from ordinary Gazans was providing the global public with an unprecedented window into the reality of Israel's assault. Despite the best efforts of Israeli propaganda to dehumanize victims, and notwithstanding selective coverage and bias on the part of traditional media, a massive growth of consciousness in Europe and America was taking place, soon leading to mass demonstrations for a ceasefire. Had the European Union chosen this moment to clarify its stance, whipping the Commission into line and removing ambiguity as to its official position, its standing in world opinion may yet have been salvageable. The EU might have rhetorically distanced itself from Israel's slaughter, while doing nothing to oppose it—this minimal step alone would have spared the EU a massive loss of reputation. The EU might even have done the right thing and employed every diplomatic and legal instrument at its disposal to press Israel for a ceasefire. None of these things happened, and in their absence, von der Leyen carried on conducting her foreign policy by public relations. By the end of the week, she and her allies had been allowed to plant the EU flag at the very center of an unfolding genocide in Gaza. Millions of citizens watched horrified as the hollowness of EU commitments to human rights and international law was definitively and irreversibly exposed.

A "solemn moment"

On the afternoon of Wednesday, October 11, a "Solemn Moment in Solidarity with the Victims of the Terror Attacks in Israel" was staged on the front steps of the European Parliament building in Brussels. This media spectacle was organized by von der Leyen's colleague in the center-right European People's Party, the president of the European Parliament, Roberta

Metsola. Flanked by von der Leyen, the European Council president Charles Michel, and the Israeli ambassador to the EU Haim Regev, Metsola stood in front of a row of EU and Israeli flags and delivered a speech to a crowd of a few hundred people, condemning Hamas for terrorism and expressing sympathy exclusively for Israeli victims. Declaring that this was "not a time for whataboutism"—i.e., mentioning or recognizing Palestinian victims, while the bombs continued to drop—Metsola addressed the official representative of the state then committing war crimes in the Gaza Strip, thanking him for his presence. "This is Europe," she said. "We stand with you!" The crowd was then asked to observe a minute's silence for Israeli victims after which a rendition of Israel's national anthem was played, followed by Beethoven's "Ode to Joy," the official anthem of the EU. As news of the stunt propagated in the press, von der Leyen and Metsola published photographs on social media. "Europe stands with Israel and its people. 🟦🇮🇱," Metsola tweeted.

This event was an orchestrated insult to Palestinians all over the world. While Israel demolished block after block of apartments in Gaza, it was made to appear as if the EU was alive to the humanity of Israeli civilians only; as if European eyes could not see Palestinians, except as "terrorists." The event also gave the impression that this was the position not just of the European Commission but of the European Parliament too. The problem with this was that the European Parliament did not yet have a position, because it had not met. There would not be a sitting until the following week, at which a position would be formally decided. But that no longer mattered. Few people follow the plenary sessions of the European Parliament or read its resolutions. Democratic procedure had been short-circuited. Metsola and von der Leyen had created a picture that spoke a thousand words. This was the image that would endure.

My parliamentary colleague Mick Wallace and I had con-
tacted Metsola beforehand, warning against a one-sided display and urging her to make sure that the event mourned *all*
innocent civilian victims, both Palestinian and Israeli. This
was ignored until after the event had taken place. We were
approached privately by other European parliamentarians
(MEPs), who expressed agreement with our concerns but stayed
silent in public. Such was the climate of EU politics in the wake
of October 7 that MEPs were terrified of voicing any objection.
The presence of Council president Charles Michel at Metsola's
photo-op can probably be explained in a similar way. The event,
organized outside of any normal procedure, amounted to moral
blackmail; the invitations sent out were effectively ultimatums.
Many decided to go with the flow rather than risk having to
explain their absence after the fact. This is how the institutions
and parties of the EU were bounced by a hardline faction of
pro-Israel politicians into a propaganda performance that overshadowed the official EU position, and from which it would
subsequently become difficult to retreat.

"Hamas alone is responsible"
The "solemn moment" was a showstopper but von der Leyen
and Metsola had an even more spectacular finale planned for
Friday 13, the end of that week. As of that morning, the death
toll in Gaza stood at 1,500, including some 500 children, with
an additional 6,600 people wounded. Fully 6,000 bombs had
been dropped, destroying 752 buildings, comprising 2,835
housing units. More than 423,000 people had been forced to
flee their homes. But Israel was just getting started. The Israeli
military now issued an order to the 1.1 million Palestinians living in the northern half of Gaza. They were given twenty-four
hours to move, en masse, to the southern half of the Strip.
A ground invasion was predicted to follow. The evacuation

order was immediately condemned by human rights and humanitarian organizations. The UN urged that the directive be rescinded as it could not be obeyed "without devastating humanitarian consequences." Tens of thousands of Gazans began to move; dozens were killed by Israeli air strikes as they fled.

As the Israeli military ramped up its assault, accompanied by statement after statement of genocidal intent from Israel's political establishment,[14] Israel should have been the last place any EU leader wanted to be seen. But that very afternoon, Presidents Metsola and von der Leyen chose to touch down in Tel Aviv and insert themselves directly into the situation, participating in a propaganda tour of the sites of the October 7 attacks. Clad in bulletproof vests, they stood awkwardly amidst crowds of men, peering off camera and expressing horror at events that had happened a week ago, but making no comment whatsoever on the catastrophe that was unfolding even while they spoke. That evening, the pair gave a joint statement with Israeli president Isaac Herzog, who ran through the customary list of Israeli lies about "human shields" and Palestinians blowing up their own infrastructure, before Metsola assured him, "We stand with you."[15] Separately, in a joint statement with Netanyahu, von der Leyen described the October 7 attacks as "acts of war," asserting not only Israel's unqualified right but also its "duty" to "defend itself," while absolving it of any responsibility for the consequences: "Hamas alone is responsible for what is happening."[16]

This was a far cry from the Council's "in line with international humanitarian law" proviso. At this point, von der Leyen's actions were best described as unauthorized diplomacy. Alarm bells belatedly rang in Brussels. Now, finally, senior officials began to brief anonymously against von der Leyen. The *Financial Times* reported on concerns that she "could look as if she is endorsing military actions that will cause mass civilian casualties—and that will swiftly be labelled as war crimes." One senior diplomat told the paper that "[w]e may be about to see massive ethnic cleansing." Another expressed fear that the EU would "pay a heavy price in the global south because of this conflict."[17]

Too little, too late. There was still no explicit institutional rebuke. The Council was in disarray: with the pro-Israel member states unwilling to chastise von der Leyen, there was no prospect of a unanimously agreed joint statement that called her out directly. The result was that von der Leyen got her way. It didn't matter what the formal Council position was. It was invisible. Any hope of the EU acting as a restraint on Israel was eliminated. By the time the institutions could develop a position through the proper procedures, a political climate had been created that made it inconvenient to walk back the positions von der Leyen had already committed to. At this point, political cowardice kicked in and institutional inertia did the rest: the EU continued down a path of no return, failing week after week to call for a permanent ceasefire, contrary to the wishes of many European citizens. As of November 30, Israel had killed at least 15,000 people in Gaza, with many more thousands buried under rubble. Von der Leyen was successful. She railroaded the European Union into unconditional support for an extreme right-wing government in Israel, at the exact moment it embarked on a campaign of genocidal terror against a defenseless civilian population.

A "leader" nobody asked for
This does not just fly in the face of EU law. It is also an affront to any notion of EU democracy. There is a reason why the Commission was not invested with the power to make foreign policy. Member state governments are elected. The president of the Commission is not. She is appointed for a five-year term by

a collective decision of the member states and confirmed by the Parliament. No citizen ever voted for President von der Leyen. For her to attempt to dictate EU foreign policy is like the US secretary of commerce trying to override the White House on an issue of national security.

In fact, even von der Leyen's appointment stank. For some years, as a sop to democracy, there has been an informal understanding that the Council should pick the head of the largest party in the Parliament as their appointee. But after the European elections in 2019, the "lead candidate" Manfred Weber was blocked by Orbán and the rest of the Visegrád Four (i.e., Czechia, Poland, and Slovakia). So was the second option, the Dutch social democrat Frans Timmermans. After several rounds of horse trading, an alternative was found that Orbán and company could support: a German center-right defense minister, unknown to the rest of Europe, once touted as a successor to Chancellor Angela Merkel before her ministry became so embroiled in scandal that many of her party colleagues reportedly wanted her ejected from German politics altogether. That is the story of how Ursula von der Leyen found herself as the president of the European Commission.

Installed in the post, von der Leyen quickly consolidated power around herself, centralizing control in a small team. She launched her tenure in 2019 by announcing that she would lead the first "geopolitical Commission."[18] She employed a slick PR machine and a keen sense of political theater to present herself as *the* leader of the EU. She has been aided in this by the Biden administration, which has rewarded her robust Atlanticism by treating her as a counterpart and favored interlocutor. Her hand thus strengthened, she has developed a habit of trespassing on the foreign policy prerogatives of the Council, often in ways that serve US interests. She has mercilessly exploited Russia's invasion of Ukraine for visibility, making routine visits to Kyiv for photo opportunities with President Volodymyr Zelensky, earning her the plaudit of "unexpected wartime leader" from the *New York Times*.[19] In 2023, she unilaterally concluded a migration pact with Tunisia on behalf of the EU, without the agreement of most member states, prompting them to express "incomprehension" at her actions.[20] On other occasions, her attempts to usurp the Council have been contained, as appears to have happened when French president Emmanuel Macron preempted her bid to sabotage EU relations with China by inviting her on his own state visit to Beijing, in which she was positioned in a subordinate role.[21]

But a consensus between twenty-seven governments for reprimanding this kind of bad behavior is slow to materialize, and there is normally an aversion to kicking up too much of a fuss in EU politics, out of fear of undermining "European unity." Most of the time, von der Leyen's chicanery is shown an astonishing degree of indulgence by people who should know better. Rather than being exposed and held to account, she is embraced and enabled by the press for making the role "more presidential." EU politics has always been prosaic by comparison with Washington. The press in Brussels struggles to make the EU's byzantine procedures and large cast of bureaucrats work as a news product. In the first female Commission president—pant-suited, coiffured to within an inch of her life, and leaning hard into the reactionary clichés of liberal feminism—they found a girl-boss protagonist they could run with. She has thus been extended every benefit of the doubt while she brazenly swipes roles and responsibilities that do not belong to her. Her power grabs are reported as if it was not a question of black letter law but rather *anyone's guess* who is supposed to be in charge, and to the winner go the spoils.

The struggle ahead

All of this is symptomatic of a chronic rule of law and democratic legitimacy crisis in European politics. The official ideology of European politics presents the EU as a world historical actor for democracy, besieged by "authoritarian regimes." But the higher you get in European politics, the less decision-making has anything to do with the preferences of ordinary people, and the more it is dominated by a squalid brand of realpolitik. Is this what we want? Do citizens want a system where a high-handed, born-to-rule European elite, elevated to power without a single vote, can swoop in and override the preferences of elected governments? On the evidence of mass protests in recent weeks, it does not appear that they do.

For many people, the past several weeks have been a moment of nightmarish clarity. We are confronted by one of the greatest and most visible crimes against humanity in living memory, as citizens all over Europe and the West scroll through social media feeds bearing witness to the most unimaginable cruelties, even as their leaders robotically insist, "we must stand with Israel." In 2009, during Operation Cast Lead, the EU called for a ceasefire. It did likewise in 2014, during Operation Protective Edge. So why, then, has Europe so enthusiastically and brazenly cheered the current assault on Gaza?

Many factors have been in play. The long ideological hangover from the "War on Terror" in European security discourse. The readiness-to-hand of an official EU propaganda script for the war in Ukraine, all flag-waving and fatuous sloganeering, carelessly copy-pasted onto a settler-colonial occupation in Palestine. The United States' restored hegemony in Europe, through NATO, in the wake of that war. The pathological, racist form that Holocaust guilt has taken in Germany, Europe's largest economy, contributing to an embrace of Islamophobia and anti-Arabism among political and media elites as well as unconditional support, across the political spectrum, for the stupefying foreign policy dogma of "Israel right or wrong." But none of these fully explains it. Bigger wheels are turning.

In the margins of our world order—in the anticipation of climate breakdown and the mounting brutality of Western border policy, in the global lurch toward ultra-nationalism and the bonfire of international law—something has been taking form, and is now being summoned into the world. The mask of liberal respectability is dropping and the barbarism of old Europe is coming back into the open. Israel has been given a role in the vanguard of a wider assault on the norms and standards that have existed since the Second World War. The rules of a much more deeply unfair and violent world are being written. In Gaza, and in the callous indifference of Europe's political class to its fate, we catch a glimpse of the darkness ahead. That is why the emergence of mass consciousness from these events is so important. Palestine is our future. Its people are ours. We have to fight for them.

"If I must die / let it bring hope"

—Refaat Alareer, poet and professor
from Gaza, killed by an Israeli
airstrike on December 6, 2023

Notes

Introduction

1. Giora Eiland quoted in US ambassador to Israel Daniel C. Kurtzer, "Israeli Officials Brief Djerejian on Improved Regional Security Situation; Unilateral Disengagement Plans," 04TELAVIV1952_a (31 March 2004), WikiLeaks.
2. Sara Roy, "'A Dubai on the Mediterranean'," *London Review of Books* 27.21 (3 November 2005) ("depression"). United Nations Special Rapporteur John Dugard, *Situation of Human Rights in the Palestinian Territories Occupied Since 1967* (27 September 2006), para. 70 ("sanctions").
3. Sara Roy in this volume.
4. Dov Weissglas quoted in Conal Urquhart, "Gaza on Brink of Implosion as Aid Cut-Off Starts to Bite," *Observer* (16 April 2006).
5. Amnesty International et al., *The Gaza Strip: A Humanitarian Implosion* (6 March 2008), p. 4 (food). World Bank, *Economic Report to the Ad Hoc Liaison Committee* (27 May 2015), pp. 5, 21 (unemployment). UN Country Team in the Occupied Palestinian Territory (UNOPT), *Gaza Ten Years Later* (July 2017), p. 20 (water). Medical Aid for Palestinians, "New Film from MAP's Team in Gaza: Combatting Child Malnutrition," map.org.uk (4 February 2020) (stunted). Larry Elliott, "UN Report: 80% of Gaza Inhabitants Relied on International Aid Before War," *Guardian* (25 October 2023) (assistance). Oxfam, "The World Cannot Stand By as Starvation Is Used as a Weapon of War in Gaza," oxfam.org (19 November 2023) ("acute"). Most Gazans had to rely on more expensive sources of water—desalinated, bottled—including from Israel.
6. Karen Koning AbuZayd, "This Brutal Siege of Gaza Can Only Breed Violence," *Guardian* (23 January 2008).
7. Amnesty International, *Implosion* ("implosion"). UN Conference on Trade and Development, *Report on UNCTAD Assistance to the Pales-*

tinian People: Developments in the Economy of the Occupied Palestinian Territory (6 July 2015), p. 12 ("unlivable"). "IDF Intel Chief Warns Despair in Gaza Could Explode Toward Israel," timesofisrael.com (24 February 2016) (agreed). UNOPT, *Gaza*, pp. 2-3, 28 (optimistic). The UN had sounded the alarm over Gaza's viability already in 2012, before Israel's 2014 offensive. UN Country Team in the Occupied Palestinian Territory, *Gaza in 2020: A Liveable Place?* (August 2012).

8.   Editorial, "It's Been a Decade. Open the Palestinian Ghetto," *Ha'aretz* (17 May 2016). Editorial, "How to End the Endless Conflict Between Israel and the Palestinians," *Economist* (17 May 2018). Stephanie Nebehay, "Red Cross Sends War Surgeons to 'Sinking Ship' Gaza," *Reuters* (31 May 2018).

9.   Tom Miles, "U.N. Sets Up Human Rights Probe into Gaza Killings, to Israel's Fury," *Reuters* (18 May 2018).

10. International Crisis Group, *After Gaza* (2 August 2007), p. 24n210.

11. Mouin Rabbani, "Israel Mows the Lawn," *London Review of Books* 36.15 (31 July 2014).

12. R. J. in this volume.

13. Norman G. Finkelstein, *Gaza: An Inquest into Its Martyrdom* (University of California Press, 2018), pp. 17–38, 212–214. Cf. Colter Louwerse and Khaled Hroub in this volume.

14. Finkelstein, *Gaza*, p. 311. Six Israeli civilians were killed and one house in Israel was destroyed.

15. Cf. John Dugard et al., *Report of the Independent Fact Finding Committee on Gaza Presented to the League of Arab States* (30 April 2009), para. 27. *Report of the United Nations Fact-Finding Mission on the Gaza Conflict* (25 September 2009), para. 75.

16. "IDF Intel Chief."

17. Yaakov Amidror, "Finding a Humanitarian Solution to the Gaza Problem," jiss.org.il (8 July 2018) ("operations") [Hebrew]. Yaakov Amidror, "Yaakov Amidror: 'Whoever Proposes to Occupy Gaza Is Talking Nonsense'," *Ma'ariv* (15 August 2018) ("rise") [Hebrew].

18. Shlomo Brom, "The Crisis Shows the Failure of Israeli Policy Towards Palestinians, Says Shlomo Brom," *Economist* (10 October 2023).

19. Amnesty International, "Israel/OPT: Civilians Must Be Protected After Unprecedented Escalation in Violence," amnesty.org.uk (7 October 2023).

20. B'Tselem, "Fatalities Since the Outbreak of the Second Intifada and Until Operation 'Cast Lead'," btselem.org (n.d.).

21. UN OCHA, "Hostilities in the Gaza Strip and Israel: Reported Impact, Day 64," ochaopt.org (9 December 2023).

22. Based on Save the Children, "Gaza: 3,195 Children Killed in Three Weeks Surpasses Annual Number of Children Killed in Conflict Zones Since 2019," savethechildren.org.uk (29 October 2023).

23. Kate Nicholson, "Doctor Reveals New Medical Acronym 'Unique to Gaza' to Describe Particular War Victim," huffingtonpost.co.uk (6 November 2023). Mai Khaled et al., "How the Loss of Entire Families Is Ravaging the Social Fabric of Gaza," *Financial Times* (13 December 2023).

24. UN OCHA, "Day 64."

25. Jean-Philippe Rémy, "Inside Gaza With the Israeli Army As It Hunts for Hamas Tunnels," *Le Monde Diplomatique* (19 November 2023) (Beit Hanoun). Isabel Debre, "Gaza Has Become a Moonscape in War. When the Battles Stop, Many Fear It Will Remain Uninhabitable," apnews.com (23 November 2023).

26. HRW, "Gaza: Unlawful Israeli Hospital Strikes Worsen Health Crisis," hrw.org (14 November 2023) (hospitals). "Gaza: UN Expert Condemns 'Unrelenting War' on Health System Amid Airstrikes on Hospitals and Health Workers," ohchr.org (7 December 2023) ("obliterated").

27. UN OCHA, "Hostilities in the Gaza Strip and Israel: Flash Update 30," ochaopt.org (5 November 2023). Human Rights Watch (HRW), "Israel: Starvation Used as Weapon of War in Gaza," hrw.org (18 December 2023).

28. UN World Food Programme, "WFP Palestine Emergency Response: Situation Report 11," wfp.org (19 December 2023) ("hunger"). Henry Mance, "UN Aid Chief Martin Griffiths: 'The War in Gaza Isn't Halfway Through'," *Financial Times* (18 December 2023) ("multiples").

29. Musa Abuhashhash in this volume.

30. Benny Gantz, a member of Israel's emergency war cabinet, quoted in Jamie Stern-Weiner, "Gaza's Last Stand? The Dangers of a Second Nakba," bylinetimes.com (16 October 2023).

31. Yaniv Cogan in this volume.

32. Mouin Rabbani and Nathan J. Brown in this volume.

33. Colter Louwerse in this volume.

34. Mitchell Plitnick and Talal Hangari in this volume.

35. Jacopo Barigazzi and Gregoria Sorgi, "Internal EU Discontent Grows at Von Der Leyen's Neglect of Palestinian Statehood," politico.eu (20 October 2023). Ellen Knickmeyer, "Dissent Over US Policy in the Israel-Hamas War Stirs Unusual Public Protests From Federal Employees," apnews.com (19 November 2023). Tara Suter, "Biden Administration Staffers Call for Cease-Fire While Protesting Outside White House," thehill.com (13 December 2023).

Chapter Two. Sara Roy

1. World Health Organization, "Gaza Faces Widespread Hunger as Food Systems Collapse, Warns WFP," wfp.org (16 November 2023).

2. I define it differently from Seymour Drescher who coined the term in his book *Econocide: British Slavery in the Era of Abolition* (University of Pittsburgh Press, 1977). Drescher argued that econocide occurs when decisions are made that have detrimental consequences for an economy and a nation's economic interests. I also borrow from Baruch Kimmerling's brilliant concept of politicide. Baruch Kimmerling, *Politicide: Ariel Sharon's War Against the Palestinians* (Verso, 2006).

3. Parts of this section are taken from Sara Roy, "Introduction to the Third Edition—De-development Completed: Making Gaza Unviable," in *Gaza Strip: The Political Economy of De-development*, third edition (Institute for Palestine Studies, 2016), pp. xxi-xxxvii & lxvi (where all references can be found).

4. Restrictions on imports from Israel, notably for the construction sector, led to the creation of a tunnel economy to Egypt, which provided Gaza with construction materials, fuel, and other consumer products. There were over 1,000 tunnels built, and while the tunnel trade could not compensate for the loss of exports to the Israeli and West Bank markets, the restoration of imports stimulated the economy and the construction sector in particular for several years. The economic situation began to deteriorate further with Israel's assault in November 2012, Egypt's destruction of the tunnels in 2013, and Israel's intensification of the blockade.

5   Karim Nashashibi et al., *Palestinian-Israeli Economic Relations: Trade and Economic Regime* (Palestine International Business Forum, International Council of Swedish Industry, and Office of the Quartet Representative Tony Blair, 2015), pp. 22 ("robbed"), 23 ("hollowed").

6. United Nations Economic and Social Commission for Western Asia (UNESCWA) and United Nations Development Program (UNDP), *Gaza War: Expected Socioeconomic Impacts on the State of Palestine—Preliminary Estimations until 5 November 2023* (November 2023), p. 9.

7. UNESCWA and UNDP, *Gaza*, p. 12.

8. Yonatan Mendel, "If Israel Aspires to Life, It Must Change Its Approach to Palestinians," *Ha'aretz* (15 November 2023). Cf. Yaniv Kubovich, "Israel Completes Vast, Billion-Dollar Gaza Barrier," *Ha'aretz* (7 December 2021).

Chapter Three. Colter Louwerse

1. Quoted in Jerome Slater, *Mythologies Without End: The US, Israel, and the Arab-Israeli Conflict, 1917–2020* (University of Oxford Press, 2021), p. 285.

2. Saed Bannoura, "Livni Calls for a Large-Scaled Military Offensive in Gaza," *IMEMC News* (8 December 2008).

3. Some commentators also suggested that the brutality displayed on October 7 itself disqualified Hamas from any political process; like ISIS, the group had to be destroyed. Given that Israel has inflicted much greater atrocities on Palestinians and Lebanese, this reasoning straightforwardly implies that Israel must be eliminated. As this obvious inference was not drawn, it is doubtful the argument was intended seriously.

4. Joe Biden, "The US Won't Back Down from the Challenge of Putin and Hamas," *Washington Post* (18 November 2023).

5. Ed Pilkington, "Bernie Sanders Calls for End to Israeli Strikes and Killing of Thousands," *Guardian* (5 November 2023).

6. Timothy H.J. Nerozzi, "Hillary Clinton Says Those Demanding Ceasefire 'Don't Know Hamas'," foxnews.com (31 October 2023) ("understand"). Hillary Rodham Clinton, "Hamas Must Go," *Atlantic* (14 November 2023) ("sabotage").

7. Editorial, "Why Israel Must Fight On," *Economist* (2 November 2023).

8. Influential Israeli officials collapsed any distinction between Hamas and Gaza's civilian population while Israeli forces inflicted destruction in Gaza indiscriminately. Insofar as Hamas was theoretically or practically inseparable from Gaza's population, the claim that Hamas could not be bargained with but only eliminated implied, in practice, the mass expulsion or extermination of Gaza's inhabitants.

9. Quoted in Ze'ev Maoz, *Defending the Holy Land: A Critical Analysis of Israel's Security and Foreign Policy* (University of Michigan Press, 2006), p. 386.

10. United Nations Security Council (UNSC), S/RES/242 (22 November 1967). United Nations General Assembly (UNGA), A/RES/3236 (22 November 1974).

11. Norman G. Finkelstein, *Knowing Too Much: Why the American Jewish Romance With Israel Is Coming to An End* (OR Books, 2012), pp. 203–221.

12. Shlomo Ben Ami, *Prophets Without Honor: The Untold Story of the 2000 Camp David Summit and the Making of Today's Middle East* (Oxford University Press, 2022), p. 13. The author was Israel's foreign minister.

13. Gershom Gorenberg, *The Accidental Empire: Israel and the Birth of the Settlements, 1967–1977* (Times Books, 2006), chap. 4. Idith Zertal and Akiva Eldar, *Lords of the Land: The War Over Israel's Settlements in the Occupied Territories, 1967–2007* (Nation Books, 2009), pp. 10–12. UNSC, S/RES/476 (30 June 1980). UNSC, S/RES/478 (20 August 1980).

14. Benny Morris, *Righteous Victims: A History of the Zionist-Arab Conflict, 1881–2001* (Vintage, 2001), p. 341.

15. Norman G. Finkelstein, *Image and Reality of the Israel-Palestine Conflict* (Verso, 1995), pp. 151–162. Kathleen Christison, *Perceptions of Palestine: Their Influence on US Middle East Policy* (University of California Press, 1999), p. 132. Hilde Henriksen Waage and Hulda Kjeang Mørk, "Mission Impossible: UN Special Representative Gunnar Jarring and His Quest for Peace in the Middle East," *The International History Review* 38.4 (2016), pp. 830–853.

16. William B. Quandt, *Peace Process: American Diplomacy and the Arab-Israeli Conflict Since 1967* (Brookings Institution Press, 2005), pp. 55–130.

17. In this chapter, "rejectionism" designates opposition to the international consensus two-state settlement while "accommodationism" and "moderation" designate acceptance of it.

18. "Palestine National Council: The Palestinian National Charter," in Walter Laqueur, ed., *The Israel-Arab Reader: A Documentary History of the Middle East Conflict* (Penguin Books, 2008), pp. 117–121.

19. See "Minutes of a Combined Senior Review Group and Washington Special Actions Group Meeting," 15 October 1970, *Foreign Relations of the United States (FRUS), 1969–1976*, vol. XXIII, *Arab-Israeli Dispute, 1969–1972* (US Government Printing Office, 2015), pp. 580–588.

20. Paul Thomas Chamberlin, *The Global Offensive: The United States, the Palestine Liberation Organization, and the Making of the Post-Cold War Order* (Oxford University Press, 2012), pp. 66, 218.

21. Colter Louwerse, *The Struggle for Palestinian Rights: The Palestinian Campaign for Self-Determination and Statehood at the United Nations, 1967-1989*, PhD thesis (University of Exeter, 2022), pp. 80–86, 91–92, 95, 99.

22. UK Embassy Amman to UK Foreign and Commonwealth Office (FCO), "Rabat Summit," FCO 93/332 (2 November 1974), UK National Archives (TNA).

23. Colter Louwerse, "'Tyranny of the Veto': PLO Diplomacy and the January 1976 United Nations Security Council Resolution," *Diplomacy & Statecraft* 33.2 (2022), pp. 318–319.

24. Ibid., p. 316.

25. Noam Chomsky, *Fateful Triangle: The United States, Israel, and the Palestinians*, updated edition (Haymarket Books, 2015), p. 78.

26. Nathan Thrall, *The Only Language They Understand: Forcing Compromise in Israel and Palestine* (Metropolitan Books, 2017), pp. 13–18. Jørgen Jensehaugen, *Arab-Israeli Diplomacy Under Carter: The US, Israel and the Palestinians* (I.B. Tauris, 2018), pp. 36–50, 68–76.

27. Colter Louwerse, *Struggle, pp. 198–248. Cf.* Salim Yaqub, *Imperfect Strangers: Americans, Arabs, and US-Middle East Relations in the 1970s* (Cornell University Press, 2016), pp. 307–315.

28. Quoted in Alan Hart, *Arafat: Terrorist or Peacemaker?* (Sidgwick & Jackson Limited, 1987), p. 440.

29. UNSC, S/13911 (30 April 1980). Louwerse, *Struggle*, pp. 260–263.

30. UNSC, S/15317 (28 July 1982). Cf. Rashid Khalidi, *Under Siege: PLO Decision-Making During the 1982 War* (Columbia University Press, 2014), pp. 135–154.

31. "Apart from a few extremist Arab states," the US intelligence assessment added, "the leaders of most other Arab states privately agree that the only viable solution is a settlement that includes ultimate Israeli withdrawal from all territory occupied in 1967 . . . and self-determination for the Palestinians, coupled with realistic security agreements and some form of Arab recognition of Israel." Special National Intelligence Estimate, "Core Positions of Parties to the Palestinian Dispute," CIA-RDP00T02041R000100100001-4 (12 December 1981), CIA Records Search Tool (CREST).

32. Ibid. Cf. Louwerse, "Tyranny," p. 321.

33. Robert Fisk, *Pity the Nation: Lebanon at War* (Oxford University Press, 2001), chaps. 4–6. Chomsky, *Fateful Triangle*, pp. 199–373.

34. Rowland Evans and Robert Novack, "Israel's New Isolation," *Washington Post* (3 August 1979). Louwerse, *Struggle*, pp. 221–222.

35. Chomsky, *Fateful Triangle*, p. 209 ("preventive"). Report, "National Intelligence Bulletin," CIA-RDP79T00975A028400010008-8 (4 December 1975), CREST, p. 3 (civilians). Louwerse, "Tyranny," p. 309 ("reflection").

36. Embassy Beirut, "(U) Israeli Air Raids on July 22 in Lebanon," 1979BEIRUT04070 (23 July 1979), WikiLeaks ("unprovoked'). "Memorandum From the Deputy Assistant to the President for National Security Affairs (Aaron) to Vice President Mondale" (23 July 1979), *FRUS, 1977-1980*, vol. IX, *Arab-Israeli Dispute, August 1978-December 1980*, second revised edition (US Government Printing Office, 2018), p. 896 ("bloody").

37. Embassy Washington to FCO, "Tel Aviv Tel 376: US/Israel Relations," FCO93/2176 (3 August 1979), TNA.
38. Louwerse, *Struggle*, pp. 259–261.
39. Azriel Bermant, "Israel, the United States, Saudi Arabia and the Fahd Plan of 1981: An Historic Missed Opportunity," *British Journal of Middle Eastern Studies* 50.4 (2022), p. 14.
40. E. G. M. Chaplin to Mr. Miles, "Israel/Lebanon Ceasefire," FCO 93/2779 (16 November 1981), TNA.
41. J. C. Moberly to Sir J. Graham, "Contacts With the PLO," FCO 93/2806 (26 August 1981), TNA. Cf. "Note of Discussions Between Mr J C Moberly and Mr J E Holmes, FCO, and Mr Ahmed Dajani, PLO. London, 24-25 August 1981," FCO 93/2806 (26 August 1981), TNA.
42. "Meeting Between Prime Minister Begin and Foreign Minister Shamir with Philip Habib the Prime Minister's Residence Jerusalem" (21 July 1982), Virtual Reading Room Documents Search (VRRDS). Peter Constable, "Habib Conversation Today With Begin" (21 July 1981), VRRDS.
43. Uri Ben-Eliezer, *War Over Peace: One Hundred Years of Israel's Militaristic Nationalism* (University of California Press, 2019), p. 158.
44. Embassy Tel Aviv, "Habib Mission: Meeting With Foreign Minister Shamir" (5 December 1981), VRRDS.
45. Embassy Washington to FCO, "Israel/Lebanon," FCO 93/3110 (2 April 1982), TNA.
46. Avner Yaniv, *Dilemmas of Security: Politics, Strategy, and the Israeli Experience in Lebanon* (Oxford University Press, 1987), p. 70 ("peace offensives"). Ze'ev Schiff and Ehud Ya'ari, *Israel's Lebanon War* (George Allen & Unwin, 1985), pp. 66, 220 ("wipe out").
47. Ronen Bergman, *Rise and Kill First: The Secret History of Israel's Targeted Assassinations* (Random House, 2018), pp. 243–244 ("goad"). E. G. M. Chaplin to Mr. Miles, "Israel/Lebanon Ceasefire," FCO 93/2779 (16 November 1981), TNA ("manufacture"). Embassy Tel Aviv to External Affairs Ottawa, "Southern Lebanon: Ceasefire on the Brink," FCO 93/3110 (9 February 1982), TNA ("propaganda base").
48. Chomsky, *Fateful Triangle*, pp. 217–219 (villages). Bergman, *Rise*, pp. 225-247 (car bombs at 242–243, stadium at 244–246).
49. Finkelstein, *Image*, p. xxiii.
50. FCO to Embassy Bonn, "Following for Private Secretary," FCO 93/3113 (9 June 1982), TNA. Emphasis added.
51. FCO to Embassy Washington, "Implications of Israeli Invasion of Lebanon," PREM 19/824 (22 June 1982), TNA. The JIC is respon-

sible for oversight of the Secret Intelligence Service, Security Service, GCHQ, and Defence Intelligence.

52. Memorandum, "The Fatah Mutiny: Implications for the Peace Process," CIA-RDP85T00287R000800130001-1 (10 June 1983), CREST.
53. Ibid. Cf. Chomsky, *Fateful Triangle,* pp. 224–225.
54. Wendy Pearlman, *Violence, Nonviolence, and the Palestinian National Movement* (Cambridge University Press, 2011), pp. 105–107.
55. "Israel Declines to Study Rabin Tie to Beatings," *New York Times* (12 July 1990).
56. Norman Kempster, "US to Talk With PLO as Arafat Meets Terms: Ambiguities Eliminated, Shultz Says," *Los Angeles Times* (15 December 1988).
57. Memorandum, Peter Rodman to Colin L. Powell, "Dealing With the PLO" (16 December 1988), 2003-0261-F, Nicholas Rostow Files, Bush Presidential Records, George Bush Presidential Library [GBPL]. Rodman, Special Assistant to the President for National Security Affairs, added that the US would "continue to reject a Palestinian state."
58. Edward Said, "The Morning After," *London Review of Books* (21 October 1993).
59. Quoted in Jimmy Carter, *Palestine Peace Not Apartheid* (Simon & Schuster, 2006), pp. 136–137.
60. Lev Luis Grinberg, *Politics and Violence in Israel/Palestine: Democracy Versus Military Rule* (Routledge, 2010), p. 96.
61. Yitzhak Rabin, "Speech to the Knesset," jewishvirtuallibrary.org (5 October 1995). B'Tselem, *Land Grab: Israel's Settlement Policy in the West Bank* (May 2002), p. 8.
62 Finkelstein, *Knowing,* pp. 221–248. Norman G. Finkelstein, *How to Resolve the Israel-Palestine Conflict* (unpublished, 2014), chap. 3.
63. Charles Enderlin, *Shattered Dreams: The Failure of the Peace Process in the Middle East 1995–2002* (Other Press, 2002), p. 202.
64. Maayan Lubell, "Netanyahu Says No Palestinian State as Long as He's Prime Minister," *Reuters* (16 March 2015). Tovah Lazaroff, "Netanyahu: A Palestinian State Won't Be Created," *Jerusalem Post* (8 April 2019). Mohammed Al-Kassim, "Palestinians Furious Over Netanyahu Claims That Israel Must 'Crush' Statehood Ambitions," *Jerusalem Post* (1 July 2023).
65. B'Tselem, *A Regime of Jewish Supremacy from the Jordan River to the Mediterranean Sea: This Is Apartheid* (12 January 2021).
66. Yesh Din et al., "Policy Paper: What Israel's 37th Government's Guiding Principles and Coalition Agreements Mean to the West Bank," ofekcenter.org.il (January 2023).

67. UN Office for the Coordination of Humanitarian Affairs (OCHA), *The Humanitarian Impact on Palestinians of Israeli Settlements and Other Infrastructure in the West Bank* (July 2007). "West Bank Split into Isolated Enclaves: World Bank," *Reuters* (9 August 2007). UN OCHA, "Closure Update: Main Findings and Analysis (30 April–11 September 2008)," un.org (September 2008), para. 8.

68. "Hamas: Charter," in Laqueur, ed., *Reader*, pp. 341–349.

69. Human rights organizations and legal experts overwhelmingly insisted that, despite the redeployment, Israel remained the occupying power in Gaza. Human Rights Watch, "'Disengagement' Will Not End Gaza Occupation," hrw.org (29 October 2004). Gisha, *Disengaged Occupiers: The Legal Status of Gaza* (January 2007). Cf. Yoram Dinstein, *The International Law of Belligerent Occupation* (Cambridge University Press, 2009), p. 277.

70. Former US president Jimmy Carter, quoted in Norman G. Finkelstein, *Gaza: An Inquest into Its Martyrdom* (University of California Press, 2018), p. 11.

71. Sara Roy, *Failing Peace: Gaza and the Palestinian-Israeli Conflict* (Pluto Press, 2007), p. 221.

72. Paul Owen, "Hamas Sets Out Conditions for Peace," *Guardian* (8 February 2006). Lally Weymouth, "We Do Not Wish to Throw Them into the Sea," *Washington Post* (26 February 2006).

73. Ahmed Yousef, "Pause for Peace," *New York Times* (1 November 2006).

74. Quoted in Slater, *Mythologies*, p. 288.

75. Eric Silver, "Hamas Softens Israel Stance in Calls for Palestinian State," *Independent* (11 January 2007). Avi Issacharoff, "PM Dismisses Meshal Comments That Israel's Existence Is a Reality," *Ha'aretz* (11 January 2007). In private, Hamas also expressed tacit support for the Arab League's 2002 Peace Initiative, which unambiguously endorsed a two-state outcome. Donald Macintyre, *Gaza: Preparing for Dawn* (Oneworld Publications, 2017), p. 149.

76. Medea Benjamin, "Hamas Delivers Peace Letter to President Obama," huffpost.com (5 July 2009).

77. "Obama Inspires Possible Shift in Hamas," *Israel Policy Forum* (11 June 2009). Cf. Gianni Perrelli, "Con Israele Non Sarà Mai Pace," *L'Espresso* (26 February 2009) [Italian]. "Hamas 'Will Not Obstruct' 1967 Borders Deal," *BBC News* (10 June 2009). Ofri Ilany, "Carter: I Believe Gilad Shalit Is Alive," *Ha'aretz* (16 June 2009). Jay Solomon and Julien Barnes-Dacey, "Hamas Chief Outlines Terms for Talks on Arab-Israeli Peace," *Washington Post* (31 July 2009).

78. Mel Frykberg, "Hamas Parliamentarian: 'We Accept Existence of Israel Within 1967 Borders'," *Electronic Intifada* (1 February 2010). "Hamas Renews Offer to End Fight if Israel Withdraws," Reuters (30 May 2010). Ethan Bronner, "Hamas Leader Calls for Two-State Solution, but Refuses to Renounce Violence," *New York Times* (5 May 2011). Eyder Peralta, "Hamas Foreign Minister: We Accept Two-State Solution With '67 Borders," *NPR* (17 May 2011). "Israel-Hamas Cease Fire; Interview With Hamas Political Leader Khaled Meshaal," *CNN* (12 November 2012). Shlomi Eldar, "Ghazi Hamad: Hamas Agrees to Accept State Within '67 Borders," *Al-Monitor* (4 April 2013). Adam Ciralsky, "Hamas's Khalid Mishal on the Gaza War, Tunnels, and ISIS," *Vanity Fair* (21 October 2014). Entsar Abu Jahal, "Hamas Says It Does Not Oppose a State Along the 1967 Borders," *Al-Monitor* (26 July 2019). Elior Levy, "In Letter to Biden, PA and Hamas Commit to Two-State Solution on 1967 Lines," *Ynet* (21 February 2021).

79. Paul Scham and Osama Abu-Irshaid, *Hamas: Ideological Rigidity and Political Flexibility* (United States Institute of Peace, June 2009).

80. Colter Louwerse, "Efraim Halevy: Hamas Is Ready to Negotiate," colterlouwerse.wordpress.com (20 December 2023).

81. "Hamas Vows to Honor Palestinian Referendum on Peace With Israel," *Reuters* (1 December 2010). Cf. Chris McGreal, "Hamas Falters in Effort to Achieve Unity," *Guardian* (13 March 2006).

82. Khaled Hroub, "A Newer Hamas? The Revised Charter," *Journal of Palestine Studies* 46.4 (2017), pp. 102, 107 ("outdated . . . de-facto"). "Hamas in 2017: The Document in Full," middleeasteye.net (2 May 2017) ("formula").

83. Hamas has repeatedly upheld ceasefire agreements with Israel and tacitly acquiesced in elements of the Oslo Accords. Tareq Baconi, *Hamas Contained: The Rise and Pacification of Palestinian Resistance* (Stanford University Press, 2018), pp. 104, 119, 183–185, 206–208, 224, 229.

84. Tareq Baconi, "Against Anti-Hamas Dogmatism," in Jamie Stern-Weiner, ed., *Moment of Truth: Tackling Israel-Palestine's Toughest Questions* (OR Books, 2018), p. 200. Cf. Baconi, Hamas, pp. 229–232.

85. UN Special Coordinator for the Middle East Peace Process Álvaro de Soto, *End of Mission Report* (May 2007), p. 46.

86. "Report: Recording Released of Clinton Suggesting Rigging 2006 Palestinian Election," *Jerusalem Post* (29 October 2016).

87. Finkelstein, *Gaza*, pp. 15, 139. *Report of the United Nations Fact-Finding Mission on the Gaza Conflict* (25 September 2009), p. 26.

88. De Soto, *Report*, p. 19.

89. Shortly after Hamas won electoral power, Israel's director of military intelligence Amos Yadlin asserted that Israel would be "happy" if Hamas took over in Gaza "because the IDF could then deal with Gaza as a hostile state." Embassy Tel Aviv, "Military Intelligence Director Yadlin Comments on Gaza, Syria and Lebanon," 07TELAVIV1733_a (13 June 2007), WikiLeaks.

90. Cf. Gisha, *Area G: From Separation to Annexation: Israel's Isolation of the Gaza Strip and How it Serves Annexationist Goals in the West Bank* (June 2020). Gidi Weitz, "Another Concept Implodes: Israel Can't Be Managed by a Criminal Defendant," *Ha'aretz* (9 October 2023).

91. Cf. Jamie Stern-Weiner, "Did Israel Thwart Another Palestinian 'Peace Offensive'?" jamiesternweiner.wordpress.com (29 March 2017).

92. International Crisis Group (ICG), *Enter Hamas: The Challenges of Political Integration* (18 January 2006).

93. Ahmed Yousef, "Why Hamas Supports Armed Struggle," in Stern-Weiner, ed., *Moment*, p. 164. Barak Ravid, "In 2006 Letter to Bush, Haniyeh Offered Compromise With Israel," *Ha'aretz* (14 November 2008).

94. Human Rights Watch, *Indiscriminate Fire: Palestinian Rocket Attacks on Israel and Israeli Artillery Shelling in the Gaza Strip* (30 June 2007), pp. 84–93 (family picnicking). ICG, *Palestinians, Israel, and the Quartet: Pulling Back from the Brink* (13 June 2006), p. 20 ("largely maintained"). In a separate incident a day earlier, Israel assassinated a high-level Hamas official.

95. Concurrent with these arrests, Israel launched Operation Summer Rains (2006) against the Gaza Strip. Between June and November, the IDF killed some four hundred Palestinians, "including many unarmed civilians." Two Israeli civilians were killed in the same period. Israel claimed it was retaliating against Hamas's June 26 capture of an Israeli soldier, Gilad Shalit, and killing of two others. But this pretext did not bear scrutiny. Hamas's military operation was launched *after* Israel refused to negotiate a reciprocal ceasefire or terminate attacks, and *after* months of "daily" indiscriminate IDF shelling which killed "more than 100 Palestinians." Moreover, just two days before the capture of Shalit, Israel kidnapped a pair of civilians in Gaza, imprisoning them "without trial" and with "no time limit" under its longstanding and illegal practice of "administrative detention." Indeed, at the moment of Shalit's capture, some eight hundred Palestinians were already languishing in Israeli administrative detention. Considering that kidnapping civilians is plainly more egregious than capturing a soldier, was Hamas entitled to "retaliate" by arresting Israeli parliamentarians, indiscriminately shelling Israel, and killing hundreds

of Israelis? All told, the UN Special Rapporteur for Human Rights in the Occupied Palestinian Territory, John Dugard, concluded that "[r]egime change, rather than security, probably explains Israel's punishment of Gaza." Noam Chomsky, "Comments on Dershowitz," chomsky.info (17 August 2006) (kidnapped). John Dugard, "Despite the 'Withdrawal,' the Siege of Gaza Goes On," *Independent* (5 October 2006) ("punishment"). Amnesty International, *Road to Nowhere* (December 2006), pp. 8–9 ("unarmed," "100"). Richard Falk and Howard Friel, *Israel-Palestine on Record: How the New York Times Misreports Conflict in the Middle East* (Verso, 2007), pp. 135–142 ("daily"). B'Tselem, *Without Trial: Administrative Detention of Palestinians by Israel and the Internment of Unlawful Combatants Law* (October 2009) ("without trial"). B'Tselem, "Statistics on Administrative Detention in the Occupied Territories," btselem.org (20 November 2023) (800). B'Tselem, "Administrative Detention: Background," btselem.org (n.d.) ("time").

96. David Rose, "The Gaza Bombshell," *Vanity Fair* (3 March 2008). Daniel E. Zoughbie, *Indecision Points: George W. Bush and the Israeli-Palestinian Conflict* (The MIT Press, 2014), pp. 125–127. Björn Brenner, *Gaza Under Hamas: From Islamic Democracy to Islamist Governance* (I.B. Tauris, 2017), pp. 35–40. De Soto, *Report*, pp. 21–22, 45–46. For a slightly divergent but informative account of the Hamas takeover, see Victor Kattan, "The 2007 Hamas-Fatah Conflict in Gaza and the Israeli-American Demands," in Peter Sluglet and Victor Kattan, eds., *Violent Radical Movements in the Arab World: The Ideology and Politics of Non-State Actors* (I.B. Tauris, 2019), pp. 93–120.

97. ICG, *Ending the War in Gaza* (5 January 2009).

98. Finkelstein, *Gaza*, p. 32 ("careful"). Embassy Tel Aviv, "Defense Minister Barak's Discussions in Egypt Focus on Shalit, Tahdiya, Anti-Smuggling, and Iran," 08TELAVIV1984_a (29 August 2008), WikiLeaks ("measure"). Cf. Amnesty International, "Gaza Ceasefire at Risk," amnesty.org (5 November 2008).

99. Quoted in Henry Siegman, "Israel Lies," *London Review of Books* (29 January 2009).

100. Finkelstein, *Gaza*, p. 35.

101. Rory McCarthy, "Gaza Truce Broken as Israeli Raid Kills Six Hamas Gunmen," *Guardian* (5 November 2008). Israel purported that it was pre-empting a Hamas attack via a tunnel running beneath the Gaza border. But as a prominent Israeli columnist pointed out, the tunnel "was not a clear and present danger": if it truly passed into Israeli territory, the IDF could just have easily destroyed it from the Israeli side. Israel's decision to launch an assault within Gaza was clearly directed

at "shattering" the ceasefire. Zvi Ba'arel, "Crushing the Tahadiyeh," *Ha'aretz* (16 November 2008).

102. Macintyre, *Gaza*, pp. 150–153. Finkelstein, *Gaza*, pp. 36–37 (re-establish). "Hundreds Die in Gaza Air Raids," *Toronto Star* (27 December 2008) (100 tons). Amnesty International, *Operation "Cast Lead": 22 Days of Death and Destruction* (2 July 2009), pp. 6, 100 (hundreds).

103. "UN Official Says Israel Responsible for Breaking Truce With Gaza," *Ha'aretz* (30 December 2008).

104. Amnesty International, *Cast Lead*. Finkelstein, *Gaza*, p. 68.

105. Nir Hasson, "Israeli Peace Activist: Hamas Leader Jabari Killed Amid Talks on Long-Term Truce," *Ha'aretz* (15 November 2012). Cf. Gershon Baskin, "Assassinating the Chance for Calm," *Daily Beast* (15 November 2012). Reuven Pedatzur, "Why Did Israel Kill Jabari?" *Ha'aretz* (4 December 2012). Gershon Baskin, *The Negotiator: Freeing Gilad Schalit from Hamas* (The Toby Press, 2013), pp. 273–276.

106. *Report of the United Nations High Commissioner for Human Rights on the Implementation of Human Rights Council Resolutions S-9/1 and S-12/1* (13 March 2013), p. 4n4.

107. Jack Khoury, "Abbas: Palestinian Unity Government Will Recognize Israel, Condemn Terrorism," *Ha'aretz* (26 April 2014). Rami Khouri, "The Palestinian Unity Government Will Shape Its Own Fate," *Jordan Times* (5 June 2014).

108. Barak Ravid, "Amid Wave of Endorsements, PM 'Troubled' by US Decision to Work With Palestinian Gov't," *Ha'aretz* (3 June 2014). Barak Ravid, "Israel 'Deeply Disappointed' US Will Work With New Palestinian Government," *Ha'aretz* (3 June 2014).

109. Finkelstein, *Gaza*, pp. 212–214.

110. Hamas additionally demanded that Gaza residents be given access to the Al-Aqsa Mosque in Jerusalem and that an international seaport and airport be established under UN supervision. Yasser Okbi and Maariv Hashavua, "Report: Hamas Proposes 10-year Cease-Fire in Return for Conditions Being Met," *Jerusalem Post* (16 July 2014). Asaf Gabor, "Hamas Conditions for Pacification: Airport, Seaport and Entrance to Al-Aqsa," *Ma'ariv* (7 July 2014) [Hebrew]. This July 16 Hamas offer responded to a ceasefire proposal tabled by the Egyptian president Abdel Fatteh el-Sissi two days earlier. Hamas's rejection of the Egyptian ceasefire proposal was cast by Washington as proof of its obstinacy and justification for Israel's ensuing offensive. And yet, whereas previous ceasefire agreements incorporated international demands that Israel take steps to lift its illegal siege, Cairo's 2014 proposal stipulated that "the security situation [become] stable on the

ground" *prior to* the opening of Gaza's border crossings. As the leading authority on Israel's military operations in Gaza pointed out, "[i]nsofar as Israel designated Hamas a terrorist organization, the security situation in Gaza could only stabilize when Hamas either was defeated or disarmed itself, in the absence of which the siege would continue." Was it then incumbent on Hamas to acquiesce in Israel's infliction of a crime against humanity against the people of Gaza? By contrast, *all* the demands in Hamas's counteroffer were either validated by international law or consistent with it. "TEXT: Cease-fire Agreement Between Israel and Hamas," *Ha'aretz* (21 November 2012) (previous). "The Full Text of the Egyptian Ceasefire Proposal," *Ha'aretz* (15 July 2014) ("stable"). Francesca Albanese, "The Deafening Silence Around the Hamas Proposal for a 10-year Truce," *Mondoweiss* (22 July 2014) (validated). Finkelstein, *Gaza*, p. 214 ("disarmed").

111. UN OCHA, *Fragmented Lives: Humanitarian Overview 2014* (March 2015), p. 6.
112. Ecclesiastes 1:9.
113. Baconi, *Hamas*, pp. 223, 236.

Chapter Four. R. J.

1. Baruch Kimmerling, *Politicide: Ariel Sharon's War Against the Palestinians* (Verso, 2003), p. 169.
2. Permanent Observer of Palestine to the UN Riyad Mansour, "Letter from Palestine," un.org (8 April 2011).
3. Sharif Abdel Kouddous, "Palestinians Engaged in Nonviolent Protest. Israel Responded With a Massacre," *The Nation* (17 May 2018).
4. Amira Hass, "Along the Gaza Border, They Shoot Medics (Too), Don't They?" *Ha'aretz* (28 May 2018).
5. *Report of the Detailed Findings of the UN Commission of Inquiry on the Protests in the Occupied Palestinian Territory*, A/HRC/40/CRP.2 (18 March 2019), pp. 160–163. Hereafter: UN Report II.
6. Hilo Glazer, "'42 Knees in One Day': Israeli Snipers Open Up About Shooting Gaza Protestors," *Ha'aretz* (6 March 2020).
7. UN Office for the Coordination of Humanitarian Affairs (OCHA), "Humanitarian Bulletin: Occupied Palestinian Territory," ochaopt.org (May 2018), pp. 1, 3.
8. See below.
9. International Crisis Group, *The Gaza Strip and COVID-19: Preparing for the Worst*, Middle East Briefing No. 75 (1 April 2020), p. 5.

10. Amira Hass, "It's Not a 'Hamas March' in Gaza. It's Tens of Thousands Willing to Die," *Ha'aretz* (15 May 2018).

11. Efraim Inbar and Eitan Shamir, "Mowing the Grass in Gaza," *Jerusalem Post* (22 July 2014).

12. Norman G. Finkelstein, *I'll Burn That Bridge When I Get to It: Heretical Thoughts on Identity Politics, Cancel Culture, and Academic Freedom* (Sublation, 2023), p. 212.

13. Arundhati Roy interviewed by Jeremy Scahill, theintercept.com (11 April 2018).

14. *New York Times, Wall Street Journal,* and *USA Today.* "Top 10 US Newspapers by Circulation," agilitypr.com (January 2020).

15. Fox News, CNN, and MSNBC. "Leading Cable News Networks in the United States in April 2020, by Number of Primetime Viewers," *Statista* (18 May 2020).

16. By the end of May, it was clear the nonviolent strategy was not working. The center of gravity accordingly shifted to armed attacks occurring away from the demonstrations.

17. This chapter relies on documentation by Adalah, Al-Haq, the Al Mezan Center for Human Rights, Amnesty International, B'Tselem, Human Rights Watch (HRW), the Palestinian Center for Human Rights (PCHR), Yesh Din, and an Independent Commission of Inquiry appointed by the UN Human Rights Council (UN Commission of Inquiry).

18. Israel Ministry of Foreign Affairs, "MFA Statement Regarding Events in Gaza," embassies.gov.il (31 March 2018).

19. Tovah Lazaroff, "'There Are No Innocents in Gaza,' Says Israeli Defense Minister," *Jerusalem Post* (8 April 2018).

20. Ronen Manelis, "The Truth About Hamas and Israel," *WSJ* (20 May 2018). To his credit, the brigadier general, though wanting in fact, did provide excellent fiction. The former chief intelligence officer claimed that "Hamas hired [innocent civilians, women, and children] as extras, paying $14 a person or $100 a family for attendance—and $500 if they managed to get injured. Hamas forced all of their commanders and operatives to go to the border dressed as civilians, each serving as a director of an area—as if to direct their own stage of the operation." In addition, "anyone with a video camera" was given "front-row access to the show and free Wi-Fi." The brigadier general did not clarify whether the cast was provided with complimentary snacks and AK-47s.

21. "Celebrations, Protests Mark US Embassy Move to Jerusalem," *Fox News* (14 May 2018). Associated Press, "Israeli Jets Bomb Gaza After Mortar Shells Fired from Strip," *USA Today* (29 May 2018). Iyad

Abuheweila and Isabel Kershner, "A Woman Dedicated to Saving Lives Loses Hers in Gaza Violence," *NYT* (2 June 2018). Cf. *NYT*, 4.5.18, 4.6.18, 4.13.18, 4.15.18. *USA Today*, 7.19.18. *Fox News*, 5.11.18, 5.15.18.

22. "US Opens Embassy as Dozens Killed in Gaza," *CNN* (14 May 2018). Cf. *CNN*, 5.15.18, 5.29.18. *WSJ*, 4.2.18, 4.4.18, 4.7.18, 4.13.18, 5.15.18.

23. Ali Velshi, "Inside the Israeli-Palestinian Conflict: Why It's a Decades-Long Conflict That Evades Solution," *MSNBC* (14 May 2018). Quoted is Ronen Bergman, an Israeli journalist who appeared on the show. His assertion was not challenged.

24. HRW, "Don't Blame Hamas for the Gaza Bloodshed," hrw.org (22 May 2018).

25. UN Report II, para. 200. Cf. ibid., para. 201.

26. PCHR, "Question and Answer: 1st Year Anniversary of the March of Return Demonstrations," pchrgaza.org (28 March 2019). PCHR, *Annual Report 2018* (July 2019), p. 12. Cf. Al-Haq, "Al-Haq Sends a Letter to the High Representative of the Union for Foreign Affairs and Security Policy Regarding the EU Response to the Mass Killings in the Occupied Gaza Strip," alhaq.org (15 May 2018). Al-Haq, "Q&A The Great Return March: One Year On," alhaq.org (25 May 2019).

27. PCHR, "Weekly Report on Israeli Human Rights Violations in the Occupied Palestinian Territory (26 April-02 May 2018)," pchrgaza.org (3 May 2018). This observation was reiterated in PCHR field observations throughout the period examined.

28. *Report of the Independent International Commission of Inquiry on the Protests in the Occupied Palestinian Territory* (25 February 2019), para. 24. Hereafter: UN Report I.

29. UN Report II, para. 240. According to the Commission of Inquiry, it wasn't until early October that Hamas sought to "exert more control over the protest movement" as it sought to "capitalize on the negotiations with Israel facilitated by Egypt and UNSCO." Ibid., para. 245.

30. Ibid., para. 248. Cf. paras. 242–245, 247.

31. Yesh Din, "HCJ Petition: Revoke Rules of Engagement Permitting Live Fire at Non-Dangerous Demonstrators Near Gaza Fence," yesh-din.org (15 April 2018). Al Mezan Center for Human Rights and Adalah, "Briefing Paper on Israeli Supreme Court Petition Challenging the Israeli Military's Use of Lethal Force Against Gaza Protestors and the State of Israel's Response," adalah.org (15 May 2018).

32. Yesh Din, "HCJ."

33. UN Report I, para. 32. Cf. UN Report II, para. 398.

34. UN Human Rights Office of the High Commissioner, "Basic Principles on the Use of Force and Firearms by Law Enforcement Officials," ohchr.org (7 September 1990), principle 9.
35. "Videos Showing Gaza Violence Stir Outrage," *CNN* (1 April 2018). Cf. *CNN*, 3.31.18, 4.30.18.
36. "Deadly Protests Erupt in Gaza," *MSNBC* (14 May 2018). The human rights organizations did not report any "human wave attacks" in their documentation.
37. Felicia Schwartz and Rory Jones, "Scores Killed as Palestinians Protest US Embassy Opening in Jerusalem," *WSJ* (14 May 2018) ("[n]umerous shots were fired"). Cf. *WSJ*, 3.30.18, 4.2.18, 4.20.18, 4.27.18.
38. Yardena Schwartz, "Israeli Farmers Scorched by Latest Attacks, Coping With Ecological Disaster," *USA Today* (24 July 2018). Cf. *USA Today*, 4.27.18, 4.30.18, 5.4.18, 5.15.18.
39. "Tensions Escalate on Israel, Gaza Border," *Fox News* (11 May 2018).
40. UN Report II, para. 370. In November 2018, B'Tselem reported that a "small number" of protesters "threw hand grenades," but did not provide details or evidence. B'Tselem, "Seven Months of Protests by Gaza Fence: Over 5,800 Palestinians Wounded by Live Israeli Gunfire," btselem.org (22 November 2018).
41. UN Report II, para. 693.
42. Al Mezan and Adalah, "Briefing."
43. PCHR, *Annual*.
44. PCHR, "Weekly Report on Israeli Human Rights Violations in the Occupied Palestinian Territory (29 March-04 April 2018)," pchrgaza.org (5 April 2018).
45. HRW, "Israel: Apparent War Crimes in Gaza: Accountability Needed for Officials Who Authorized Lethal Force," hrw.org (13 June 2018).
46. Muhammad Shehada and Jamie Stern-Weiner, "Debunking Myths About the Palestinian Protests," vice.com (12 June 2018).
47. Al-Haq, "Great Return March: Four Killed, Including a Child, and 295 Injured in 11th Week of Peaceful Protests," alhaq.org (10 June 2018). Al-Haq reaffirmed the "unarmed" nature of the protesters in numerous reports.
48. Amnesty International, "Gaza: Fears of Further Bloodshed as Israel Adopts 'Zero Tolerance' Policy," amnesty.org (19 October 2018).
49. B'Tselem, "Seven."
50. UN Report I, para. 101. Cf. UN Report II, paras. 94, 702.
51. Gardiner Harris, "Mike Pompeo Expresses Support for Israeli Response to Gaza Protests," *NYT* (30 April 2018). Cf. *NYT*, 4.6.18, 4.13.18.

52.   Felicia Schwartz and Abu Bakr Bashir, "Tens of Thousands Gather at
      Gaza Border to Mark Protest Anniversary," *WSJ* (30 March 2019). Cf.
      WSJ, 4.2.18, 4.27.18, 5.14.18, 5.15.18.

53.   Oren Dorell, "40 Hurt as Israel Warns Against Burning Kites at Pal-
      estinian Demonstration in Gaza," *USA Today* (4 May 2018). Cf. *USA
      Today*, 5.14.18.

54.   "Israel Opens Fire on Palestinian Protesters that [*sic*] Breached Gaza
      Border Fence: Report," *Fox News* (5 April 2019). Cf. *Fox News*,
      4.27.18, 5.11.18, 5.14.18, 5.16.18.

55.   Amnesty International, "Israel: Arms Embargo Needed as Mili-
      tary Unlawfully Kills and Maims Gaza Protesters," amnesty.org
      (27 April 2018).

56.   Al-Haq, "Q&A."

57.   HRW, "Apparent."

58.   B'Tselem, "Seven."

59.   PCHR, *Annual*.

60.   UN Report II, para. 692. Cf. UN Report I, para. 95.

61.   In any event, human rights organizations agreed that attempts to
      breach the fence did not inherently pose an "imminent threat to life"
      such as would entitle Israel to use lethal force in response. HRW,
      "Apparent." Cf. UN Report II, *Summary*, para. 694.

62.   Iyad Abuheweila and Isabel Kershner, "Flaming Kites from Gaza
      Thwarted by Winds," *NYT* (4 May 2018). Cf. *NYT*, 4.1.18, 4.6,
      2018, 4.7.18, 4.20.18, 4.22.18.

63.   "Sun Sets on Deadly Day Along Gaza Border," *Fox News* (14 May
      2018). Cf. *Fox News*, 5.11.18, 5.15.18, 5.16.18.

64.   Associated Press, "Israel Asked to Avoid Lethal Force as Gaza Protest
      Resumes," *USA Today* (27 April 2018). Cf. *USA Today*, 5.14.18.

65.   Al-Haq, "30 March: 15 Palestinians Killed, More Than a Thousand
      Injured, as IOF Violently Suppress Palestinian Protestors in the Gaza
      Strip," alhaq.org (31 March 2018).

66.   HRW, "Gaza Killings Unlawful, Calculated: Officials Green-Light
      Shooting of Unarmed Demonstrators," hrw.org (3 April 2018).

67.   PCHR, "Accountability Guarantees End of International Law Viola-
      tions Against Peaceful Demonstrators," pchrgaza.org (17 May 2018).

68.   Amnesty International, "Embargo."

69.   UN Report II, paras. 518–519, 526, 536, 537, 692; emphases added.

Chapter Five. Yaniv Cogan

1. "Statement From Secretary of Defense Lloyd J. Austin III on the Attacks Against Israel," defense.gov (7 October 2023).
2. Israeli prime minister, post on X (formerly Twitter), 7 October 2023.
3. UN Office for the Coordination of Humanitarian Affairs (OCHA), "Hostilities in the Gaza Strip and Israel: Reported Impact, Day 64," ochaopt.org (9 December 2023).
4. Human Rights Watch (HRW), "Gaza: Unlawful Israeli Hospital Strikes Worsen Health Crisis," hrw.org (14 November 2023). "WHO Director-General's Opening Remarks at the Media Briefing—15 November 2023," who.int (15 November 2023).
5. Molly Blackall, "Patients in Gaza 'Covered in Flies' With 'Worms Coming Out of Wounds,' Says Surgeon," inews.co.uk (6 November 2023).
6. Isabel Debre and Wafaa Shurafa, "Little Light, No Beds, Not Enough Anesthesia: A View from the 'Nightmare' of Gaza's Hospitals," apnews.com (21 October 2023). Nidal Al-Mughrabi, "In Gaza, Hospital Procedures without Anaesthetics Prompted Screams, Prayers," Reuters (10 November 2023). The Daily (podcast), "The Doctors of Gaza," nytimes.com (13 November 2023).
7. UN OCHA, "Hostilities in the Gaza Strip and Israel: Flash Update 9," ochaopt.org (15 October 2023).
8. "Israel Must Stop Using Water as a Weapon of War: UN Expert," ohchr.org (17 November 2023).
9. Fares Akram and Jodi Rudoren, "Raw Sewage and Anger Flood Gaza's Streets as Electricity Runs Low," New York Times (20 November 2023).
10. Julia Conley, "Disease, Fueled by Blockade, Could Be Bigger Killer Than Bombs in Gaza: WHO," commondreams.org (28 November 2023).
11. "Babies Dying from Preventable Causes in Besieged Gaza," oxfam.org (23 November 2023).
12. Amira Hass, "Gaza's Unfolding Disaster: When Humanitarian Aid Is Your Last Meal," Ha'aretz (28 November 2023).
13. "What Happens to Gaza After the War?" economist.com (19 November 2023). Isabel Debre, "Gaza Has Become a Moonscape in War. When the Battles Stop, Many Fear It Will Remain Uninhabitable," apnews.com (23 November 2023). "British-Palestinian Surgeon Fears Gaza Will Become an 'Uninhabitable Death World'," globalnews.ca (28 November 2023).

14.   Yinon Magal and Ben Caspit, "In All the Wars, We Are Careful Not to Hit Civilians," *103fm* (9 October 2023), 00:06:42 [Hebrew].
15.   "Yinon Magal from the Heart of Gaza: 'There Should Be a Sign Here: "Welcome to Hell," by How Things Look'," *Channel 14 News* (16 November 2023) [Hebrew].
16.   Ron Ben Yishai, "Between Machine Guns and Mortar Shells, IDF Soldiers Operate in Captured Hamas Strongholds," ynet.co.il (4 November 2023) [Hebrew].
17.   Brett Samuels, "'Obvious to Us' Israel Trying to Minimize Civilian Casualties, Kirby Says," thehill.com (31 October 2023).
18.   "Mark Regev: Israel Making 'Maximum Effort' to Safeguard Gaza's Civilian Population," *Morning Joe—MSNBC* (31 October 2023).
19.   Hannan Greenberg and Diana Bachur-Nir, "The Cabinet Approved a Limited Operation; Lapid: Shall We Reenforce Roofs in Sderot?" ynet.co.il (1 October 2004) [Hebrew].
20.   "Halutz: The Palestinian Population Must Throw Up the Rocket Launchers," walla.co.il (4 November 2006) [Hebrew].
21.   Yaniv Kubovitch, "Israel's Targeting Policy Changes: Residential Neighborhoods Instead of Military Sites," haaretz.co.il (9 August 2018) [Hebrew]. One of the airstrikes in that particular bombardment killed 18-month-old Bayan Khamas and her mother Enas, who was pregnant at the time. Another one targeted and destroyed the Said al-Mishal Cultural Center. Bethan McKernan, "Israeli Airstrikes Kill Pregnant Woman and One-Year-Old Daughter as Fighting With Hamas Escalates," *Independent* (9 August 2018). Hazem Balousha and Oliver Holmes, "'Our Memories Have Vanished': The Palestinian Theatre Destroyed in a Bomb Strike," *Guardian* (22 August 2018).
22.   Alex Fishman and Ariela Ringel-Hoffman, "I Have Enormous Power, I Won't Have Any Excuses," *Yediot Aharonot* (3 October 2008) [Hebrew].
23.   Giora Eiland, "The Third Lebanon War: The Target—Lebanon," *INSS Strategic Update* 11.2 (October 2008).
24.   Giora Eiland, "Who's the Real Enemy?" ynetnews.com (24 July 2008).
25.   Michael Uriah, "This Is What the New Concrete Wall at the Northern Border, Which Will Stop Hizballah's 'Radwan' Force, Looks Like," idf.il (6 September 2018) [Hebrew].
26.   Ya'acov Eilon and Miki Haimovich, *Channel 10 News* (27 December 2008), 00:54:13 [Hebrew].
27.   Yossi Yehoshua and Reuven Weiss, "So I Don't Have Any Dilemma," *Yediot Aharonot* (23 January 2009) [Hebrew].

28. Fisher Institute for Air and Space Strategic Studies, "Major General (Res.) Yoav Gallant—On Operation Cast Lead," *Lecture to the Institute's "Cast Lead" Conference* (7 July 2012), 00:38:20 [Hebrew].

29. Amiram Bareket, "Netanyahu: The IDF Has the Operational Capacity to Wipe Out Gaza," *Ha'aretz* (22 June 2006) [Hebrew].

30. *Report of the United Nations Fact-Finding Mission on the Gaza Conflict* (25 September 2009), paras. 62, 1893. Goldstone later recanted certain findings but presented no new evidence to justify his change of mind. Richard Goldstone, "Reconsidering the Goldstone Report on Israel and War Crimes," *Washington Post* (1 April 2011).

31. University of Haifa, "The Characteristics of a Possible Conflict in the Northern Front and Home Front," haifa.ac.il (30 November 2010), 00:40:09 [Hebrew]. Emphasis added.

32. Ibid., 01:14:14.

33. Ran Dagoni, "Deputy Chief of Staff Benny Gantz: 'We Will Win the Third Lebanon War; When We Take the Horses Out of the Sheds, It Will Be Very Painful for Lebanon'," globes.co.il (2 June 2010) [Hebrew].

34. Peter Beaumont, "Israeli Soldiers Cast Doubt on Legality of Gaza Military Tactics," *Guardian* (4 May 2015).

35. Benny Gantz, "6,231 Targets Destroyed. Parts of Gaza Returned to the Stone Age," post on Facebook (20 January 2019).

36. Guy Elster, "Sinwar Warns: If the IDF Invades Gaza—Its Forces Will Be Crushed," walla.co.il (13 August 2019) [Hebrew]. Benny Gantz, post on X (formerly Twitter), 31 August 2019.

37. Galit Hemi and Attila Somfalvi, "Lapid: 'My Assessment Is That the Operation Will End in an Agreement With Egypt, There Is No Talk With Hamas'," ynet.co.il (31 July 2014) [Hebrew].

38. Yossi Yehoshua, "Former Security Officials and a Strategic Consultant: The 'Cabinet' Gallant Has Set Up for Himself," ynet.co.il (27 October 2023) [Hebrew].

39. Some elements of Israel's conventional military doctrine were maintained. For instance, Israeli officials repeatedly drew a connection between the level of destruction inflicted on Gaza and Israel's deterrence capacity vis-á-vis Hezbollah. Defense Minister Gallant, for example, threatened: "What we are [currently] doing in Gaza we will know how to do in Beirut." Giora Eiland, an advisor to Gallant, argued that "Hezbollah will only be deterred if they see in Gaza City not just destruction, but also a humanitarian disaster." Amir Bohbot, "Gallant: What We Are Doing in Gaza, We Know How to Do in Beirut," walla.co.il (11 November 2023) [Hebrew]. Giora Eiland, "The Mili-

tary, Moral, and Diplomatic Challenge," *Yediot Aharonot* (29 October 2023) [Hebrew].

40. Ran Dagoni, "Deputy Chief of Staff Benny Gantz: 'We Will Win the Third Lebanon War: When We Take the Horses Out of the Stable, It Will Be Very Painful for Lebanon'," globes.co.il (2 June 2010) [Hebrew].

41. Yaniv Cogan and Jamie Stern-Weiner, "Fighting Amalek in Gaza: What Israelis Say and Western Media Ignore," normanfinkelstein.substack.com (12 November 2023; updated regularly).

42. Anna Barsky, "Netanyahu in a Dispatch to Soldiers: 'Remember What Amalek Did to You, We Will Defeat the Evil'," maariv.co.il (3 Novem-ber 2023) [Hebrew].

43. "'We Are Fighting Human Animals—and We Act Accordingly. We Are Laying Siege to Gaza City'—Minister of Defense, Yoav Galant," The Knesset Channel (9 October 2023) [Hebrew]. Yoav Zitun, "Gallant: 'We Will Change the Face of Reality in Gaza 50 Years Going Forward'," ynet.co.il (7 October 2023) [Hebrew]. Yoav Zitun, "Gallant Toured the North: 'If Nasrallah Makes a Mistake—He Will Seal the Fate of Lebanon'," ynet.co.il (4 November 2023) [Hebrew].

44. Ariel Weitmann, "Giora Eiland: If We Want to Ever See the Kidnapped Alive—This Is What Has to Be Done," globes.co.il (8 October 2023) [Hebrew].

45. Rino Tzror, GLZ Radio (10 October 2023), 00:45:40 [Hebrew]. Nadav Eyal, "How One Should React to a Massacre of Hundreds," *Yediot Aharonot* (9 October 2023) [Hebrew].

46. Giora Eiland, "Getting into a Routine of War," *Yediot Aharonot* (25 October 2023) [Hebrew].

47. Giora Eiland, "It's Not Revenge, It's Either Us or Them," *Yediot Aharonot* (11 October 2023) [Hebrew]. Giora Eiland, *Channel 12 News* (6 November 2023) [Hebrew].

48. Giora Eiland, "Not to Be Deterred by the World," *Yediot Aharonot* (19 November 2023) [Hebrew].

49. For example, Israel claimed to have offered incubators to Al-Shifa Hospital. A Medical Aid for Palestinians representative termed this PR stunt "weird propaganda" because "Shifa already has incubators"—what the hospital lacked was the fuel to operate them. Erin Kilbride and Bill Van Esveld, "Birth and Death Intertwined in Gaza Strip," hrw.org (1 December 2023). Einav Halabi and Elisha Ben Kimon, "IDF Offered Incubators to Gaza's Shifa Hospital, But Was Refused," ynetnews.com (14 November 2023). Rohan Talbot, post on X (formerly Twitter), 14 November 2023.

50. "Lapid: 'It Will Take as Long as It Has to Take'," ynet.co.il (20 July 2014) [Hebrew].

51. Shirit Avitan Cohen, "A Proposal in the Likud: The Disengagement Cancellation Law—in Gaza as Well," *Israel Hayom* (1 November 2023) [Hebrew].

52 Jonathan Lis and Ben Samuels, "Israeli Intel Ministry Suggests Relocating Gazans to Sinai After Hamas War," *Ha'aretz* (30 October 2023).

53 *Channel 12 News* (1 November 2023) [Hebrew].

54 Ron Ben Yishai, "Outline of the War Plan to Change the Situation in Gaza," ynet.co.il (19 October 2023) [Hebrew]. The United Nations Interim Force in Lebanon (UNIFIL) is a UN peacekeeping mission deployed in southern Lebanon.

55. Nir Gontarz, "Miki Zohar: The Gaza Strip Should Be Placed Under the Care of the Palestinian Authority," *Ha'aretz* (24 October 2023) [Hebrew].

56. Gideon Sa'ar MK, post on Facebook, 14 October 2023 [Hebrew].

57. *Ha'aretz* reported that "dozens of members of the military government unit, which the IDF operated in the past after wars in Lebanon and the [occupied Palestinian territories], were also called upon to the join the reserves." The paper also quoted former Major General Ya'acov Or saying: "As time passes, the IDF will be drawn in and become responsible for the population in the territory under its control, as an occupied territory . . . The practical meaning will be a return to a partial military rule, even if this [transition] is done through the back door." Amos Harel, "The International Attention Is Directed at Shifa, and Every Complication Might Harm a Hostage Exchange," *Ha'aretz* (16 November 2023) [Hebrew].

58. A notable example being US secretary of state Antony Blinken's admission that he asked Arab leaders about the possibility of relocating the population of Gaza into Sinai. Jacob Magid, "Blinken Says Efforts to Relocate Palestinians from Gaza to Sinai a 'Non-Starter'," timesofisrael.com (15 October 2023).

59. The *Washington Post* reported, citing anonymous sources in Western intelligence agencies, that Hamas originally envisioned a much deeper attack, and that militants were ordered to "[k]ill as many people and take as many hostages as possible." *Middle East Eye*, on the other hand, cited claims by anonymous sources within Hamas that "[t]he plan was to assault the Gaza Division and not the kibbutz" and "the strike was supposed to be tactical, not strategic." A report by the *Guardian* noted a consensus among "many experts" including "Israeli security sources" that Hamas was surprised by the success of the

assault. David Hearst, "Israel-Palestine War: Hamas and Israel Were 'Inches' Away from Deal on Hostages," middleeasteye.net (1 November 2023). Jason Burke, "A Deadly Cascade: How Secret Hamas Attack Orders Were Passed Down at Last Minute," *Guardian* (7 November 2023). Shira Rubin and Joby Warrick, "Hamas Envisioned Deeper Attacks, Aiming to Provoke an Israeli War," *Washington Post* (13 November 2023).

60. Avi Issacharoff and Amos Harel, *The Seventh War: How We Won and Why We Lost the War With the Palestinians* (Yedioth Ahronoth, 2004), p. 142 [Hebrew].

61. Four Mothers was a protest movement launched by mothers of IDF soldiers stationed in Israeli occupied South Lebanon. It was set up in response to mounting casualties as a result of the Hezbollah insurgency. The movement is widely credited for making withdrawal from Lebanon a politically viable (and eventually overwhelmingly popular) position within Israeli society.

62. Hezbollah's secretary-general Hassan Nasrallah has noted the significance of the Four Mothers movement to the liberation of Lebanon and suggested that a similar dynamic might catalyze the end of Israeli control over the occupied Palestinian territories. "Quote of the Week," israelnationalnews.com (15 February 2002) [Hebrew]. "Israel Agrees to Include Palestinians in the Prisoner Exchange with Hezbollah," albawaba.net (16 February 2002) [Arabic].

63. Israeli decision-makers and the Israeli public might have been convinced that maintaining an on-the-ground occupation of the Strip was not in their interest. But they chose to act upon that realization by implementing a regime of "occupation by remote control." Amir Oren, "Occupation Without Presence," *Ha'aretz* (14 July 2004).

64. Sabri Jiryis, "The 'Dialogue' and National Unity," translated by Edna Dahari Davidovitch, *Dialogue Quarterly Magazine on Palestinian Affairs*, Issue 1 (January 1988), p. 27 [Hebrew]. Originally printed in *Shu'un Filastiniyyah*, Nos. 170–171.

65. Guy Bechor, "A Split in the PLO. The Next Generation Goes to War," *Hadashot* (11 February 1988) [Hebrew].

66. "The Names of the Hostages That Have Been Published: Entire Families, Elderly, Children, and Soldiers," *Ha'aretz* (23 November 2023) [Hebrew].

67. "Demonstrations in the Cities Calling for an Immediate Hostage Deal; In Tel Aviv There Are Still Protests Against Netanyahu," zoha.org.il (11 October 2023) [Hebrew]. Free Jerusalem, post on Facebook (12 October 2023). B'Tselem, "Hamas Must Release All

Captives Immediately; Israeli Government Must Advance Deal to Release Them," btselem.org (11 October 2023).

68. Oren Ziv, "For the First Time Since the War Began: A Demonstration in Kaplan Calling for a Ceasefire," mekomit.co.il (29 October 2023) [Hebrew].

69. Various measures were put in place to depress turnout to anti-war protests. Israel's police commissioner Kobi Shabtai declared that "anyone who wishes to show solidarity with Gaza—I'll put him on buses [and deport him] there." The Israeli government approved changes to the open fire policy of the police, allowing for live-ammunition to be used against protesters blocking roads—a decision widely understood to be targeted at the Palestinian population of Israel and a veiled threat to repeat the massacre of Palestinian protesters known as the "October 2000 events." The Israeli High Court of Justice has similarly barred Palestinian citizens from holding anti-war protests even as it approved a similar protest in Tel Aviv. Ran Shimoni, Deiaa Haj Yahia, and Adi Hashmonai, "Israel Police Commissioner: Those Who Identify With Gaza Can Be Escorted There on Buses," Ha'aretz (19 October 2023). Suleiman Maswadeh and Moshe Steinmetz, "The Government Will Authorize Live Shooting of Protesters Blocking Roads in an Emergency," kan.org.il (26 October 2023) [Hebrew]. Gilad Morag, "The High Court of Justice Sides With the Police: Bans Anti-War Demonstrations Scheduled in Arab Cities," ynet.co.il (8 November 2023) [Hebrew]. Chen Maanit, "Following a Petition to the High Court, the State Will Allow Hadash to Hold a Demonstration in Tel Aviv Against the War," Ha'aretz (16 November 2023) [Hebrew].

70. "Clashes at the Government Meeting: We Need to Be Cruel," kan.org.il (8 October 2023) [Hebrew].

71. At one point Hamas claimed that over 60 hostages, representing nearly 25 percent of the total number of captives held in Gaza, had been killed in Israeli airstrikes. Ahmed Asmar, "Hamas Says 60 Hostages Killed in Israeli Airstrikes on Gaza Strip Since Oct. 7," aa.com.tr (5 November 2023). A specific claim by the Palestinian Islamic Jihad alleging that a hostage died in captivity was later revealed as false. Chao Deng, "Hostage Hanna Katzir Was Released Alive After Militants Said She Was Dead," Wall Street Journal (28 November 2023).

72. Tamar Hermann and Or Anabi, "'Swords of Iron' Flash Survey: Public Trust in the IDF and the Police Is Higher Than in June 2023," idi.org.il (23 October 2023).

73. A separate group, The Abducted and Missing Families Forum, represented a smaller group of families. Unlike the HQ, the Forum endorsed the Israeli government's policy and advocated for

"[e]liminating all Hamas terrorists wherever they are and rescuing the kidnapped." Reports in the English media have often confused one organization for the other. Atara German, "With a Good Atmosphere: Two Headquarters of the Families of the Kidnapped, Different Messages," *Makor Rishon* (16 October 2023) [Hebrew]. Sivan Chilai, "'Staying Until They Return': A Singing Circle and Performances of Support in the 'Kidnapped Square' in Tel Aviv," ynet.co.il (5 Novem-ber 2023) [Hebrew].

74.   Yaron Abraham, "The Charged Conversation Between Gallant and the Families of the Abductees," mako.co.il (29 October 2023).

75.   See for example the statement made by a speaker at a November 11 demonstration organized by the HQ: "Mr. Prime Minister, members of the cabinet, don't speak to us about destroying [Hamas], don't speak to us about occupying [Gaza], don't speak to us about 'flatten-ing.' As far as I'm concerned—don't speak at all, just do everything required to bring my father and the rest of the hostages back home." "Bring Them Home Now! Live from the Demonstration in the Hos-tages Square in Tel Aviv," *DemocratTV* (11 November 2023), 01:18:23 [Hebrew].

76.   The HQ for Bringing Back the Kidnapped and the Missing, post on Facebook, 18 October 2023 [Hebrew].

77.   Lee Naim, "'No Pause—Without Their Return': The Hostages' Families Are Protesting in Front of the Kirya 'With No Time Limit'," mako.co.il (3 November 2023) [Hebrew].

78.   Roee Rubinstein, "The Families' March Ended in a Mass Demonstra-tion in Front of Netanyahu's Office: 'If We Have To—We'll Walk to Gaza'," ynet.co.il (18 November 2023) [Hebrew].

79.   Netanyahu: "[W]e will implement and exhaust every possibility to bring them home." Benny Gantz: "[W]e'll do anything to return the hostages." Merav Sever and Avi Cohen, "Netanyahu in the Meeting: 'We Will Implement and Exhaust Every Possibility to Bring Them Home,' the Families of the Kidnapped: 'You Must Bring Them Back, That's on You'," *Israel Hayom* (28 October 2023) [Hebrew]. "Gantz: We Will Do Everything to Bring Back the Hostages. We Will Fight Whoever We Have to and Speak With Whoever We Can," mako.co.il (7 November 2023) [Hebrew].

80.   Tamar Hermann and Or Anabi, "'Swords of Iron' Flash Survey: Most of the Jewish Public Believes the Most Important War Aim Is Releas-ing the Hostages, Followed by the Destruction of Hamas," idi.org.il (24 November 2023).

81.   Itamar Eichner and Reuters, "Report: Negotiations for the Release of Children and Women from Hamas Captivity—in Exchange for the

Release of Female Prisoners from Prison in Israel," ynet.co.il (9 October 2023) [Hebrew].

82. The IDF reportedly estimated that 1,000 to 3,000 Hamas fighters were killed in Gaza prior to the temporary ceasefire, far from a fatal blow to the organization's military capabilities. Various claims were made by the Israeli government and its supporters in order to create the impression that the military assault led to significant concessions by Hamas and to a deal more favorable to Israel. These assertions were not backed by any evidence and were inconsistent with multiple press reports regarding the terms of the proposed exchange. Nadav Frankovitch, "The Public Is Being Told That Military Pressure Led to the Release of the Hostages. Is That So?" mekomit.co.il (22 November 2023) [Hebrew]. Dan Sabbagh, "IDF Messaging Suggests Gaza Truce Unlikely to Last Much Beyond Tuesday," *Guardian* (26 November 2023).

83. Avi Dabush, "Starting This Week, I'm Also a Massacre Survivor. This Is What Has to Be Done Now," *Ha'aretz* (17 October 2023) [Hebrew].

84. Ofer Cassif, posts on X (formerly Twitter), 10 October 2023 and 17 November 2023. Zeeshan Aleem, "A Leftist Israeli Lawmaker Makes His Case for an Immediate Ceasefire," msnbc.com (22 October 2023).

85. Ofer Cassif, posts on X (formerly Twitter), 17 October 2023 and 20 October 2023.

86. An early and consistent critic of Netanyahu's supposedly pro-Hamas policy was former Israeli foreign minister Tzipi Livni, who played an instrumental role in diplomatically isolating Hamas, thus ensuring that its diplomatic overtures for a peace settlement would fail. Ksenia Svetlova, a former Member of the Knesset representing Livni's political party, HaTnua, praised the Netanyahu government's decision to "heed the call by Palestinian Authority President Abu Mazen [Mahmoud Abbas] to decrease the electricity supply to Gaza," noting that it may "bring about a very great hardship" for the Gazan population and was a "positive step as part of a policy aimed at removing Hamas from power." Ksenia Svetlova, post on Facebook, 12 June 2023. Alona Ferber, "Tzipi Livni: 'A Ceasefire Isn't a Solution'," *New Statesman* (2 November 2023).

87. Egyptian and Syrian atrocities included the execution (including large-scale massacres) of Israeli soldiers who were captured or surren-dered, as well the torture of soldiers who were taken hostage, while Israeli atrocities included the carpet bombing of cities, burning down of villages, and execution of civilians. Protocol 334 of the Knesset's Foreign Affairs and Security Commission (31 October 1973) [He-

brew]. Oslo News Agencies, "At the Outset of the War There Were 500-600 Soldiers at the Bar-Lev Line," *Yediot Aharonot* (27 November 1973) [Hebrew]. US House of Representatives, "Problems of Protecting Civilians Under International Law in the Middle East Conflict," *Hearing, 93rd Congress, 2nd session* (4 April 1974).

88.   Tommy Lapid (father of Israeli opposition leader Yair Lapid) wrote: "Our retaliation must be so harsh, so overwhelming, so devoid of mercy, and so cruel—that it will inflict a national trauma upon the collective consciousness of the Arabs. The Arabs require, perhaps even want, for their souls to be shocked into accepting the existence of the State of Israel." Yosef 'Tommy' Lapid, "Break Them," *Ma'ariv* (9 October 1973) [Hebrew].

89.   AFP, "Sadat's Wife: I Have the Feeling We Are Standing on the Threshold of Peace," *Yediot Aharonot* (20 November 1973) [Hebrew]. Eliezer Be'eri, "Instead of Stagnation—the Beginning of a Development Towards Peace?" *Al HaMishmar* (17 October 1973) [Hebrew]. "Golda: In Favor of Peace and a Territorial Compromise," *Yedioth Aharonot* (30 December 1973) [Hebrew].

90.   Daoud Kuttab, "Opinion: After a Cease-Fire in Gaza, There Is Only One Answer for What Happens Next," *Los Angeles Times* (9 November 2023).

91.   The Flagship Bulletin, *Kol Hai Radio* (22 November 2023), 00:15:00 [Hebrew].

92.   Adam Ragson and David D. Kirkpatrick, "What Was Hamas Thinking?" *New Yorker* (13 October 2023).

93.   Associated Press, "Hamas Official in an Interview to the AP: Hezbollah Is Currently Acting Against the Occupation, but We Expect More From It," *Ha'aretz* (26 October 2023) [Hebrew]. Uriel Levy, "Hamas Officials Are Not Seeking a Deescalation and Call for the War to Be Widened," davar1.co.il (9 November 2023) [Hebrew].

94.   As indicated by Hamas's head of international relations Bassem Naim: "[W]e didn't choose this road while having other options. We have no options." Rubin and Warrick, "Deeper."

Chapter Seven. Khaled Hroub

1.   Speech broadcast on Al Jazeera Arabic [Arabic].

2.   Mohammed Deif, "We Launched 5,000 Rockets on the Enemy's Settlements and Cities," *Al Jazeera Arabic* (7 October 2023) [Arabic]. It is noteworthy that Deif's speech made repeated reference to the United Nations and international law. This cuts against reductive distinctions

made by some commentators on Hamas between diplomatic "moderates" outside Gaza and military "hardliners" within. Based on close observation over many years, this author can confidently state that both moderates and hardliners in Hamas are distributed across the board. Cf. Nour Abu Aisha, "'Operation Al-Aqsa Flood' Proceeding According to Plan: Palestinian Group," aa.com.tr (7 October 2023).

3. Already five years ago, this author joined many observers in warning of "a large-scale explosion in the Strip." Khaled Hroub, "Palestine's Impasse: Israeli Occupation, Regional Conflicts and Internal Division," *IEMed Mediterranean Yearbook 2018* (IEMed, 2018), p. 238.

4. Amnesty International, "Israel/OPT: Civilians Must Be Protected After Unprecedented Escalation in Violence," amnesty.org.uk (7 October 2023). UN Secretary-General António Guterres, "Secretary-General's Remarks to the Security Council—On the Middle East," un.org (24 October 2023).

5. At the outset of the second intifada, Hamas was suspicious that the revolt did not reflect a genuine change of strategy by Fatah but rather a short-lived popular mobilization aimed at pressuring Israel to concede more in negotiations. A couple of weeks later, Hamas joined in full force. Hani Awwad, "How Arafat Planned for the Second Intifada, Then Turned Against It," *Metras* (25 October 2018) [Arabic].

6. Cf. Basem Ezbidi, *Hamas and Governance: Entering the System or Revolting Against It?* (PCPSR, 2010), pp. 55–56 [Arabic].

7. On suicide attacks, cf. Farhad Khosrokhavar, *Suicide Bombers: Allah's New Martyrs* (Pluto Press, 2002), pp. 113–119, 152.

8. Frode Løvlie, "Explaining Hamas's Changing Electoral Strategy, 1996-2006," *Government & Opposition* 48.4 (2013), pp. 570–593.

9. Hamas contested the election as the Change and Reform List and won 76 out of 132 seats. The Fatah bloc secured 43 seats and the remainder were distributed among smaller groups. For discussion of Hamas's electoral platform, cf. Khaled Hroub, "A 'New Hamas' Through Its New Documents," *Journal of Palestine Studies* 35.4 (2006), pp. 6–27.

10. Khaled Hroub, *Hamas: A Beginner's Guide* (Pluto Press, 2010), pp. 136–143.

11. David Rose, "The Gaza Bombshell," *Vanity Fair* (April 2008).

12. Interviews with Hamas affiliates, Ramallah, August 2009 and July 2012.

13. The Quartet was established in 2002 to help mediate Middle East peace talks and deliver economic and institutional support for the Palestinians. In practice, it was dominated by the US.

14. Yezid Sayigh, "Policing the People, Building the State: Authoritarian Transformation in the West Bank and Gaza," *Carnegie Papers* (Carnegie Endowment for International Peace, February 2011).
15. Björn Brenner, *Gaza Under Hamas: From Islamic Democracy to Islamist Governance* (I.B. Tauris, 2017), chap. 7.
16. UN Conference on Trade and Development, *Report on UNCTAD Assistance to the Palestinian People: Developments in the Economy of the Occupied Palestinian Territory* (6 July 2015), para. 60. UN Country Team in the OPT, *Gaza Ten Years Later* (July 2017), pp. 3, 28.
17. For a debate on the efficacy of armed struggle in Gaza, cf. As'ad Abu-khalil et al., "Can Armed Struggle End the Siege of Gaza?" in Jamie Stern-Weiner, ed., *Moment of Truth: Tackling Israel-Palestine's Toughest Questions* (OR Books, 2018), pp. 131–174.
18. In most aspects monitored by the Palestinian Independent Commission for Human Rights—e.g., freedom of assembly, freedom of expression, illegal arrests—Hamas fares better than the PA. See, e.g., its annual report for 2022. It is also evident that Fatah operates almost freely in the Gaza Strip whereas Hamas is banned in the West Bank.
19. Palestinian Center for Policy and Survey Research, "Public Opinion Poll No (80)," pcpsr.org (15 June 2021).
20. "Palestinian Factions Hamas and Fatah End Split on Gaza," *bbc.co.uk* (12 October 2017).
21. Adnan Abu Amer, "Palestinian Elections: Fatah's Fragmentation and Hamas Vigilance," carnegieendowment.org (24 March 2017) [Arabic].
22. Ala'a Lahlouh and Waleed Ladadweh, "The Challenges that Forced the Fatah Movement to Postpone the General Elections," pcpsr.org (July 2021).
23. Cf. Khaled Hroub, "A Newer Hamas? The Revised Charter," *Journal of Palestine Studies* 46.4 (2017), pp. 100–111.
24. "Netanyahu Tosses Hamas Policy Paper on Israel into Waste Bin," *Jerusalem Post* (8 May 2017).
25. Author interview with a Hamas official who spoke on condition of anonymity, 12 May 2017.
26. "IDF Intel Chief Warns Despair in Gaza Could Explode Toward Israel," timesofisrael.com (24 February 2016).
27. "Netanyahu: Israel Examining Ways to Prevent Humanitarian Crisis in Gaza," *Ha'aretz* (5 June 2018). Whereas international agencies uniformly attributed Gaza's economic plight to the Israeli blockade, Netanyahu naturally blamed Hamas.
28. Daniel Blatman, "The Israeli Lawmaker Heralding Genocide Against Palestinians," *Ha'aretz* (23 May 2017).

Chapter Eleven. Mitchell Plitnick

1. Mark Murray, "Poll: Biden's Standing Hits New Lows Amid Israel-Hamas War," *NBC News* (19 November 2023).
2. United Nations Office for the Coordination of Humanitarian Affairs (OCHA), "Hostilities in the Gaza Strip and Israel: Flash Update 42," ochaopt.org (17 November 2023).
3. Akbar Shahid Ahmed, "Biden Cast Doubt on Gaza's Death Statistics—But Officials Cite Them Internally," huffpost.com (26 October 2023). Gabrielle Tétrault-Farber, "Despite Biden's Doubts, Humanitarian Agencies Consider Gaza Toll Reliable," *Reuters* (27 October 2023).
4. Gal Beckerman, "'The Middle East Region Is Quieter Today Than It Has Been in Two Decades'," *Atlantic* (7 October 2023).
5. UN OCHA data.
6. Mitchell Plitnick, "In Latest Visit Blinken Offers Nothing to Palestinians," *Mondoweiss* (3 February 2023).
7. IHRA, "What is Antisemitism?" holocaustremembrance.com (n.d.).
8. Mitchell Plitnick and Sahar Aziz, "Presumptively Antisemitic: Islamophobic Tropes in the Palestine-Israel Discourse," *Rutgers University Center for Security, Race, and Rights* (November 2023).
9. Yousef Munayyer, post on X (formerly Twitter), 7 October 2023.
10. For a deeper examination of the history and ideology of Hamas, cf. Tareq Baconi, *Hamas Contained: The Rise and Pacification of Palestinian Resistance* (Stanford University Press, 2018).
11. Alex Gangitano, "White House Calls Lawmakers Not Backing Israel 'Wrong,' 'Disgraceful'," thehill.com (10 October 2023).
12. "Statement from Gerald Rosberg, Chair of the Special Committee on Campus Safety," *Columbia News* (10 November 2023),
13. Andrew Jack, "US Universities Lose Millions as Donors Pull Funding Over Hamas Stance," *Financial Times* (19 October 2023).
14. Anemona Hartocollis and Stephanie Saul, "After Antisemitic Attacks, Colleges Debate What Kind of Speech Is Out of Bounds," *New York Times* (9 November 2023).
15. Joyce Li, "NU Students for Justice in Palestine Leads Walkout, Calls for University Divestment and Support for Palestinians," *The Daily Northwestern* (26 October 2023).
16. "Jewish Student Tells Jake She Doesn't Feel Safe at MIT," *The Lead— CNN* (14 November 2023).
17. Cf. Sarah O'Neal, "US Media Outlets Smear Palestinians as Inherently Violent in January Coverage," palestine-studies.org (26 April 2023).

18. Bridge Initiative Team, "Factsheet: Common Anti-Muslim Tropes," *Bridge: A Georgetown University Initiative* (4 December 2018).

19. Marc Lamont Hill and Mitchell Plitnick, *Except for Palestine: The Limits of Progressive Politics* (The New Press, 2021).

20. Justin Papp, "Protesters Calling for Cease-Fire in Gaza Keep Up Drumbeat on Capitol Hill," *Roll Call* (16 November 2023).

21. "'Let Gaza Live': Calls for Cease-Fire Fill Grand Central Terminal," *New York Times* (31 October 2023).

22. "March for Israel Speaker Pastor Hagee Once Said God 'Sent Hitler to Help Jews Reach the Promised Land,'" *Democracy Now!* (15 November 2023).

23. Ali Harb, "'No Ceasefire': Israel Supporters Gather in Washington, DC, Amid Gaza War," aljazeera.com (15 November 2023).

24. For a partial list of the demonstrations and groups involved, cf. Heather Hollingsworth and David Crary, "Longtime Israeli Policy Foes Are Leading US Protests Against Israel's Action in Gaza. Who Are They?" apnews.com (16 November 2023). Ali Harb, "Group Stages 'Die-Ins' Across Washington, DC to Raise Awareness for Gaza," aljazeera.com (28 November 2023).

25. Kelly Hayes, "This Weekend's DC Protest Was Largest Pro-Palestine Mobilization in US History," truthout.org (5 November 2023).

26. "Estimated 290K Attend March for Israel in Washington DC," *ABC 7 Chicago* (14 November 2023).

27. Maha Nassar, "'From the River to the Sea'—a Palestinian Historian Explores the Meaning and Intent of Scrutinized Slogan," theconversation.com (16 November 2023).

28. Anti-Defamation League, "Allegation: 'From the River to the Sea Palestine Will be Free'," adl.org (26 October 2023).

29. "Censuring Representative Rashida Tlaib for Antisemitic Activity, Sympathizing With Terrorist Organizations, and Leading an Insurrection at the United States Capitol Complex," *H. Res. 829, 118th Congress* (1 November 2023).

30. Akela Lacy, "GOP Representative Denies Existence of 'Innocent Palestinian Civilians' and Tries to Hobble Aid to Gaza," theintercept.com (1 November 2023).

31. Mychael Schnell and Mike Lillis, "House Democrat Pulls Resolution to Censure GOP Rep. Mast," thehill.com (8 November 2023).

32. "Voters Agree the US Should Call for a Ceasefire and De-Escalation of Violence in Gaza to Prevent Civilian Deaths," dataforprogress.com (20 October 2023).

33. "Reuters/Ipsos Survey: Israel Hamas War and the 2024 Election," ipsos.com (15 November 2023).

34. Akbar Shahid Ahmed, "Exclusive: 'Mutiny Brewing' Inside State Department Over Israel-Palestine Policy," huffpost.com (19 October 2023).

35. Nahal Toosi, "US Diplomats Slam Israel Policy in Leaked Memo," politico.com (6 November 2023).

36. Michael Birnbaum and John Hudson, "Blinken Confronts State Dept. Dissent Over Biden's Gaza Policy," *Washington Post* (14 November 2023).

37. Akbar Shahid Ahmed, "Biden's Israel-Gaza Approach Sidelines State Department, and Officials Fear the Worst," huffpost.com (2 November 2023).

38. Akbar Shahid Ahmed, "'I Couldn't Shift Anything': Senior State Department Official Resigns Over Biden's Gaza Policy," huffpost.com (19 October 2023).

39. "A Statement by Journalists: We Condemn Israel's Killing of Journalists in Gaza and Urge Integrity in Western Media Coverage of Israel's Atrocities Against Palestinians," protect-journalists.com (9 November 2023). For empirical support for allegations of pro-Israel media bias, cf. Conor Smyth, "For Cable News, a Palestinian Life Is Not the Same as an Israeli Life," fair.org (17 November 2023).

40. Max Tani, "LA Times Blocks Reporters Who Signed Open Letter Criticizing Israel From Covering Gaza," semafor.com (17 November 2023).

41. "'No Ceasefire, No Votes': Arab American Support for Biden Plummets Over Gaza Ahead of 2024 Election," democracynow.org (7 November 2023).

42. National Muslim Democratic Council, "2023 Ceasefire Ultimatum," muslimdems.org (30 October 2023).

43. Kathy Frankovic and David Montgomery, "Americans Support Ceasefires in Both Israel-Hamas and Russia-Ukraine Wars," yougov.com (29 November 2023),

44. Sharon Zhang, "Biden Approval Hits Low With 70 Percent of Young Voters Opposing His Gaza Policy," truthout.org (21 November 2023).

45. "Modest Backing for Israel in Gaza Crisis," pewresearch.org (13 January 2009).

Chapter Twelve. Talal Hangari

1. On October 26, 2023, the UN General Assembly adopted by 121 votes to 14 a resolution condemning "all acts of violence aimed at Palestinian and Israeli civilians" and calling for "an immediate, durable

and sustained humanitarian truce leading to a cessation of hostilities." Britain was among the 44 delegations that abstained. On December 12, 2023, the UN General Assembly adopted by 153 votes to 10 a resolution demanding an "immediate humanitarian ceasefire." Britain was among the 23 delegations that abstained.

2. A mid-October survey conducted by YouGov found 76 percent of British adults either "definitely" or "probably" in favor of "an immediate ceasefire."

3. Avi Shlaim, "On British Colonialism, Antisemitism, and Palestinian Rights," middleeasteye.net (1 March 2021).

4. See, e.g., Colter Louwerse, "'Tyranny of the Veto': PLO Diplomacy and the January 1976 United Nations Security Council Resolution," *Diplomacy & Statecraft* 33.2 (2022), pp. 316–318.

5. Human Rights Watch (HRW), "Memorandum," in House of Commons Foreign Affairs Committee, *Human Rights Annual Report 2007* (The House of Commons, 9 July 2008), ev. 29.

6. Norman G. Finkelstein, *Gaza: An Inquest into Its Martyrdom* (University of California Press, 2018), p. 66.

7. Owen Bowcott, "Tzipi Livni Spared War Crime Arrest Threat," *Guardian* (6 October 2011).

8. House of Commons Debates (HC Deb) 16 October 2023, vol. 738, col. 23.

9. HC Deb 23 October 2023, vol. 738, col. 598.

10. Stephen Castle, "Sunak Visits Israel in Display of British Support," *New York Times* (19 October 2023) ("demonstrate"). Prime Minister's Office, "PM Statement at Press Conference With Prime Minister Netanyahu of Israel," *gov.uk* (19 October 2023) ("win").

11. UN Office for the Coordination of Humanitarian Affairs, "Hostilities in the Gaza Strip and Israel: Flash Update 12," ochaopt.org (18 October 2023).

12. HC Deb 16 October 2023, vol. 738, col. 24.

13. Prime Minister's Office, "Press Conference."

14. HRW, "Devastating Civilian Toll as Parties Flout Legal Obligations," hrw.org (9 October 2023). B'Tselem, "Revenge Policy in Motion; Israel Committing War Crimes in Gaza," btselem.org (10 October 2023). Amnesty International, "Damning Evidence of War Crimes as Israeli Attacks Wipe Out Entire Families in Gaza," amnesty.org (20 October 2023).

15. International Committee of the Red Cross, "Evacuation Order of Gaza Triggers Catastrophic Humanitarian Consequences," icrc.org (13 October 2023). HC Deb 23 October 2023, vol. 738, col. 596.

16. "Israel-Gaza Crisis: US Vetoes Security Council Resolution," news.un.org (18 October 2023). "Security Council Fails to Adopt Either of Two Draft Resolutions Addressing Conflict and Humanitarian Crisis in Gaza," press.un.org (25 October 2023). On December 8, the United States vetoed a Security Council resolution calling for an immediate humanitarian ceasefire. Every other Security Council member voted for the resolution—except Britain, which abstained.

17. Katie Fallon, "UK Arms Israel as It Bombards Gaza," *Declassified UK* (20 October 2023).

18. HC Deb 16 October 2023, vol. 738, cols. 23–25.

19. Prime Minister's Office, "Prime Minister Deploys UK Military to Eastern Mediterranean to Support Israel," gov.uk (13 October 2023).

20. HRW, "Suspend Arms to Israel, Palestinian Armed Groups," hrw.org (6 November 2023). Cf. Amnesty International, "Unlawful Israeli Airstrikes on Gaza Have 'Decimated' Entire Palestinian Families," amnesty.org.uk (20 October 2023).

21. Andrew Ackerman, "What We Know About the Strikes at Jabalia Refugee Camp," *Wall Street Journal* (2 November 2023).

22. HC Deb 16 October 2023, vol. 738, col. 25.

23. In December, Israel's ambassador to the UK reaffirmed there was "absolutely no" prospect of Palestinian statehood while the Israeli prime minister said he was "proud" to have "prevented the establishment of a Palestinian State." "Ambassador Says Israel Will Not Accept Two-State Solution," news.sky.com (14 December 2023). "PM: I'm Proud That I Blocked a Palestinian State. Looking at Gaza, Everyone Sees What Would Have Happened," timesofisrael.com (17 December 2023).

24. UK Foreign, Commonwealth & Development Office (FCDO), "2030 Roadmap for UK-Israel Bilateral Relations," gov.uk (21 March 2023).

25. HC Deb 18 October 2023, vol. 738, col. 330.

26. Ibid., col. 334.

27. "Hamas Official Says Group Is Open to Discussions Over Truce With Israel," *Reuters* (9 October 2023).

28. Finkelstein, *Gaza*, pp. 35-36n68.

29. Colter Louwerse in this volume.

30. Finkelstein, *Gaza*, pp. 53–54, 69–72, 217, 267n75.

31. HC Deb 18 October 2023, vol. 738, col. 331.

32. Gabrielle Tétrault-Farber, "Despite Biden's Doubts, Humanitarian Agencies Consider Gaza Toll Reliable," *Reuters* (27 October 2023).

33. Percy Cradock, Foreign and Commonwealth Office planning staff, quoted in Mark Curtis, "Why Does the UK Give Israel Unqualified Backing?" *Declassified UK* (21 November 2023).

34. UK FCDO, "2030 Roadmap."

35. UN Special Coordinator for the Middle East Peace Process Álvaro de Soto, *End of Mission Report* (May 2007), paras. 63–64, 79.

36. Hayden Vernon, "UK, US, and Allies Offer Israel 'Steadfast Support' in Joint Statement," *Guardian* (10 October 2023).

37. ITV, *Good Morning Britain* (6 November 2023).

38. Polly Toynbee, "Labour Calling for a Ceasefire Would Achieve Nothing. So Why Should It Tear Itself Apart Over This?" *Guardian* (31 October 2023).

39. Taj Ali, post on X (formerly Twitter), 3 November 2023.

40. Hil Aked, *Friends of Israel: The Backlash Against Palestine Solidarity* (Verso, 2023), pp. 69–79.

41. Ibid., pp. 87-96, 102–105.

42. John McEvoy, "Two-Fifths of Keir Starmer's Cabinet Have Been Funded by Pro-Israel Lobbyists," *Declassified UK* (2 November 2023). Gabriel Pogrund and Harry Yorke, "The Secretive Guru Who Plotted Keir Starmer's Path to Power With Undeclared Cash," *Sunday Times* (12 November 2023).

43. Audrey Gillan, "Thousands of Jews Rally Against Hamas," *Guardian* (12 January 2009). Jennifer Lipman, "London Pro-Israel Rally's Turnout Far Below Support," timesofisrael.com (20 July 2014).

44. Board of Deputies of British Jews, *Navigating Workplace Issues Arising from the War in Israel: A Guide for Jewish Employees* (October 2023), p. 5.

45. Labour Friends of Israel, post on X (formerly Twitter), 17 November 2023.

46. Eliana Jordan, "Record Numbers Expected at March Against Antisemitism," *Jewish Chronicle* (23 November 2023). Cf. Berny Torre, "Pro-Palestinian Jews Distance Themselves as Tens of Thousands Join 'March Against Anti-Semitism'," *Morning Star* (26 November 2023). Michael Richmond, "A Long Way from Cable Street," *The Pickle* (1 December 2023).

47. Braverman was replaced as home secretary by James Cleverly on November 13, 2023. Cleverly was succeeded as foreign secretary by the former prime minister David Cameron.

48. Suella Braverman, "Letter to Chief Constables England and Wales," *gov.uk* (10 October 2023).

49. Suella Braverman, post on X (formerly Twitter), 16 October 2023, https://twitter.com/SuellaBraverman/status/1713897073915945089.

50. Suella Braverman, post on X (formerly Twitter), 16 October 2023, https://twitter.com/SuellaBraverman/status/1713897078923870634.

51. Robin Simcox, "Hate Marches in Britain Are a Wake-Up Call to All Decent People," *Times* (19 October 2023).

52. Douglas Murray, post on X (formerly Twitter), 2 November 2023. Murray is a director of the Free Speech Union, which according to its website is a "non-partisan . . . public interest body that stands up for the speech rights of its members and campaigns for free speech more widely."

53. Richard Tice, post on X (formerly Twitter), 6 November 2023. Isabel Oakeshott, post on X (formerly Twitter), 7 November 2023. Ewan Somerville and Daniel Martin, "Former Hamas Chief 'Behind Pro-Palestine Armistice Day Protests'," *Telegraph* (6 November 2023). Vikram Dodd and Daniel Boffey, "Met Police Chief Defies Calls to Ban Pro-Palestine Armistice Day March in London," *Guardian* (7 November 2023).

54. Campaign Against Antisemitism, "Sir Mark Rowley, Give London Back to Londoners," actionnetwork.org (n.d.).

55. These statements were parodied by a left-wing Jewish group, which exclaimed in mock outrage: "A ceasefire??? On ARMISTICE Day????" Jewdas, post on X (formerly Twitter), 3 November 2023.

56. Rishi Sunak, post on X (formerly Twitter), 3 November 2023.

57. "Statement Regarding November 11 National March," palestinecampaign.org (3 November 2023).

58. Suella Braverman, "Police Must Be Even-Handed With Protests," *Times* (8 November 2023).

59. Simon Childs, "The Far-Right Observed Remembrance Day by Fighting the Police," *Novara Media* (11 November 2023).

60. Tom Watling, "Six People Charged by Police after Pro-Palestinian Protest in London," *Independent* (6 November 2023).

61. Metropolitan Police, "We Ask You to Urgently Reconsider" (6 November 2023). Although the police asked that the march planned for November 11 be postponed, they suggested that violence and disorder was "often perpetrated by breakaway groups who have no interest in demonstration causes."

62. On November 18, the Metropolitan Police reported 253 arrests during protests and public gatherings since October 7. This figure was not limited to pro-Palestine protesters, and it should not be assumed that all arrests were legitimate. "Further Arrests as Officers Investigate Offences Linked to Israel/Hamas Conflict," news.met.police.uk (18 November 2023).

63. Richard Adams, "Williamson Accuses English Universities of Ignoring Antisemitism," *Guardian* (9 October 2020). Cf. Jamie Stern-Weiner, *The Politics of a Definition: How the IHRA Working Definition of Antisemitism Is Being Misrepresented* (Free Speech on Israel, 2021).

64. Eleanor Busby, "Universities May Face Cuts If They Reject Definition of Antisemitism, Says Education Minister," *Independent* (9 October 2020).

65. Department for Levelling Up, Housing and Communities, "UK Public Bodies Banned From Imposing Their Own Boycotts Against Foreign Countries," gov.uk (19 June 2023).

66. UK FCDO, "2030 Roadmap."

67. HC Deb 16 October 2023, vol. 738, col. 25.

68. "Labour Conference: Members Fill Hall With Palestinian Flags," bbc.co.uk (25 September 2018). "Palestine Motion," Labour Party Conference 2021, labourandpalestine.org.uk.

69. Ell Folan, "The Public Supports Palestine. Why Don't Our Politicians?" *Novara Media* (13 July 2023).

70. HC Deb 16 October 2023, col. 26.

71. The interview was broadcast on LBC radio.

72. Jonathan Cook, "Lawless in Gaza: Why Britain and the West Back Israel's Crimes," *Declassified UK* (13 October 2023).

73. Shehab Khan, "Exclusive: Labour Leaders Tell MPs and Council Leaders Not to Attend Palestine Protests," *ITV News* (14 October 2023).

74. Early Day Motion 1685, "Protecting Civilians in Gaza and Israel," edm.parliament.uk (17 October 2023). Muslim Census, "Labour and Conservatives Losing the Muslim Vote," muslimcensus.co.uk (26 October 2023). Dania Kamal Aryf and Sam Gelder, "Over 250 Muslim Councillors Demand Keir Starmer Calls for Ceasefire in Gaza," *openDemocracy* (26 October 2023). Aubrey Allegretti, "Sarwar and Khan Add to Pressure on Starmer Over Israel-Hamas Ceasefire," *Guardian* (27 October 2023). Early Day Motion 1, "Protecting Civilians in Gaza and Israel," edm.parliament.uk (7 November 2023).

75. Sam Blewett, "Starmer Denies Backing Israel on Withholding Humanitarian Aid From Gaza," *Independent* (20 October 2023).

76. Sir Keir Starmer, "Speech on the International Situation in the Middle East," labour.org.uk (31 October 2023).

77. "Israel-Palestine War: UK Poll Finds 76 Percent Want an Immediate Ceasefire," middleeasteye.net (19 October 2023). Eleni Courea, "Keir Starmer Defies Gaza Cease-Fire Calls Despite Labour Backlash," politico.eu (31 October 2023).

78. Starmer, "Situation."

79. Katie Neame, "Keir Starmer Says Instant Judgements 'Unwise' on Whether Israel Breaking Law," *Labour List* (31 October 2023).

80. Adam Forrest, "Keir Starmer Calls for Nuremberg-Style War Crimes Tribunal for Putin," *Independent* (7 March 2022). Starmer called for a

tribunal to prosecute "Vladimir Putin and his criminal cronies" twelve days into Russia's invasion.

81.   Tom Belger and Katie Neame, "Ceasefire Vote: Full List of Labour MPs Who Voted for SNP Pro-Ceasefire Motion," *Labour List* (15 November 2023).

82.   Paul Seddon, "Keir Starmer Suffers Major Labour Rebellion Over Gaza Ceasefire Vote," bbc.co.uk (16 November 2023).

83.   Tim Baker, "Andy McDonald: Senior Labour MP Suspended Over 'Deeply Offensive' Comments at Pro-Palestine Rally," *Sky News* (30 October 2023).

84.   Richard Kuper and Naomi Wimborne-Idrissi, "11th November Demonstration for Gaza—A Superb Event," jewishvoiceforlabour.org.uk (12 November 2023). The report noted that the Jewish bloc at the march "had its biggest presence to date."

Chapter Thirteen. Clare Daly MEP

1.   *Legal Consequences of the Construction of a Wall in the Occupied Palestinian Territory,* Advisory Opinion, ICJ Reports (2004), para. 139.

2.   Max Fisher, "This Chart Shows Every Person Killed in the Israel-Palestine Conflict Since 2000," vox.com (14 July 2014).

3.   "EU Trade Relations With Israel. Fact, Figures and Latest Developments," policy.trade.ec.europa.eu (n.d.).

4.   Campaign Against the Arms Trade, "Israel's Arms Suppliers," caat.org.uk (18 May 2021). Niamh Ni Bhriain, "European Complicity in War Crimes in Gaza," euobserver.com (10 November 2023).

5.   Niamh Ni Bhriain, "The EU's Funding and Support for Israeli Arms Companies," euobserver.com (24 October 2023).

6.   European Union External Action Service (EEAS), "Palestine: Statement by the Spokesperson on the Israeli Demolition of School in Masafer Yatta," eeas.europa.eu (25 November 2022).

7.   European Parliament, "Investigation of the Use of Pegasus and Equivalent Surveillance Spyware (Recommendation)," europarl.europa.eu (15 June 2023).

8.   Martin Konecny, "Textbook Hypocrisy: EU's New Low Point on Palestine," euobserver.com (15 September 2021).

9.   EEAS, "EP Plenary: Speech by High Representative/Vice-President Josep Borrell on the Situation in Israel and Palestine," eeas.europa.eu (14 March 2023).

10. "Statement by the High Representative on Behalf of the European Union on the Attacks Against Israel," consilium.europa.eu (7 October 2023).

11. "EU Backtracks on Previous Suspension of Palestinian Development Aid," aljazeera.com (9 October 2023).

12. Jorge Liboreiro "Commissioner Várhelyi Went Solo With Suspension of EU Funds for Palestinians, Prompting U-Turn," euronews.com (10 October 2023).

13. "Informal Video Conference of Foreign Affairs Ministers, 10 October 2023," consilium.europa.eu (10 October 2023).

14. Yaniv Cogan and Jamie Stern-Weiner, "Fighting Amalek in Gaza: What Israelis Say and Western Media Ignore," normanfinkelstein.substack.com (12 November 2023; updated regularly).

15. "Statement by President von der Leyen With President Metsola and Israeli President Herzog," neighbourhood-enlargement.ec.europa.eu (13 October 2023).

16. "Visit of Ursula von der Leyen, President of the European Commission, to Israel: Joint Press Briefing With Benjamin Netanyahu, Israeli Prime Minister," audiovisual.ec.europa.eu (13 October 2023).

17. Gideon Rachman, "Western Diplomats Are Walking an Impossible Tightrope With Israel," *Financial Times* (13 October 2023).

18. "Speech by President-Elect von der Leyen in the European Parliament Plenary on the Occasion of the Presentation of Her College of Commissioners and Their Programme," ec.europa.eu (27 November 2019).

19. Matina Stevis-Gridneff, "Top EU Official Is Becoming an Unexpected Wartime Leader," *New York Times* (14 September 2022).

20. Lisa O'Carroll, "EU States Expressed 'Incomprehension' at Tunisia Migration Pact, Says Borrell," *Guardian* (18 September 2023).

21. Jennifer Rankin, "Europe Must Reassess Its Relations With China, Says EU Chief," *Guardian* (30 March 2023). Jennifer Rankin, "Macron Sparks Anger by Saying Europe Should Not Be 'Vassal' in US-China Clash," *Guardian* (10 April 2023).

Further Reading

Overviews

- Norman G. Finkelstein, *Beyond Chutzpah: On the Misuse of Anti-Semitism and the Abuse of History*, updated edition (University of California Press, 2008)
- Robert Fisk, *Pity the Nation: Lebanon at War*, updated edition (Oxford University Press, 2001)
- Rashid Khalidi, *The Hundred Years' War on Palestine: A History of Settler Colonialism and Resistance, 1917–2017* (Metropolitan, 2020)
- Walid Khalidi, ed., *From Haven to Conquest: Readings in Zionism and the Palestine Problem Until 1948* (Institute for Palestine Studies, 2005)
- Zeev Maoz, *Defending the Holy Land: A Critical Analysis of Israel's Security and Foreign Policy* (University of Michigan Press, 2006)
- Benny Morris, *Righteous Victims: A History of the Zionist-Arab Conflict, 1881–2001*, updated edition (Vintage, 2001)
- Yezid Sayigh, *Armed Struggle and the Search for State: The Palestinian National Movement, 1949–1993* (Clarendon Press, 1997)
- Avi Shlaim, *The Iron Wall: Israel and the Arab World*, updated edition (Penguin, 2014)
- Jamie Stern-Weiner, ed., *Moment of Truth: Tackling Israel-Palestine's Toughest Questions* (OR Books, 2018)

Gaza

- Tareq Baconi, *Hamas Contained: The Rise and Pacification of Palestinian Resistance* (Stanford University Press, 2018)
- Norman G. Finkelstein, *Gaza: An Inquest into Its Martyrdom* (University of California Press, 2018)
- Amira Hass, *Drinking the Sea at Gaza: Days and Nights in a Land Under Siege* (Metropolitan, 1999)
- Khaled Hroub, *Hamas: Political Thought and Practice* (Institute for Palestine Studies, 2000)
- International Crisis Group:
  - *Enter Hamas: The Challenges of Political Integration* (January 2006)
  - *After Mecca: Engaging Hamas* (February 2007)
  - *After Gaza* (August 2007)
- Shaul Mishal and Avraham Sela, *The Palestinian Hamas: Vision, Violence, and Coexistence*, updated edition (Columbia University Press, 2006)
- Sara Roy, *The Gaza Strip: The Political Economy of De-development*, third edition (Institute for Palestine Studies, 2016)
- Álvaro de Soto (UN Special Coordinator for the Middle East Peace Process), *End of Mission Report* (May 2007)

Some Key Terms

Abraham Accords A series of agreements to normalize relations between Israel and Bahrain (September 2020), the United Arab Emirates (September 2020), Morocco (December 2020), and Sudan (January 2021). The agreements were promoted by the US administration of President Donald Trump.

Al-Aqsa intifada *See* Second intifada.

Al-Aqsa Mosque *See* Temple Mount/Al-Haram Al-Sharif.

Apartheid Between 1948 and the early 1990s, South Africa was governed by a formal system of racial separation or "apartheid." In international law, apartheid is defined as a crime against humanity committed when any "inhuman" or "inhumane" act is perpetrated in the context of an "institutionalized regime" of systematic "oppression" and "domination" by one racial group over another, with the intent to maintain that system. Prominent human rights organizations have argued that Israel practices the crime of apartheid vis-à-vis the Palestinians.

Arab League ("League of Arab States") A regional organization of Arab states, established in 1945. The Arab League comprises twenty-two member-states, including Palestine. In 1974, the Arab League formally recognized the Palestine Liberation Organization as the "sole legitimate representative of the Palestinian people."

Arab-Israelis *See* Palestinian citizens of Israel.

Axis of Resistance A self-styled alliance of forces opposed to US and Israeli power in the Middle East. Prominent members include Iran, Hezbollah in Lebanon, and the Houthis in Yemen.

Blockade of Gaza *See* Siege of Gaza.

Boycott, Divestment, and Sanctions (BDS) A campaign by Palestinian and international solidarity activists for consumer boycotts, institutional divestment, and state sanctions against Israel. The BDS Call, launched by Palestinian civil society groups in July 2005, demands an end to Israel's occupation, equality for Arab-Palestinian citizens of Israel, and the right of return for Palestinian refugees.

Disengagement (from Gaza) In 2005, Israel unilaterally dismantled its military bases and civilian settlements in the Gaza Strip. Most international observers continued to regard Gaza as either occupied or unlawfully annexed by Israel. Four settlements in the northern West Bank were also evacuated.

East Jerusalem That part of Jerusalem which was militarily occupied by Israel in the course of the June 1967 War. Immediately after the 1967 War, Israel unilaterally expanded the municipal borders of East Jerusalem and de facto annexed this expanded territory. The annexation is not recognized under international law or by the international community. Palestinians living in East Jerusalem hold permanent residency status in Israel. This entitles them to live and work in Israel and East Jerusalem, receive state benefits, and vote in municipal (but not national) elections. East Jerusalem encompasses within it the Temple Mount/Al-Haram Al-Sharif and the Old City.

Fatah A Palestinian nationalist organization founded in 1958–1959 by, among others, Yasser Arafat. It is the largest faction in the Palestine Liberation Organization and effectively controls the Palestinian Authority.

First intifada A mainly nonviolent civil revolt against Israel's occupation that erupted in December 1987. Tactics deployed by Palestinians included general strikes, demonstrations, economic self-sufficiency, tax boycotts, and stone-throwing. The uprising was led by grassroots organizations based in the Occupied Palestinian Territory, which wrested the initiative from the external Palestine Liberation Organization (PLO) leadership based in Tunis. As a result of the intifada, Jordan disengaged from the West Bank and the PLO formally endorsed the two-state solution.

Great March of Return A predominantly nonviolent protest movement against the siege of Gaza and for Palestinian refugee rights that began in Gaza on March 30, 2018.

Green Line The armistice demarcation line of 1949 which has been accepted by the international community as marking the legal boundary between Israel and Occupied Palestinian Territory.

Hamas The Islamic Resistance Movement. Established during the first intifada as the military arm of the Muslim Brotherhood in Palestine, Hamas is one of the two largest Palestinian factions (alongside Fatah). Hamas won a majority of seats in the 2006 Palestinian legislative election and consolidated its control of Gaza the following year.

Judea and Samaria The official Israeli government designation for what is internationally termed the West Bank, excluding East Jerusalem.

Mandatory Palestine ("Historical Palestine") The area now comprising the State of Israel and the Occupied Palestinian

Territory, which was administered by the United Kingdom as a League of Nations mandate between 1922 and 1948.

Nakba Arabic for "Catastrophe." Refers to the 1947–1948 expulsion of approximately 750,000 Palestinians from what is now the State of Israel.

Occupation The status under international law of a territory that is under the effective control of foreign armed forces. The International Court of Justice determined in 2004 that the West Bank, including East Jerusalem, and Gaza constitute Occupied Palestinian Territory. Some observers have concluded that Israel's protracted rule over Palestinian territories and declared intention to permanently incorporate them have transformed what was an occupation into an illegal annexation.

Occupied Palestinian Territory (OPT) The West Bank, including East Jerusalem, and Gaza Strip. These areas came under Israeli military occupation in the course of the June 1967 War. The designation "unlawfully annexed" is arguably more precise than "occupied" given that Israel has formally annexed East Jerusalem and, according to Israel's most prominent human rights organization, de facto annexed the rest of the West Bank and the Gaza Strip.

Occupied Territories *See* Occupied Palestinian Territory (OPT).

Operation Cast Lead A military offensive by Israel against Gaza conducted between December 27, 2008, and January 18, 2009. In the course of hostilities, Israeli forces killed approximately 1,400 Palestinians, of whom up to four-fifths were civilians and 350 children. Thirteen Israelis were killed, including three civilians and four combatants killed by friendly fire. Israeli forces destroyed or severely damaged 6,300 homes in Gaza. Palestinian projectiles destroyed one house in Israel.

Operation Protective Edge A military offensive by Israel against Gaza conducted between July 8 and August 26, 2014. Approximately 2,200 Palestinians were killed, of whom some 70 percent were civilians and 550 children. Seventy-three Israelis were killed, including six civilians. Eighteen thousand homes in Gaza and one house in Israel were destroyed or rendered uninhabitable.

Oslo Accords Two agreements—the Oslo I Accord (1993) and Oslo II Accord (1995)—reached between Israel and the Palestine Liberation Organization (PLO), which together established the framework for the Oslo peace process. These provided inter alia for the establishment of an interim Palestinian self-government authority in the Occupied Palestinian Territory (the Palestinian Authority); the sub-division of the West Bank into three areas—A, B, and C—with different levels of Palestinian autonomy; and the commencement of negotiations between Israel and the PLO toward a conflict-ending agreement within five years. This permanent status agreement was never concluded. The Oslo Accords did not commit Israel to dismantling settlements, freezing settlement construction, or recognizing a Palestinian right to independent statehood.

Palestine Liberation Organization (PLO) An organization established in 1964 at the initiative of the Arab League to represent Palestinians. In 1969, the PLO came under the control of Palestinian forces led by Yasser Arafat. It eventually incorporated the major Palestinian factions (excluding Hamas) and was internationally recognized as the "sole legitimate representative of the Palestinian people." The PLO was led by Arafat from 1969 until his death in 2004, when he was succeeded by Mahmoud Abbas.

Palestinian Authority (PA) A Palestinian interim self-government body established in 1994 as part of the Oslo peace process. The PA was invested with limited authority over the Gaza Strip and the 40 percent of the West Bank not under direct Israeli rule. Mahmoud Abbas was elected president of the PA in 2005. In June 2007, the PA lost de facto control in Gaza as a result of factional conflict between Fatah and Hamas.

Palestinian citizens of Israel Most Palestinians living in what became the State of Israel were expelled in 1947–1948. Those who remained became Israeli citizens. Israel's Palestinian minority lived under formal military rule until 1966 and remains subject to various forms of legal and de facto discrimination.

Palestinian Legislative Council (PLC) The legislature of the Palestinian Authority.

Qassam Brigades The military wing of Hamas.

Quartet on the Middle East ("Middle East Quartet") The Quartet comprises the European Union, Russia, the United Nations, and the United States. It was established in 2002 to facilitate diplomacy on the Israel-Palestine conflict.

Refugees (Palestinian) Palestinians who were forced into exile in the run-up to and during the 1948 and 1967 wars, and their descendants. Approximately 70 percent of the population of Gaza are refugees.

Right of return The right under international law of Palestinian refugees to return to their homes. Amnesty International has upheld this right for "Palestinians who fled or were expelled from Israel, the West Bank or Gaza Strip, along with those of their descendants who have maintained genuine links with the area."

Second intifada A Palestinian uprising against Israel's occupation that erupted in September 2000 after the failure of the Camp David peace talks and following a provocative visit to the Temple Mount/Al-Haram Al-Sharif by the right-wing Israeli politician Ariel Sharon. Between September 2000 and February 2005, approximately 1,000 Israelis and 3,000 Palestinians were killed in the violence.

Settlement An Israeli colony established in Occupied Palestinian Territory in violation of international law.

Siege of Gaza After Hamas won the 2006 Palestinian Authority legislative elections, Israel along with the US and European Union imposed various forms of economic sanctions. When Hamas consolidated control of Gaza in June 2007, Israel closed Gaza's border crossings and sharply reduced the passage of goods and people across its borders. This effectively eliminated Gaza's economy and caused sharp increases in poverty, unemployment, and aid dependence. International human rights bodies have characterized the siege as a collective punishment and consequently a violation of international law.

Temple Mount/Al-Haram Al-Sharif A Muslim and Jewish sacred site located in Jerusalem's Old City. Jewish tradition holds it to be the location of the destroyed First and Second Jewish Temples, while the Al-Aqsa Mosque, situated within the compound, is considered among the holiest sites in Islam. The Temple Mount/Al-Haram Al-Sharif came under Israeli military occupation in June 1967, but Israel left the Jordanian authorities to administer the compound and prohibited Jews from worshipping in it, directing them instead to pray at the site's retaining wall (the "Western Wall" or "Kotel"). This arrangement is known as the "status quo." Hamas cited encroachments on this status quo by Israeli Jewish nationalists as a motivating grievance for its participation in the May

2021 "unity intifada" as well as Operation Al-Aqsa Deluge of October 2023.

Two-state solution A framework for resolving the Israel-Palestine conflict by establishing an independent State of Palestine alongside the State of Israel on the Green Line. The two-state solution has been near-unanimously endorsed by the General Assembly of the United Nations.

UN General Assembly Resolution 181 (II) In November 1947, the General Assembly resolved by a vote of thirty-three to thirteen (with ten abstentions) to endorse the partition of Palestine into a Jewish and an Arab state.

UN General Assembly Resolution 194 In December 1948, the General Assembly resolved by a vote of thirty-five to fifteen (with eight abstentions) that "the [Palestinian] refugees wishing to return to their homes and live at peace with their neighbors should be permitted to do so at the earliest practicable date."

UN Security Council Resolution 242 In November 1967, following the June 1967 War, the Security Council affirmed the "inadmissibility of the acquisition of territory by war"; called for a "just and lasting peace in the Middle East" based on the "[w]ithdrawal of Israeli armed forces from territories occupied in the recent conflict"; and simultaneously called for the "[t]ermination of all claims or states of belligerence and respect for and acknowledgement of the sovereignty, territorial integrity and political independence of every State in the area and their right to live in peace within secure and recognized boundaries free from threats of acts of force."

Unity Uprising In May 2021, Palestinians across the OPT and inside Israel participated in protests, unrest, and strikes alongside a military escalation between Hamas and Israel in Gaza. The latter was initiated by Hamas in declared response to Israeli raids on the Al-Aqsa Mosque in East Jerusalem and the attempted expulsion of Palestinians from their homes in that city's Sheikh Jarrah neighborhood.

Zionism A movement for a Jewish national home or state in the Land of Israel/Palestine, originating in nineteenth-century Europe.

List of Contributors

Musa Abuhashhash worked for many years as Hebron field researcher for B'Tselem, the Israeli Information Center for Human Rights in the Occupied Territories. He grew up in Fawwar refugee camp.

Ahmed Alnaouq is a journalist from Gaza. He co-founded We Are Not Numbers, which helps young people in Gaza share their stories, and Border Gone, which publishes stories from Gaza in Hebrew. He works as an advocacy officer for the Euro-Med Human Rights Monitor.

Nathan J. Brown is professor of political science and international affairs at George Washington University and nonresident senior fellow at the Carnegie Endowment for International Peace. He wrote this while a visiting fellow at the Hamburg Institute for Advanced Study in Germany.

Yaniv Cogan studies computer science at Tel Aviv University.

Clare Daly MEP is an Irish politician, currently serving as a member of the European Parliament, representing the constituency of Dublin. Elected as an independent socialist, she is affiliated to the Left in the European Parliament, and works across a range of policy areas, including migration and human rights, data protection, home affairs, transport, and defense. She is a vocal advocate for peace and a critic of EU foreign policy.

Talal Hangari is a socialist who lives in London and has written for several left-wing publications. His website is talalhangari.com.

Khaled Hroub is professor of Middle Eastern studies at Northwestern University/Qatar and the author of two books on Hamas.

R. J. is an independent researcher and humanist living in the United States.

Colter Louwerse is an academic researcher focused on the diplomatic history of the Palestine Question. His Ph.D. dissertation, *The Struggle for Palestinian Rights: The Palestinian Campaign for Self-Determination and Statehood at the United Nations, 1967-1989*, shed new evidentiary light on the relationship between Palestinian popular struggle, diplomacy, and development of proposals for "resolving" the Israeli-Palestinian conflict under international auspices.

Mitchell Plitnick is president of ReThinking Foreign Policy and co-author, with Marc Lamont Hill, of *Except for Palestine: The Limits of Progressive Politics*. His earlier positions included co-director of Jewish Voice for Peace and founding director of the US office of B'Tselem, the Israeli Information Center for Human Rights in the Occupied Territories.

Mouin Rabbani is co-editor of *Jadaliyya* and host of its *Connections* podcast.

Sara Roy is an associate of the Center for Middle Eastern Studies at Harvard University. Her most recent book is *Unsilencing Gaza: Reflections on Resistance* (Pluto Press, 2021).

Avi Shlaim is an emeritus professor of international relations at Oxford University, a fellow of the British Academy, and the author of *The Iron Wall: Israel and the Arab World* (Penguin, 2014) and *Israel and Palestine: Reappraisals, Revisions, Refutations* (Verso, 2009).

Jamie Stern-Weiner is an associate editor at OR Books and a doctoral candidate at the University of Oxford. His previous publications include *Moment of Truth: Tackling Israel-Palestine's Toughest Questions* (OR Books, 2018), *Antisemitism and the Labour Party* (Verso, 2019), and *How the EHRC Got It So Wrong* (Verso, 2021).

When history is written as it ought to be written, it is the moderation and long patience of the masses at which men will wonder, not their ferocity.

—C. L. R. James, *The Black Jacobins*